The NEW Launch Plan

152 Tips, Tactics and Trends from the Most Memorable New Products

The NEW
Launch Plan

152 Tips, Tactics and Trends from the Most Memorable New Products

JOAN SCHNEIDER AND JULIE HALL

BNP Media II, LLC
Custom Media Group
Troy, Michigan

Printed in the United States of America

Published in 2010 by BNP Media II, LLC, Troy, MI 48084

The NEW Launch Plan: 152 Tips, Tactics and Trends from the Most Memorable New Products
Joan Schneider
Includes footnotes and index
ISBN 0-615-32678-1

Photos reprinted with permission

Cover illustration by: Michael Demmons
Jacket, book design and layout by: Breanna Fong

DEDICATION:

To Ronald Egalka, my husband, who never ceases to amaze me with his understanding of and respect for who I am and what makes my world go round. A big thank you to our clients, who give us the privilege of launching their products, and to my talented colleagues who make it all happen.
—*Joan Schneider*

To Joan Schneider, my mentor and inspiration. She makes launching into everything we do an adventure, not to mention a lot of fun. And to my husband, Howard Hall, and the best launches we've worked on together, Oliver Bean and Linus Hamilton.
—*Julie Hall*

MISSION:

To motivate consumer product companies and their marketing communication partners to always be flexible in their approach to launching new products by adopting new methodologies and technologies. Our goal is to identify and introduce new and effective ways to successfully bring products to market.

CONTENTS:

ACKNOWLEDGMENTS

from Joan Schneider:

It's a pleasure to acknowledge the many people who helped me bring this second book on launching new products to fruition. First, I want to thank Steve Beyer, director of the BNP Custom Media Division, who believed in the value of writing a second book on launching new products and took the concept to management. Next, a big thank you goes to Marti Smye, Ph.D., my friend and mentor, who encouraged me to continue researching and writing about launch as a way to sustain visibility and intellectual property for my firm, Schneider Associates. There is no amount of thanks that will convey my admiration and gratitude to Jeanne Yocum, who is always there to help me write, edit and think about launch in innovative ways. And a special thanks to my husband, Ron Egalka, who gave up a summer of motorcycle, boat and vintage car rides to be sure I met my deadlines. His unending belief in my abilities keeps me sane.

I'd also like to thank John McIndoe, vice president of global media & analyst relations, and Char Partelow, senior vice president, Consumer and Shopper Insights Group, from IRI; Joan Holleran, director of research, Lynn Dornblaser, director of CPG Trend Insight, Diana Sheehan, director of research for Comperemedia, and Joanna Gueller, public relations executive, from Mintel; Lynda Gordon, co-founder of Decision Metrics; Aaron Reid, chief behavioral scientist, and Meghan Van Horn, market research manager, from Sentient Decision Science, LLC; and Julie Hall and Patrick Richardson from Schneider Associates for continually improving and expanding how we promote the Most Memorable New Product Launch Survey. Conducting this research enables us to keep our pulse on what motivates consumers to try and buy new products. We use this important information daily in our quest to develop innovative, compelling launch campaigns.

I am blessed with knowing so many smart people in marketing communications. I'd like to thank the numerous experts I spoke with about their insights on launching new products. It is amazing how quickly the art and science of new product launch is changing. Being able to talk with the many people who shared their knowledge brought real insight to this book.

My Gratitude to:

Rob Adelstein of R solutions, LLC, Colin Angle of iRobot Corporation, Jason Baer of Convince & Convert, Dave Balter of BzzAgent, Jens Bang of Cone, CPG consultant Eric Baty, Liz Bigham of Jack Morton Worldwide, Thom Blischok of IRI, Ken Braaten of Radiator Specialty Company, Dr. Walter J. Carl of ChatThreads, Deborah Cassell of *Candy Industry* and *Retail Confectioner* magazines, Ed Chansky of Greenberg Traurig, Olivier Cheng of Olivier Catering and Events, Carol Cone of Cone, Zak Dabbas of Punchkick Interactive, Dan Danielson of Mercury Media, Dave Dickinson of Zeo, Iain Dodsworth of TweetDeck, Chris Donnelly of A&G Brand Promotion, Lynn Dornblaser of Mintel, Elissa Elan of *Nation's Restaurant News*, Justin Esch of Bacon Salt, Jeff Falkowski of R solutions, LLC, Ryan FitzSimons of Gigunda, Steve Garfield, consultant and author of *Get Seen*, Randy Golenberg of R solutions, LLC, Lynda Gordon of Decision Metrics, Mike Guggenheimer of Radiator Specialty Company, Jackie Hague of New England Confectionery Company, media relations coach Louisa Hart, Dana Harville of Domino's Pizza, Burt Helm of *BusinessWeek*, Joan Holleran of Mintel, Michelle King of Dunkin' Brands, Dave Lefkow of Bacon Salt, Dror Liwer of Zemoga, Eric Mankin of Harvard Business School Publishing, Rick Maynard of KFC, Pat McGauley of Anheuser-Busch, John McIndoe of IRI, Nicole Murra of Baskin-Robbins, Heather Oldani of McDonald's, Katie Paine of KDPaine & Partners, LLC, Teresa Panas of KY Brands, Chris Pape of Genuine Interactive, Char Partelow of IRI, Mark Phillips of the USO, Dave Puner of Dunkin' Brands, Dany Sfeir of DS&A Consulting, Clair Sidman of Ian's, Marcy Singer of Jack Morton Worldwide, Jeff Snyder of Inspira Marketing, Charles StClair of KFC, Laura Sturaitis of Business Wire®, Cindy Syracuse of Burger King, Mike Troiano of Holland-Mark Digital, Ryan Unger of Punchkick Interactive, Beth Vendice of Mercury Media, Susan Viamari of IRI, Stanford Weiner of Sterling Inc., Mary Wiggins, Chief Mommy Organizer of Mommies Clique, and Jeanne Yocum of Tuscarora Communications.

Of course, I could not have written this book without the help of my partner Julie Hall, EVP of the Consumer Group of Schneider Associates, who is dedicated to learning the latest tips, tactics and trends when it comes to introducing new products. A special thanks goes to Patrick Richardson, the launch director at Schneider Associates, who is always on top of the latest technology whether it be blogs, streaming video, online communities—you name it, Patrick and Julie know about it. Special thanks also to Michael Dowding, B.L.S., M.S., MBA, president of Wordscape Communications, Inc., who brought clarity and insight to sort out challenges in the final edits. And what would I have done without the help of Tom Ryan, our marketing associate; Michael Demmons, our designer; Caitlin Daley, our relentless graphics coordinator; Brett Pohlman, who stayed on top of emerging social media technologies; and Rachel Yanofsky, our summer launch intern, who kept me scheduled, focused and armed with the latest research. Also, the editing skills of Ron Egalka, CEO of Rampart Investment Management, need to be commended.

I'd also like to thank the team from the BNP Custom Media Division who helped get this book produced, including Steve Beyer, director; Kathy Colwell, senior project manager; Irena Gerdova, custom media coordinator; Maya Dollarhide, managing editor; Elizabeth Brewster, freelance editor/writer; Breanna Fong, custom media art director; and Melanie Kuchma, copy editor.

The NEW Launch Plan

152 Tips, Tactics and Trends from the Most Memorable New Products

INTRODUCTION:

A Tough Task Gets Tougher

Successfully launching a new product gets tougher every year. Today's new product cacophony is brought to consumers via news flashes and competing messages broadcast 24 hours a day, seven days a week, virtually everywhere we go. Let us count the ways we're bombarded with marketing messages: There are the usual print and broadcast media. Venture onto the Internet and you'll find marketing everywhere, from search engine results to blogs, from news sites to shopping sites, and from corporate to product sites. When we pass a store, a text message may be sent to our mobile phone telling us the Gap has a sale or Whole Foods is running a special. When we enter a store, we're exposed to increasingly sophisticated point of purchase devices that, in some cases, talk to us as we walk by a specific shelf. There are billboards along highways and on buildings, and posters in mass transit stations and bus shelters, and in just about any other public spot where you can post a message. Watch baseball on TV and

you'll be treated to a revolving display of promotional signs behind home plate throughout the game. Go to the movies and you'll see ads before the previews and then product placements in the films themselves. The carton your Chinese take-out comes in may feature an ad. Seatback dining trays on airplanes have been used for advertising, as have turnstiles. There are even signs in the restroom stalls at restaurants, highway rest stops, office buildings, sports arenas and hotels. Talk about not being able to escape!

From the time we get up in the morning and turn on the radio or TV to catch up on the news over breakfast to the time we turn off Letterman or Leno at night, all of us are being exposed to hundreds of marketing messages, most of which are designed to get us to try a new product or service. Of course, some of the estimates of the number of marketing messages we're exposed to per day or year are total guesswork, yet have obtained the status of urban legends. Researchers at the Advertising Internet Media Center, a leading Web site for media and marketing professionals, have tried to debunk the higher estimates that are frequently cited:

"There are about 245 ad exposures daily: 108 from TV, 34 radio and 112 print. Others estimate 3,000, 5,000 or more. Even the 245 is 'potential' and perhaps only half are real exposures. The higher estimates probably include all marketing exposure including being in the vicinity of product labels or actual products with trademarks visible, such as your car, computer, fax, phone, shirt, pencil, paper towel in the bathroom, etc. Just think, if we were really exposed to 3,000 advertising messages per day, at an average of just 10 seconds apiece (accounting for radio 60's and brief exposure to billboards) these exposures would consume 8.33 hours out of our 16 waking hours per day."[1]

No matter how many marketing messages we're actually exposed to each day, there is no arguing that the figure is growing exponentially as marketers develop ever more inventive and intrusive ways to grab our attention. No wonder the battle for mindshare rages on and manufacturers struggle to get their new products noticed. This fact was confirmed over the seven-year period that we at Schneider Associates conducted the annual Most Memorable New Product Launch Survey (MMNPLS) in conjunction with partners such as Mintel and Information Resources, Inc. (IRI).

To understand more about what motivates consumers to try and buy new products, we polled 1,000 adult consumers online to name the most memorable new product launched during the year in the grocery, personal and beauty care, fast-food, technology, and toy categories.

Increasingly we have found significant erosion of the public's ability to name new products. In our first survey, 33 percent of survey respondents could not name a single new product launched that year without needing a list of new products to aid with recognition. Eight years later, the lack of consumer new product recall had reached an alarming 51 percent.

In 2009, 51% of respondents could not name a new product, compared with 33% in 2002

Are consumers paying less attention than they used to or are they so overwhelmed with the masses of marketing clutter that it's impossible to get through to them? Or have they become so cynical about marketing that they believe it is all hype and buzz and has no substance? Whatever the case, launch campaigns now require even more-sophisticated planning and execution that can be delivered in several different dimensions. No longer can you use solely editorial coverage, advertising, radio, television or just the Internet, because consumers are now fragmented into so many different economic, ethnic, geographic, societal and special interest groups that companies must consider multiple methods and delivery vehicles to introduce new products.

"About half of all new products launched in a given year fail after two years on the market," according to Char Partelow, senior vice president, Consumer and Shopper Insights Group at IRI, who conducted an analysis of Food/Drug/Mass distribution and dollar sales for new brands and form/flavor extensions. So what do those of us engaged in new product launch need to do to increase our success rates in this crazy media environment?

How can we deliver integrated launch campaigns that work harder and smarter in this new technological era? What tips, tactics and trends can be employed to improve the odds for introducing blockbuster products—or incremental product improvements—in today's changing environment?

We've written this book to help marketing professionals navigate the sometimes murky and often dangerous waters of new product launch.

Since our last book, *New Product Launch: 10 Proven Strategies*, was published, we've found that many of the tried and true tactics we recommended are now being replaced by a coterie of brand new tips, tactics and trends. In fact, the launch landscape is changing so rapidly that many of the bedrock strategies we all depend on may soon be obsolete. When newspaper institutions like the *Boston Globe* are in jeopardy of closing and broadcast favorites like *The Ellen DeGeneres Show*, and *The Martha Stewart Show* are offering so-called branded segments on a "pay-for-play" basis, we realize the importance of exploring new ways to introduce new products that go beyond traditional media.

In the following pages we will:

- **Discuss the trends that are hindering the ability of consumer product companies to break through the clutter and provide consumers with information about new products that encourage trial and purchase.** As we plan and execute new product introductions, it is vital to understand as much as possible about the ever-shifting environment that will surround your market launch. Keeping abreast of trends in media, retailing, and consumer behavior will help you avoid making costly mistakes on launch tactics that aren't going to work in today's new normal.

- **Create and execute what we are calling the New Launch Plan, a method for developing, implementing and tracking launch strategies.** Now more than ever, it's critical for your launch plan to be strategic, creative, comprehensive and totally buttoned-up to succeed. The days when you could "wing" the launch plan or repeat what you've done before are gone. No longer can you expect a new product to succeed without the passion, proficiency, product planning and performance required to beat the odds.

- **Examine the marketing basics required to make every launch a success.** Each launch plan needs a blend of tried and true and brand new launch techniques to succeed. In our original research, conducted in conjunction with Boston University, we identified 10 launch success factors, many of which still hold true today.

BOSTON UNIVERSITY

We've built on those strategies and added many more that we believe are critical to successfully launching new products today.

- **Delve into launch issues that need to be resolved during the product development stage. Decisions that are made while the product is still being shaped can greatly impact launch success.** More often than not, companies are inviting consumers to be an integral part of the new product development process to be sure that what is being created is vetted by the very audience that will ultimately buy the product. This not only speeds the research and time to market process but ensures that the launch phase is based on consumer insights. This type of in-depth market research confirms market needs and consumer receptivity, thus significantly boosting the chances for launch success.

- **Explore ways to work effectively with retailers to obtain shelf space or to launch your product through e-tailing.** Getting your product placed in brick-and-mortar stores, online, or in virtual environments where it can actually be purchased is no easy task. Understand the many ways you can impact shelf space and consumer purchasing behavior and move your product from a retail startup to a retail star seller.

- **Discuss the all-important topics of branding and launch messaging.** Deciding how you are going to describe your new product and making sure it matches your brand's image and ethos is important work. Do a good job on branding and messaging and your product will not only speak to consumers but will stay in their minds and shopping carts for years to come.

- **Identify ways to gear up your buzz-generating machine.** The media world is undergoing dramatic changes, and so should the strategies and tactics you include in the New Launch Plan. We'll talk about what works and what doesn't work in this altered new media landscape.

- **Examine real world and virtual launch tactics such as social media.** To succeed, a new product launch has to reach people multiple times in both the real and online worlds. We'll discuss tactics that work in both of these realms, with particular emphasis on the growing importance of Web 2.0 launch tactics.

- **Discuss how and why it is critical to measure launch progress and success. Make no mistake; launch is a high-stakes game.** Metrics need to be established prior to launch so you can track whether your launch campaign is succeeding or requires a tune-up. How can you succeed if you haven't defined what success looks like? Get those metrics on paper; you will be pleased to see how many benchmarks you can meet or exceed with a strategic and creative launch plan.

- **Offer real world examples of how companies have put various strategies and tactics to work to achieve launch success.** To create memorable launch campaigns, we believe it's important to monitor introductory campaigns in all different types of industries. Tracking launches both inside and outside your product category will provide a wealth of new ideas that might warrant inclusion in your next new product launch campaign.

- **Learn from the masters whose products have made it onto the Top 10 lists of the MMNPL Survey over the past seven years.** We've interviewed brand and product managers from the most memorable new product companies to understand how they orchestrate and activate award-winning launch campaigns. You'll hear how companies like Anheuser-Busch, McDonald's, and KFC make their new products memorable. Whether you're

COURTESY OF KFC CORPORATION

an experienced launch pro with a well-established brand or conducting your first launch for a start-up company, you can learn something from what these launch experts have to say.

- **Conclude with a few all-purpose gems of new product launch advice to help you avoid launch pitfalls and stay on course throughout the frenzy that often surrounds new product introductions.** With so much riding on the successful commercialization of your new product, it is easy to let product pitfalls, production problems and sales snafus delay and potentially derail your mission. We'll offer practical advice to put your launch back on track by focusing on critical success factors.

Our goal with this book is to help fill the information void that continues to exist around this important business topic of new product launches. In a world where companies routinely share best practices about a wide range of operational areas, it is surprising that many marketers remain highly secretive about how they launch new products. Based on our agency's 30 years of launch experience and our extensive study of launch, we know that marketers could learn a lot from each other that would help improve the abysmal launch success ratio. We hope our book helps start more conversations around this topic, and we thank the marketers who were willing to share their expertise with our readers.

We hope that after reading this book, you'll feel even more confident about creating a launch campaign that will beat the odds. Nothing would thrill us more than to see your new product make it into the ranks of our annual Most Memorable New Product Launch Survey. Please let us know if the axioms we describe here help make it happen!

CHAPTER 1:

The Ever-Changing Launch Environment

It's hard to keep up with the rapid pace of change in today's world. But successfully launching a new product into a constantly shifting environment requires tracking a wide range of variables where change can affect your ability to achieve launch objectives.

Accept it. The days when you could simply replicate the launch strategies and tactics that worked the last time around are long gone. The odds are great that something significant has changed in your environment since your last new product launch, even if it took place just last year. There is little that even the most experienced launch team can take for granted— except how hard it is to achieve launch success.

New marketing platforms, such as mobile devices of all types, are rapidly evolving. Competitors are determined to grab market share by outspending you with bigger or better

marketing campaigns, or by outsmarting you to quickly deliver super-innovative products to market in record time. Social media platforms are giving customers the power to reach others with their opinions—both positive and negative—about new products and services.

At the same time that consumers are making their voices heard, they are tuning out marketing messages through the use of TiVos, DVRs, the Do Not Call Registry and the Direct Marketing Association's Do Not Mail list. Retailers are demanding more from manufacturers than ever before as they struggle to achieve margins that will keep them afloat in the toughest retail environment in decades.

These and many other developments raise fundamental questions about traditional launch tactics. Why spend money on pricey Free Standing Insert coupons (FSIs) when newspaper circulation is drastically decreasing? Why continue to buy packages of 60-second commercials at the upfront meeting when consumers are online and watching their favorite shows on Hulu? Why continue to transport your entire marketing team and take a $100,000 booth at a trade show, when attendance is declining and you can create a community of value on Facebook or Ning, and interact with your key customers 365 days a year at a fraction of the cost?

In short, *everything* needs to be looked at with fresh eyes to make sure you're making smart launch choices that are based on today's reality instead of on how the world operated yesterday.

Here is a quick review of some of the significant shifts in the launch landscape that every marketer needs to consider when fashioning new product launch campaigns:

A New Paradigm–No Longer B2B or B2C, But B2E

The omnipresence of the Internet in everyday life has been a prime game-changing phenomenon for new product launches, and has created a new paradigm for marketers—the arrival of business-to-everyone, or B2E. In the United States, 74.7 percent of the population has Internet access; that's over 304 million people.[1] Overall, the Internet is the medium with which users spend the most time (32.7 hours/week), according to IT market intelligence giant International Data Corporation (IDC). This is equivalent to almost half of the total time spent each week using all media (70.6 hours), almost twice the time spent watching television (16.4 hours), and eight times more than reading newspapers and magazines (3.9 hours).[2]

When literally anyone around the world can visit your Web site, you are no longer aiming your messages at only your carefully targeted business-to-business (B2B) or business-to-consumer (B2C) customers. Instead, you are talking to everyone—B2E. This may have broader implications for those in the B2B market since B2C companies are more accustomed to thinking of virtually anyone as a potential customer. In the more

B2B + B2C = B2E

tightly controlled B2B arena—particularly in the business service sector—companies usually talk to a carefully selected group of target customers and prospects. Now anyone, including your competition, can visit your Web site and see your products, pricing, and case studies, and learn how you are positioning your wares. No one cares whether you characterize your product, service or company as B2C or B2B; all they want is information available 24/7 brought to them by Google, Yahoo, Bing or other search engines that provide rapid search access.

Whether you're in the B2C or B2B realm, you don't have a choice about developing an informative Web site—it's a marketing must. The fact that your Web site might enable prospective customers to do their own comparison shopping or allow competitors to gain valuable insight into your company is part of doing business. Everyone expects you to provide detailed information online. If you do not provide relevant information, customers may get frustrated and move to the next company that comes up in their Internet search. Your only choice is how much information you make accessible to everyone and how much data you put behind a firewall where only customers or prospects who agree to register can access it.

And here's the other big B2E change being created by the Internet. With the evolution of Web 2.0, you're not just talking to customers or potential customers—they are talking back, through social media and consumer-generated media such as blogs and video blogs. In fact, video blogs, known as vlogs, have grown so common that *Merriam-Webster* added the word *vlog* to its dictionary in 2009.

If you're lucky, these consumer journalists and bloggers are writing glowing reviews of your new product and how it was just what they needed. If you're not so lucky, they are telling the world your new product is substandard, doesn't match up to competitive products, or is too expensive. Or they're complaining about a service issue like how their homeowners or health insurance company didn't come through for them in the clutch. Or maybe they're venting about a bad experience they had with your company's tech support people. If consumers are thinking something positive or negative about your company, product or service, they are also writing about it online. Get used to it and be prepared to deal with the ramifications.

The emergence of Web 2.0 has crumbled the media gates formerly patrolled by journalists who have tightly controlled product news. Now products are often given to bloggers or "mommy bloggers," who try new products, and generate and share reviews, photos, videos, and other content. This new paradigm gives marketers complete freedom to think carefully and creatively about who is best to break the news about a product or service. But Web 2.0 also allows consumers to offer unbridled feedback, making launching a new product more complex than ever before.

The Blurring of the Lines between B2B and B2C Launches

As marketers, we've all been taught that B2B and B2C are two distinct markets that use very different tactics when launching new products or services. B2C launches employed splashy events, celebrity endorsements, scads of TV advertising, point of purchase materials and retail promotions or contests. The five Ps were product, price, place (distribution), promotion and people. Launching a new B2B product involved the usual five Ps, but also had its own set of launch rules of engagement: beta testing of the product, sales force preparation, distributor/dealer/retailer education, customer seminars, and trade shows, to name a few favored B2B tactics.

A few years ago B2B clients started asking our opinion about using different types of consumer strategies to launch their new products or services. They were interested in trying some of the sexy consumer launch campaigns we created for clients like SUBWAY®, Colgate-Palmolive, and Baskin-Robbins. We started looking "outside the B2B box" and wondered why B2B companies introduced new products using relatively dull launch ideas. Where was it written that we couldn't employ consumer tactics for B2B clients? After all, everyone is a consumer and in our experience, most respond favorably to sound strategies, clever ideas and flawless execution.

Concurrent with the B2B executives asking about consumer techniques, B2C companies started taking a page out of the B2B playbook. Realizing the growing importance of influencers and early adopters, consumer companies began using product seeding programs and outreach to key influencers. They also began seeking awards to add credibility to their new products and launch campaigns as well as beta testing to be sure consumers liked the products before they were officially launched to a broad audience.

This blurring of the lines between B2B and B2C launch tactics opens up the opportunity for marketers to test all kinds of innovative launch methods. Of course, these new methods can come with a steep learning curve. By all means, explore new tactics for your industry but don't go overboard. Trying to master one or two new tactics at a time is probably a better approach than trying to totally revise all aspects of your launch approach in one fell swoop. There's no question that studying B2C launch strategies will lead to a host of new discoveries that can bring B2B marketers full circle to a B2E approach.

The Shifting FMOT

Many will tell you the holy grail of consumer packaged goods marketing is based in Cincinnati. For decades, The Procter & Gamble Company has been known for leading the charge in innovative, consumer-facing marketing. From inventing the "soap opera" in the 1930s to support its soap brands to creating the Tremor network in 2001 designed to understand the dynamics of word-of-

mouth marketing, P&G has consistently led the consumer products pack when it comes to effective consumer marketing. Former CEO A.G. Lafley is known for his insistence on always remembering the "First Moment of Truth" for P&G brands when developing programs. That FMOT is the three to seven seconds companies have when a mom is standing at the supermarket shelf to entice her to choose your product. The "Second Moment of Truth" is when she gets that product home and uses it. But the FMOT has always been seen as the absolutely crucial time for companies to assert brand dominance.

We realized that the FMOT had moved out of the store and into the home when we listened to a panel of several well-known "mommy bloggers" speak at an IRI Summit in Las Vegas about what influences them to try and buy new products. Moms like these represent over 80 percent of household purchases—an incredibly large and powerful number.

Do you know where she is finding out about new products and services? Do you know where she is spending the majority of her time? At home,

on her computer. She is on Facebook; she is tweeting on Twitter and uploading photos to Tumblr. She is creating bookmarks for things she likes on Digg or Delicious and sharing them with her network of thousands of other moms.

Thus, the "First Moment of Truth" is no longer at retail…it's at home! Marketers need to realize this change in FMOT and begin using social media strategies and tactics to reach Mom at home, where she lives, shops and interacts with other moms online.

Tens of thousands of other moms— and dads—religiously follow what these influential moms have to say on their blogs. Walmart realized the power of these bloggers when it created "Elevenmoms," a group of 11 influential mommy bloggers who visited corporate headquarters to learn about Walmart and its products. They were then asked to create content, including information on how to save money, to be posted on a YouTube brand channel. By December 2008, the group had grown to 21, including a green-focused mom and its first Canadian member. Now other companies have joined in this trend, ranging from McDonald's, which has launched "Moms' Quality Correspondents" who report on their visits behind the scenes at McDonald's outlets and events—to Hanes, whose "Comfort Crew" includes not just moms but other bloggers who write about parenting, fashion and lifestyle outlets.

Is there a silver bullet for reaching consumers at this FMOT when launching new products? While there is no one tactic that functions as a silver bullet, there are several rounds of powerful ammunition you can use in reaching moms online and at home. In Chapter 3, we'll talk about Immersion Marketing™ and the importance of surrounding your target consumer with messages that, over time, will reach him or her at different times and places.

Retailers Cope with Fundamental Changes in How People Shop

Economists today are predicting that the effects of the worst economic downturn in decades are likely to linger for as long as five to seven years, which is devastating news for a retail sector that has already experienced considerable consolidation with the prospect of more to come.

Retailers are trying to cope with relearning how people shop, according to Thom Blischok, IRI's president of consulting and innovation. "We are in a transformation in which the new normal is a conservative shopper," he said. "This is an economic transformation that will last between four to eight years and the new normal coming out of this timeframe will be centered on less use of credit and more living within one's means, looking hard at how to save differently. We may see the re-emergence back to the 1950s when people selectively chose to buy things they could afford."

"We've seen a lot of consumers, even well-off consumers, rethink their buying habits," said Joan Holleran, director of research at Mintel. "They're shopping at Walmart. But Walmart still caters to its core paycheck-to-paycheck consumers, while at the same time appealing to higher-end consumers with products like electronics."

Blischok reports that the average shopper today shops five stores and is looking for deals. "The new sport in America," he said, "is shopper hunting. We're going to go find where we can make the dollar stretch the best. We start with the Sunday morning papers and we decide the three stores where we're going to buy. Fundamentally, the decisions regarding meals for this week are made at home before they [we] go to the store." (Again, this is another powerful indication the FMOT has moved from store to home.)

"You only get one chance to be 'new' on the market so making any corrections to the product needs to be done as soon as possible," added Char Partelow, senior vice president, Consumer and Shopper Insights

Group at IRI. "By talking to consumers through new 'trier surveys' [triers are consumers who have tried the product once], we can help manufacturers understand how consumer perceptions of a new product differ among known products or 'trier-repeaters' versus 'trier-non-repeaters.' We can identify the product's strengths and weaknesses and take appropriate action to position the product for a positive launch," she said.

How are retailers coping with this changing shopper behavior and these new economic realities? They are leveraging their power to demand more from manufacturers in terms of the deals they can pass through to customers. And—in a move of great interest to anyone who is marketing a new product—major retailers are adopting a "less is more" mentality, cutting back on variety and offering bargain-hunting consumers a simplified, less confusing and more affordable shopping experience.

As reported in *The Wall Street Journal*, retailers who thought variety was the spice of life when consumer dollars were flowing freely now "are cleaning up the clutter. They are trying to cater to budget-conscious shoppers who want to simplify shopping trips and stick to familiar products. Retailers have found that eliminating certain products can lift sales and profits."[3]

As *The Wall Street Journal* also points out, loyalty card databases are helping retailers decide what consumers really want; with fewer products to stock, they hope to lower labor costs and increase their leverage to drive deals with manufacturers. The overall goal is to drive more sales per store rather than adding new stores, the strategy that drove growth during boom times but doesn't work in the tightened economy.[4]

Retailers are also responding to the high levels of consumer price consciousness by devoting more space to private label brands. This trend was already moving forward before the recession and has gained momentum since, as retailers try to wring out every penny of margin. And research shows that the trend is unlikely to abate any time soon. According to the NPD Group, a leading market research firm, 97 percent of all households consume private label food on a regular basis. A 2009 consumer survey conducted for the Private Label Manufacturers Association found that 91 percent of U.S. shoppers said they will continue to purchase store brand products as the economy recovers.[5]

The implications here are huge for those launching a new product. When both retailers and consumers are going for the tried and true, how do you interest both of these critical audiences in your new flavor or widget?

In this environment, you have less time to gain consumer attention and prove the value of your new product—that is, if you can convince retailers to take it on in the first place. Retailer expectations—and therefore the performance obligations they are building into slotting fees and promotional agreements—are getting even tougher.

Another factor not to be overlooked is that retailers are cleaning out the clutter by mandating "clean store" rules that prohibit signage and promotional information, thus making it more challenging to sell a new product. In addition, they are devoting more shelf space to house brands that provide higher margins.

Clearly, this gives new product launchers a lot to think about in terms of introductory strategies. Are line extensions really the way to go in this environment? Possibly not. Should more time be spent in research and development (R&D) to create and test new product concepts? Should manufacturers do consumer insight testing to learn what products are really needed and would be welcomed by consumers? Absolutely. Should marketers develop innovative ways to work in closer partnership with retailers who counter their new "less is more" focus? And should you explore other modes of distribution such as the Internet, just in case you run into a brick wall at brick-and-mortar outlets? Definitely.

In 2009, 93% of respondents could not name one new product launch from a list of 50

The Slow Death of Traditional Media

You know things are going badly for traditional media when someone on Twitter using the handle "themediaisdying" is able to report almost daily to 20,000-plus followers that yet another newspaper or magazine has shut its doors. It is ironic that this bad news is being delivered via the instrument that is causing so many publishing death knells—the Internet, which is rapidly becoming the dominant news source.

At the end of 2008, a survey done by the Pew Research Center for the People & the Press found—for the first time ever—that more people (40 percent) got most of their international and national news from the Internet than from newspapers (35 percent). While TV still led the pack, with 70 percent overall, it was losing ground among the key younger demographic, with the Internet now rivaling TV as a main source of national and international news for Americans under age 30. Fifty percent of the younger generation said they get most of their national and international news online, while an equal number of that demographic said they rely on TV for international and national news.[6]

As a result of the failure of daily newspapers to find a business model that replaces the ad revenues lost to the Internet, the future of major dailies across the nation is in doubt. And one only has to sign on to Twitter or Facebook when there is major news breaking anywhere around the world to understand the popularity of the Internet as a news vehicle. Every day the value of social media sites as a news medium is being acknowledged by cable news channels as they regularly follow Twitter and Facebook chatter to add color and immediacy to their own news coverage.

So where does all this leave you, the marketer who is trying to secure news coverage for your new product? Clearly, landing a feature article in a major daily is not as valuable as it once was because the circulation and reach of even the most powerful newspapers is declining.

And if your product is geared to the under-30 crowd, even a placement on one of the network morning news shows probably won't generate the buzz among your target demographic that it used to engender.

Marketers need to understand and be on top of social media because even if you are interested in attracting an older demographic, you need to know that it, too, is migrating to the Web. The fastest-growing segment of Facebook users, according to Nielsen Online, is people aged 35 to 49.[7] Worldwide, almost a quarter of Facebook users are over 50 years of age.[8]

The same is true for Twitter, which is most popular among working adults. According to Nielsen data, people ages 35 to 49 represented the highest percentage of tweeters, with 41.7 percent in February 2009. When you include people ages 55-plus, you have 65.1 percent of Twitter users.[9] Of course, it's important to note that some of these older adults are merely dipping their toes in the social media waters in comparison to those in younger age groups who have made social media an important part of their lifestyles. Again according to Nielsen, adults with multiple social networking profiles are approximately 2.5 times more likely than average to be in the 18-20 age group and to be students. As social media fans, they are nearly three times more likely than average to publish or own a blog and more than twice as likely to visit online dating sites and other blogs.[10]

New media relations strategies that assure your story gets seen on top news sites require an in-depth understanding of how to leverage the amazing power of social media. But don't get too comfortable with Web 2.0 because just as soon as you understand how to communicate within this new normal, the media playing field will shift again as we welcome the arrival of Web 3.0.

Where Things Are Headed

To the many marketers who have not yet figured out how to embrace Web 2.0, thinking about the coming of Web 3.0 will probably induce  instant anxiety. Experts don't agree on exactly what it is that will constitute Web 3.0. Some define it as the ubiquity of the Web in all aspects of our daily lives through the increased popularity of mobile Internet devices and the merger of entertainment systems and the Web. Some believe it will be the so-called Semantic Web, a term coined by Tim Berners-Lee, inventor of the World Wide Web. The Semantic Web is a place where computers can read Web pages as humans do, only they'll do a better job of finding what we're looking for because they will eliminate the human element that now drives search engine results.

Whatever Web 3.0 emerges as down the road, prognosticators agree it will probably take about the same amount of time to evolve as Web 1.0 took to get to Web 2.0. This means we'll be seeing Web 3.0 around the year 2015. But it's not too early to start evaluating developments in this area…along with all other innovations that will drive the evolution of the Internet, the most remarkable marketing tool known to man.

Let's Get Started!

As this quick wrap-up of major trends illustrates, launching a new product or service continues to be a challenge that will not get easier over time. Our hope is that by considering our 152 tips, tactics and trends, you'll be able to craft a new product launch that is highly effective and uses a blend of tried-and-true, and brand new tactics to help propel your new product into the marketplace and sustain it over time.

CHAPTER 2:

The New Launch Plan

Let's make sure we are all on the same page when we talk about launch. Our definition, which was first unveiled in *New Product Launch: 10 Proven Strategies*, states:

> **launch** [lawnch, lahnch] - verb (used with ideas)
> Launch is the creation and implementation of a powerful, multidisciplinary process that successfully propels a new product into the marketplace...**and sustains it over time.**

The important words here are "sustains it over time." Launch is not just the introductory period. It's all the initiatives from the launch onward that impact the success of a product. If you're not supporting your launch beyond the introductory period, there's a good chance your product will not be on the market next year. Also notice the word *propel*. That means actively doing things to get your product noticed.

amazon.com

Now that we've agreed on the definition of launch, you're no doubt hoping your new product flies off the shelf. But retail is just one channel to use to market your product. Distribution channels abound, including selling on the Web (think Amazon.com, iTunes and eBay), via direct mail, through infomercials or direct-to-consumer television ads and on mobile devices.

Eight Legendary Launch Types

We've identified eight approaches companies take to launch new products. Only one usually has a happy ending.

1. Do Nothing Launch – This launch assumes "If you build it, they **will** come." That may have been true in the past, but with today's accelerated product innovation rate, the complex, fragmented media environment, and changing U.S. demographics—to name just a few factors that complicate launch—you need a comprehensive and targeted launch plan to get your products into the minds, hearts and hands of consumers. Just sending a press release will not work. If you think that's all you need to do, you are dreaming.

2. Launch on a Shoestring – How many companies spend millions on developing a new product and allow $5,000 for marketing? Before you laugh, you should know that a few years ago we met with a huge, multinational company with that exact policy in place! Needless to say, bigger spending improves launch success. A multilayered campaign that drives consumer awareness requires an adequate budget. Sure, you have to spend smart and make sure you are getting the biggest bang possible for each buck. But you have to develop a workable budget that covers your key initiatives—and finding out campaign costs requires advance planning.

3. Launch on a Wing and a Prayer – This describes a low-budget, last-minute launch where hope replaces a solid marketing plan. You'd better light candles and get out the prayer rug for this type of launch because you'll truly need divine intervention to succeed. Sadly, this type of launch occurs far more frequently than you would think. Sometimes companies get so caught up in the product development phase they fail to start planning the launch on time. And if there have been snags in the product development, they may have used up more resources than originally intended and left far fewer financial resources to devote to launch. So the company is hit with a double whammy—no plan or budget. There's no worse position to be in than as a product manager with a "zero budget" to launch one of the company's most important new products. Time to look for a new job where they allocate budgets. Or hire really creative agencies that use cost-effective social media strategies.

4. The Dribble Launch – Sometimes management is not convinced the product is a winner and they are only willing to test the waters. A small budget is allocated to market the product and surprisingly, the product starts to sell. More funds are allocated, and so on. These orphan products, which usually include only a few SKUs and have little marketing support or funding, "could have been contenders" but lacked the planned marketing investment and initiatives, hindering their long-term success. If only the company had allocated a reasonable sum of money in the beginning, these products could have become raging successes.

5. The Rocket Launch – The product is a winner, you have a launch plan, and you hit the market hard with advertising, public relations, social media—the works. The launch is successful, sales go up and all is well, except that the minute the "introductory" campaign concludes, no other support is provided and that meteoric sales rise is followed by a catastrophic fall. Launching a new product is not a short-term project—if you want that rocket to stay aloft, you need to continuously fuel the marketing fires.

6. Launch and Retreat – A certain dollar amount is attached to the launch plan during a trial period. The launch takes place and the buzz around the product is good, but less than expected. When expectation exceeds realization, doubt creeps in. The aggressive goals set during the planning phase are not being met, so management decides to pull back on supporting the product. This strategy is sad because a reasonably good product was abandoned that could have succeeded with more time and marketing support. Products that require education take longer to catch on. If you are launching a product in a new category or one that is revolutionary, remind management that consumers need time to learn about and understand the product, and this time should be built into the launch timetable and budget.

7. Languishing Launch – This launch involves products that have been introduced and are doing okay, but not well enough to warrant more marketing support nor poorly enough to be taken off the shelf or removed from the product catalog. Why pull the product if it is still bringing in sales or it hasn't been kicked off the shelf by retailers? On the flip side, why not introduce a new product in your lineup that has the possibility for greater sales and does not take up valuable shelf space as a non-performing asset?

8. Launch and Perfect the Course – This is the type of launch we strive to create. Even the best launches can be "tuned up" to be great launches. By learning as you go, you can maximize what's working and stop those activities that are not producing results. (Later in the book we will talk about how to recalibrate your launch using tactics like before-and-after action reviews.) There are numerous things you can do before and after launch to improve product sales performance beyond the introductory period. A launch is a living, breathing, organic thing. The media are changing every day; Facebook, YouTube and Twitter change instantaneously. Today's marketers have to be vigilant 24/7 to be sure they are finding new ways to perfect their launch course.

While the types of launches we've described seem tongue in cheek, they are not far from what actually happens in many companies. Our goal in writing this book is to give marketers a context and framework to use when launching new products to avoid launch disasters.

Rethinking the Launch Stage-Gate® Model

Every launch is unique—not just because the products are different, but because the strategy, timing, audience and environment into which they are being launched are constantly changing. There is truly no "one size fits all" when it comes to developing launch plans. Creating a launch plan requires discipline and a systematic approach to ensure all bases and contingencies are covered.

Over time, launching new products has become even more complex while the time to develop them has become more compressed. While it used to take a year to develop a new product, now it can take less than three months from idea to finished product. If you are outsourcing part of the product development process, it may take even less time to create a product and present it to retailers using dummy packaging, sample product and mocked-up marketing materials.

This accelerated timing also affects launch planning. Today the marketing and R&D teams think about a new idea and before you know it, the product is being manufactured. That means launch plans need to be developed quickly to react to this reality of "idea to shelf" in 90 days. The launch team and consultants need to stay close to the development team to understand what is in the pipeline and when the products are expected to launch—and then be ready to turn on a dime to develop a creative launch plan that can be implemented quickly and effectively.

You may have heard of Dr. Robert G. Cooper, the father of the Stage-Gate® model, who developed the methodology used by major consumer product manufacturing companies around the world to develop and bring new products to market. Dr. Cooper's last gate within his model is "launch" and within that gate he includes manufacturing. In *New Product Launch: 10 Proven Strategies*, we suggested that marketers using the Stage-Gate model should separate the manufacturing phase from the launch phase because the launch process is so critical that it deserves its own gate.

Since we first recommended giving launch its own phase, the launch process has become even more complex. Launching a new product is similar to assembling a highly complicated jigsaw puzzle. All the pieces of the puzzle must fit together for the new product to succeed. One large piece of that puzzle is the launch itself—and within that puzzle piece are a number of initiatives (which we are calling phases) that must be thought through and planned for to ensure launch success. And within the major puzzle pieces are lots of tasks that need to be accomplished to ensure that particular phase is successful. The more multidimensional the launch, the more important it becomes to have a sophisticated marketing campaign to reach the myriad targeted audiences that are often disparate in nature.

Basic Phases of the Launch Stage-Gate

Here are the phases of the Launch Stage-Gate:

Phase I: Pre-Launch or Validation Phase

In the Pre-Launch, often called the Validation Phase, you build the business case for creating a comprehensive launch campaign. This includes doing the detailed homework and upfront investigation leading to how you plan to launch the product, the business justification for launching the product in a specific manner, and creating a detailed plan of action for the next phases.

Tasks that need to be accomplished in the Pre-Launch Phase include surveying market conditions; creating the launch plan; investigating, confirming, testing and validating the data about the product's efficacy; honing the messaging; developing the public relations, advertising, promotional and social media campaigns; securing the spokespeople and identifying the influencers. In addition, the Web site architecture and copy are created and approved, and construction of the Web site begins to ensure it is completed in time for Soft Launch, the next phase. Planning for distribution and channel management should be discussed, and a sales plan that corresponds with the launch plan should be developed.

Phase II: Soft Launch

In this phase, tasks might include finalizing the media message guide and press materials, confirming launch event details, engaging influencers, securing an experienced media trainer to teach spokespeople how to handle media interviews, and creating a crisis plan. During this phase, another final round of consumer research can take place to test package design, campaign concepts and taglines.

During the Soft Launch Phase, the public relations team identifies the traditional and social media outlets that will break the story, and begins talking with these key media targets. The ad agency finalizes the ads and media plan, the promotional campaign is solidified, and the Web site is made ready for a test run.

This phase often includes educating the sales force so they can begin "selling-in the product" and hosting an employee event to launch the product to the internal audience. In some industries, trade media relations are conducted to build demand for the product and to help the sales force convince buyers to stock the product. Measurement parameters for the campaign are finalized so all parties are clear on what they need to deliver to make the launch a success.

In a sense, the Soft Launch Phase is where the overall launch strategy is teased out into detailed, tactical plans with each component of the launch effort mapped out. Dedicating enough time to carefully plan a launch strategy is critical to success.

Phase III: Launch

The Launch Phase is when everyone's hard work comes together as all launch tactics are deployed. Most launch campaigns typically start with the public relations team breaking the news about the new product, and often include a launch event. In conjunction with the launch, or shortly before the public relations campaign breaks, the Web site is unveiled and social media outreach begins. In addition, media relations efforts start driving consumers to the Web site for more information and to buy the product.

Concurrent with the launch, advertising and promotional activities begin to capitalize on the exposure generated by public relations. We've found that leading with public relations is far more effective in building early recognition and credibility than leading with advertising. That being said, the advertising should be ready to go once the major publications cover the story to keep the news fresh in the minds of consumers. If you are planning to use direct television or infomercials, these should be produced and ready to run once the launch publicity breaks.

Public relations should lead the charge with other marketing disciplines following closely, according to Dany Sfeir, principal, DS & Associates. "Everything has to be preceded by PR; it has to pave the way for advertising to work."

It's vital to carefully evaluate the optimum timeframe for executing the various launch plan components. One of the most common and biggest mistakes companies make is not starting launch activities early enough, and then cutting off marketing efforts too soon once the product hits store shelves. This approach does not provide enough time for launch messages to break through the clutter and reach target consumers. In addition, short campaigns allow no opportunity for tweaking strategies and messages if things do not go as planned. Remember, even though you've been working on the launch for six months to a year, consumers are just beginning to learn about your new product. Keep in mind that the launch period is not a moment in time; it is a process that takes several months. So make sure you execute all the details in the launch plan before moving on to other tactics.

"Once we educate consumers via PR in the media, longer-form media tactics like infomercials allow us to talk about the product, the industry, the needs of consumers, the features and benefits of the product, the problem and solution offered as well as testimonials from relevant consumers. While public relations educates, using an infomercial provides more time to both inform the consumer and sell the product," said Sfeir. Results during the Launch Phase can be measured in many ways:

- How many units are to be sold?
- How many hits to the Web site are expected?
- How many presentations should be given to retailers?
- Which retailers are key for sell-in?
- How many editors are to be contacted?
- Which media will drive sales?
- How many media impressions are required?
- What conversion rate should we expect from the Web and ads that translate to sales?
- What messages should be included in the launch stories?
- Which influencers are important to driving product sales and were they secured?
- Was the launch event a success? What are the criteria to determine if it was successful?

These questions are followed up on in the Post-Launch Phase, and even more questions are posed.

Phase IV: Post-Launch or Planning for Continued Success

While the Launch Phase is critical, so is the Post-Launch Phase. Even if your launch event and coverage were first-rate and your advertising is sending people to the Web for more information, and people are buying the product through various channels – if you don't continue the momentum in the Post-Launch Phase, you're in for problems, long term.

What are you doing to place additional news and feature stories after launch? How are you supporting sales? Are you selling at retail? On the Internet? Through direct television or infomercials? What are you doing to help these channels market your product? Is a new version of the product going to be introduced? How does this fit into the marketing strategy? Is the pricing strategy flexible? During this phase, social media can be helpful in keeping the buzz going. What is your ongoing social media strategy?

Mobile marketing or special events can also bring your product directly to consumers. What's planned in those areas? It's important to plan, staff and fund the Post-Launch Phase to ensure your product's ultimate success.

Over the past 8 years, Coca-Cola had the highest number of MMNPL Top 10 Launches

In the Post-Launch Phase, close evaluation of the campaign is in order before you make major decisions about the product's future. You must consider how you fared versus what you projected. What did you learn that you can use to recalibrate the campaign? A tough Post-Launch Review instills accountability for results, and at the same time, fosters a culture of continuous improvement. The performance metrics you put in place early on now come fully into play as you measure how well a specific new product performed, establish team accountability for results, and build in learning and improvement that assures the team is focused on tuning up the campaign to make it more effective, or deciding the product is not performing up to expectations and may not warrant further investment.

New Sub-Phases to Consider

Depending on the nature of your new product, we have identified several sub-phases that can extend your story beyond the initial burst of publicity. These sub-phases highlight key opportunities to reach consumers throughout the year and should be included in many—if not all—consumer launch plans. Considering each sub-phase as a separate effort assures that these important sales and media hooks will not be overlooked.

Holidays and Seasons

If the new product is a gift item (Christmas, Mother's Day, Father's Day), the launch plan must include strategies that position the product for these key selling periods. Is there a specific time of year when this product is particularly relevant? If it's a diet product, the December/January New Year's resolution timeframe is critical. Is there a specific time of year when awards are given in your industry and you need to either influence the judges or promote your product to be sure it's in contention for recognition?

Events and Specially Designated Milestones

Often, events can drive the launch plan. If you're a sneaker company, you definitely want to have a strategy to reach runners prior to and at major marathons in the spring and fall. If you are launching a consumer electronics product, you need a plan around the Consumer Electronics Show. Has a special month, week or day been designated to educate people about an issue your new product addresses? If it's a green product, of course Earth Day is a major milestone in the environmental products arena. Milestone dates are often pivotal in drawing attention to a new product, so you'll need a strategy to link your product to these special periods.

Awards

Annual awards programs in your industry or product category offer one more opportunity for garnering attention. Entering such competitions requires lots of advance planning and considerable time and effort to complete often-complicated nomination entries, but the payoff in terms of publicity can be significant. Build awards into your launch plan so you're on top of these potential bonanzas.

You get the picture. These types of specialized launch "buckets" need to be added to your basic plan to ensure you've covered all the bases.

The Planning Process

Talk about a daunting task—developing a launch plan and budget. Taking your launch timeline and transforming it into a comprehensive launch plan requires creativity and fortitude. We are often asked, "What's the best way to start crafting the plan?" Our advice is to begin with the basics and then fill in the blanks as you go along.

The goal is to use what you know as the foundation and then build from that point. Sure, there are many unknown variables, but there are many things you do know and we suggest you start with those. Here are 10 key steps to the launch planning process:

1. Developing a Strategy Statement

You can't write a plan without stating a marketing strategy. We suggest your strategy be a one-liner that begins with a verb. Think about using action words like "To launch" or "To introduce" to begin the strategy line. This is an overall statement about what you are trying to achieve in broad terms. Under each launch phase, you will summarize specific goals you are trying to achieve, so don't make yourself crazy trying to outline everything in this one statement.

Here's a very basic example:

Strategy: To launch a multilayered public relations and marketing program for Product X that results in increased sales through building visibility and awareness in key markets.

Your strategy statement is your touchstone for planning. It is used as the starting point for the next step: ideation sessions in which you develop key ideas for your launch campaign.

2. Hosting an Idea Camp^{SM}

We are firm believers that the best ideas come from assembling a group of creative, smart, interesting people from within and outside the organization. Invite the "best" account people from your creative agencies, plus a

few "ringers" or smart people or consumers who could ultimately buy the product, are the right demographic and psychographic, and have a need for what you are selling. You don't have to be a mom to suggest ideas about a new diaper, but it sure helps. Everyone loves ice cream, but if you are launching new kids' flavors, it's best to have kids and moms in your ideation session. If you are launching a flower show, it helps to tap people who love to garden and who are in the landscaping business.

Brainstorms are a great way to generate ideas–particularly big ideas that are not the usual fare. Having a group of diverse people come together to ideate makes the most sense because if you've selected the participants carefully, your group will include people from all walks of life who are creative and can think out of the box. The ideas will be fresh and, in this environment, fresh is required to not only attract consumer attention but to lure the media to cover your events.

One of our Idea Camp facilitators always said, "While all ideas are welcome, not all ideas are good ones." The goal is to write hundreds of ideas on the board and then to select the ideas the group has enthusiasm for exploring further and that make sense for the brand. Once we've filled the room with ideas, we "dot vote." Each person is given a certain number of colored dots to vote within the following categories. A green dot signals "just do it," which means the idea makes sense for the product and should be implemented no matter what. Yellow dots indicate an "interesting idea" that needs more exploration, and the last category, marked by red dots, is a "big idea" that warrants additional exploration and research to see if it is feasible. The group then continues to ideate around the interesting ideas and the big ideas to determine which ones are "winners" and should lead and/or be included in the launch campaign.

By deputizing the brand manager or other launch leader as the "client," you ensure that he or she ultimately decides on the direction for the campaign based on the ideas generated in the room. Of course, a smart launch leader will select ideas that the group has generated energy around executing. These ideas may be a little out of the brand manager's general comfort zone, as innovative ideas are often a little left or right of center and have an edge that will make the launch newsworthy. We've found that ideas tend to cluster (meaning good ideas beget other ideas that support a big idea and often a general theme).

By identifying the broad theme of the campaign, as well as the tactical ideas that support the theme, the launch leader shapes the overarching concept that will guide the work of the various disciplines involved in the launch. Ideas that have "legs" and can be extended across disciplines are the types of launch concepts that should be pursued.

At the end of the session, participants decide on five to 10 "just do its," three to five "ideas to explore" and one or two "big ideas" that could bring attention to the product, brand and launch in a major way. Before the day is over, a series of Next Steps are articulated so that everyone leaves the room with marching orders on how to make these ideas come to life. These concepts will become the bedrock of the launch plan, because if you've been successful in your ideation, you will have a "big idea" to kick off the launch, other ideas to support the launch idea, and a series of initiatives that will bring attention to the brand over time and with key audiences.

3. Developing a Budget

The good news about developing a comprehensive launch plan is that it gives you a road map for creating a comprehensive budget. Since each phase has a detailed plan, it is easy to develop a detailed budget by attaching a line item fee and expense cost to each initiative.

It's always the old chicken-and-egg story when it comes to launch budgets. When agencies ask clients how much money is budgeted for a particular launch, the response we often get is, "How much money is required for the launch?" Having a written integrated launch plan enables management and its creative agencies to develop a budget that speaks directly to the plan. Each plan element can be budgeted separately so a total number for launch can be tallied. Or a total sum can be established by management and then each launch phase or discipline is allocated a certain sum to create and execute a launch plan.

"We look at the new product launch investment as it compares to a number of organic growth options," explained Michael Guggenheimer, vice president of business development at Radiator Specialty Company. "Even though the budget may be perceived as an incremental investment in growth, at the end of the day, it has to fold back into the core business. It has to have an ROI [return on investment], so that after the investment phase, the launch has a cost structure that fits into the business. In terms of retail product, we look at what kind of distribution change is possible," he said.

"What kind of product turns might we see as an increase at major customers? Since the campaign is targeted at certain channels, are we expecting a sales lift from behavioral changes at certain accounts? Depending on the customers and the probabilities we see in increasing sales through that channel, is the outcome we are projecting realistic? It's a big math problem. It is still not precise. It is putting numbers to your own view and developing frameworks that allow people to have a conversation based on facts," he continued.

No matter how the budget is developed, the key factor is to establish a dedicated amount that is earmarked to fund a comprehensive launch campaign. The goal is for that amount to be totally dedicated to launching a particular product and not subject to being re-allocated for other programs. If the new product does well, the temptation is to pull back funding from additional phases since it is selling well. The result may be the Rocket Launch that we described earlier. On the flip side, if the product isn't selling, the question often arises, "Should we continue to fund the program?" This is the Launch and Retreat scenario that we discussed. Whichever situation arises, it is important to continue marketing as it sometimes takes a while to tweak the program to find the right message and method that attracts the target consumer.

4. Setting Milestone Dates

Within each phase, specific dates must be set to drive decisions about the launch. These dates may change, but the discipline of putting a date by each launch phase will ensure your planning is doable. We realize that people don't like to commit to dates, but when you are planning a launch, each phase builds on the other so if you miss one date, it often means you are going to miss a number of dates. Having dates by each phase forces the launch team to be realistic about what is humanly possible to accomplish in a specified amount of time.

5. Establishing Goals

Each launch phase needs its own goals. Why? Because each phase has to produce certain information for other phases to proceed. As an example, in the Pre-Launch or Validation Phase, you'll need to determine your key messages and elevator pitch—because if you don't know how to describe your new product, how are you going to market it? If you are struggling with defining your product, its category and the messaging—you may not be as far along as you think in terms of being able to launch the product quickly.

The temptation is to articulate a number of goals under each phase; our advice is to keep it to five goals per section. If you can achieve those, you'll be off to a good start.

6. Identifying Your Target Markets

Every new product has a number of target markets, whether it be the "trade" into which you are selling through retailers, wholesalers or distributors; influencers who need to know about your product so they can either recommend it, endorse it, or at least be aware of it; consumers, who are actually buying your product; and the media (which includes social media) that you hope will write about your product. Defining your audiences is incredibly important because if you don't know your target markets, you can't plan launch components to reach them.

7. Developing a Strategy for Each Audience

Once you've identified the audiences, you should create a clearly defined battle plan of how you are going to reach, educate and inform each audience about the product and determine what is going to motivate them to buy now. Different audiences will require different strategies to mobilize them to try and buy your new product. Take the time to articulate exactly what is required for each audience to have enough information, validation and motivation to purchase the product.

Burt Helm, editor of *BusinessWeek* magazine's "Best Global Brands" issue, offers sage advice for brand managers. "What's interesting is the clever way you are reaching the consumer and the keen insight you have in understanding the customer, who they are, what they like, and in what clever way you are utilizing that knowledge," he said. "If it taps into a bigger trend, that's even better. Products that launch during recessions have to be good products and you have to be smart about how they fit the sentiment of the times."

Many products will have a multitude of audiences. If it is a consumer health product, you'll have to educate medical industry influencers and physicians who are often quoted in the news about the topic your product addresses, or place papers or articles about the disease or condition in influential publications. Since many health products cross over into technology, you'll need to educate the technology editors and tech industry influencers, who may be asked about your product by others, or who may write reviews or cover new products in this category. And of course, you'll need a consumer strategy to educate consumers and the media about your product and its benefits.

8. Creating Messaging for the Product and Specific Audiences

Finding the right messages is a challenging task. By and large, today's consumers are a cynical lot. They've heard and seen it all before. They are also leading ridiculously busy lives in which they are bombarded by marketing messages no matter where they are or what they are doing. No wonder the percentage of consumers who can recall even one new product launched during the year keeps plummeting.

In some circles, "messages" have gotten a bad rap in the past few years. Especially in politics, a candidate who is staying "on message" can be seen as avoiding the truth, being overly cautious or just plain ignoring the questions a reporter wants answered. As a result, some spokespeople who are introducing your product may shy away from delivering a pre-identified series of messages, thinking that they too might be seen as devious, unresponsive or just plain uninformed.

Nothing could be further from the truth. Creating key messages is the bedrock of crafting a consumer product launch campaign. It is the basis of the communications to all your audiences: internal, the media, and anyone and everyone who might want to buy or write about your innovative new product. In a launch situation, messages should form the framework of everything that is said about your product. Put another way, they are a spokesperson's best friend.

Because developing the right messaging is so important, we've devoted the whole of Chapter 6 to this topic.

9. Developing a Crisis Plan

The last thing a manufacturer wants to do when launching a new product is to develop a crisis plan. We acknowledge that thinking about all the bad things that could possibly happen is not where the launch team wants to spend its energy. Yet, it is crucial for the entire team to sit in a room and ask, "What problems could result from this launch?" For example:

- What if the product doesn't work?
- Could a child get into the product and choke on a component?

- What if an advocacy group (environmental, child safety, animal rights, and so forth) singles out the product for attack?
- Could a recall of a similar product tarnish the reputation of all products in the category?
- Have we labeled the product properly or could we be open to action by the Food and Drug Administration?
- Is the price point too high?
- What if a competing and very similar product is launched at the same time, and creates category confusion in the consumer's mind?
- What if we get panned by the critics?
- What will we do if someone online starts making negative comments?

These questions and scores of others directly related to your product need to be asked prior to launch to be sure you have all your bases covered. For every problem that comes up during the internal "what if" scenario discussion, a solution and/or answer to the question must be developed. That way if a negative situation arises, you'll already have considered a solution so it can be resolved quickly.

10. Establishing Measurable Results

Determining what constitutes results is where the art and science of launching new products intersect. What are the desired actions and reactions for each phase? How will you measure success? What is a home run for each phase? What are the desired outcomes for the entire campaign? How will each phase and consultant on the marketing team be held accountable for their results? How will you tally where sales are coming from and why?

"In CPG, it is important to set targets that measure consumer interest and acceptance. This can be done by measuring trial/household penetration and repeat rates. Volume is determined by how many people are buying the product (trial) and how many accept it (repeat purchase). Based on the trial and repeat targets set for the new product, we can forecast volume," said Char Partelow, senior vice president, Consumer and Shopper Insights Group at IRI, who has evaluated hundreds of new product launches. "Drivers of trial are availability (distribution), price, and efforts to raise awareness and interest such as coupons, trial packs, in-store sampling, media, and cross promotions," she said. "Drivers of repeat are product quality, pack size, price, and efforts to 'remind' consumers about the product such as displays, coupons, and media. By looking at products that have been successfully launched in the category previously, we can create benchmarks and help set realistic goals."

It is critical to pore over each phase and decide what success looks like prior to beginning the launch. We'll go into this important topic in more depth when we discuss measurement in Chapter 11.

CHAPTER 3:

Launch Basics: What You Need to Do Every Time

While the strategies and tactics used for each new product launch vary according to the nature of the product, the target audience, trends in the media, retail distribution and consumer lifestyles, certain bedrock principles are required for planning and executing every new product launch. Following these launch basics will put you on the path toward success. Ignoring them will put your launch in peril, no matter how exciting or innovative your new product or service may be.

TIP 1 Assign someone who is strategic and creative to lead the launch team.

Brand or product managers make the best launch team leaders. These are people who are passionate about the product and have a single-minded focus to make it successful.

Unlike people higher up in the corporate food chain, brand or product managers are focused on the task at hand. Good brand and product managers live the product every day and know how to get things done. They also are more apt to have the requisite marketing expertise required to lead a launch, something CEOs and presidents often lack. If you're a company leader and you think that you should lead the launch team, think again. There is too much riding on the outcome not to put someone in charge who can live, eat and breathe the launch.

Our only caveat is to involve the CEO along the way in planning, as there is nothing worse than presenting a finalized launch plan the CEO doesn't like and won't support because he or she was not part of the process. In our experience, involving the CEO in key planning meetings creates the alignment necessary to ensure the launch plan is enthusiastically received.

Also, avoid putting someone in charge of the launch team who is driven solely by sales figures. Launch is an art and a science. Numbers alone don't always tell the whole story about what is happening during a launch. Someone interested only in sales figures may be apt to pull the plug too early on a launch if sales targets aren't being met. You have to be able to look behind the sales numbers to really know what's going on.

Look for a launch team leader who is skilled at:

- Bringing people together from various marketing disciplines to produce an integrated campaign.
- Communicating and reinforcing launch strategies and product messages so team members are consistent throughout the planning and implementation process.
- Fostering innovation in launch strategies and tactics.
- Generating enthusiasm, confidence and a can-do team spirit that will be required at critical moments.

TIP 2 Employ a multidisciplinary launch strategy to overcome media noise, shortened attention spans and other launch roadblocks in today's frenetic culture.

As indicated by the alarming decline in the consumer's recall of new products—uncovered by our annual Most Memorable New Product Launch Survey—the task of launching a new product has never been tougher. The old strategy that relied heavily on saturation TV advertising no longer works. Now, busy consumers are flooded with messages from an increasing number and variety of media.

With Twitter and the advent of the 140-character message, attention spans are even shorter. Information is conveyed instantaneously and there are so many media outlets, it's a challenge to keep up with the messages coming your way. The only chance marketers have to make a product stand out is to use a multidisciplinary approach that gets your launch message to consumers in numerous ways, at numerous times, and in numerous contexts.

What's happening?   140

What will be the next Most Memorable New Product Launch? Go to www.mmnpl.com and give us your ideas.

Latest: update

(sample tweet)

When we asked respondents to the Most Memorable New Product Launch Survey in 2007 how many media sources they used to learn about new products, the average was 3.3. For those all-important early adopters, the answer was even higher, at 4.5 media sources. The same figures in 2009 had increased to five sources on average, and six for early adopters.

It is almost certain that these numbers will continue to grow larger with the emergence of mobile and social media. Facebook has more than 250 million active users, with 120 million logging on daily and more than 30 million accessing it through mobile devices. Those age 35 and up, with major purchasing power, represent the fastest-growing demographic. Facebook also has more than 300,000 business pages, including 100,000 small business pages.[1] Twitter users are growing at phenomenal rates, rising from 6.1 million unique visitors in January 2009 to 9.8 million unique visitors just one month later.[2] Don't think only the younger demographics are using these sites—on Twitter, 45- to 54-year-olds make up the largest user segment.[3]

Some of the conversations going on in these online communities have to do with new products as people join fan pages on Facebook and tweet about their love (or hate) of something new they've purchased. With people turning to multiple sources for information, it's vital that you have a launch program that touches many bases. Our firm uses the term Immersion Marketing™ to describe the creative, all-encompassing approach required to surround consumers with launch messages. Immersion Marketing goes beyond the traditional marketing mix to create multiple touch points to motivate consumers to buy new products. If you think about the statistics above, you need to have anywhere from three to six ways to reach consumers for them to "register" your new product as top of mind.

MMNPL Survey respondents used 3.3 media sources in 2007 and 5 in 2009

TIP 3 | **Make sure you bring together a launch team that integrates all the disciplines you'll need from the start.**

Although companies sometimes hesitate to do this, the best approach is to get everyone you need on board from the beginning to carry out the launch. This allows people from all launch disciplines to participate in generating important campaign elements, including key launch themes, timetables, budgets and the "big idea" that will propel the campaign into consumer consciousness. Nothing is worse than bringing in key team members or agency partners after major decisions have been made, only to find that these pivotal players have fabulous ideas and it's too late to implement them.

Be crystal clear about which launch team member is responsible for each element. Launches are stressful enough without having team members waging turf wars. With many agencies now engaging in social media, it's important to designate who is going to be the lead agency handling it. Making the division of responsibilities clear from the outset should help avoid team tussles.

Also make sure the launch team stays in close contact. You don't want anyone acting like the Lone Ranger, off doing his or her own thing. They could be oblivious to decisions the team is making that affect the work, and to unavoidable changes in the launch schedule. Regularly scheduled team meetings or phone conferences are advisable.

Innovative Burger King Products Resonate with Moms and Kids

As concerns over childhood obesity have become a front burner health issue in America, moms across the country have been looking for ways to convince their kids to eat more fruits and vegetables. In 2008, Burger King developed an innovative product that squarely addressed this consumer need: BK® Fresh Apple Fries with caramel dipping sauce. At just 70 calories, this kid-pleasing alternative to french fries earned a Top 10 place in the Most Memorable New Product Launch Survey.

Here's an inside look at the launch of this extremely successful product, which is part of BK's Positive Steps® corporate social responsibility program through which the fast-food giant helps customers eat and live better by promoting balanced diets. We talked to Cindy Syracuse, senior director of cultural marketing at Burger King Corp.

What were you hearing from customers that led you to develop BK® Fresh Apple Fries?

Syracuse: There has been increasing regulation, speculation and consumer questions around children's nutrition, along with concerns about fast food and obesity rates.

When we conducted research with moms, they told us it is important for a mom to take care of her children and to feel like she is feeding them well. There is a lot of pressure around how to affordably feed your child well because ▶

fruits and vegetables are expensive. So finding a way to provide fruits and vegetables is a challenge for almost all parents. They also told us if we offer something healthy, their kids have to eat it because they don't have money to buy another meal or to throw it away. So that was an important insight for us.

We knew we needed a nutritional platform that would address our social responsibility objective as a company—providing people with healthy options. Everyone knows: Kids want fun food. The challenge was how do you make eating healthy fun, maintain your brand voice, and offer something that parents will ultimately choose when they come to the restaurant.

We immersed ourselves with a team of world-renowned nutritionists and started looking at ways to improve the BK® Kids Meal, whole fruit being one of them. We knew there was an opportunity there. We started the effort in 2007 and took about a year to launch the product.

> BK® Fresh Apple Fries tied with 5 products at #8 in 2008's MMNPL Survey

How did Apple Fries specifically come about?

Syracuse: Serving the fruit as a whole apple wasn't necessarily appealing to kids or to moms; some want them peeled, others want the skin and so on. McDonald's was already in the market with apple slices, and we weren't interested in replicating that product. One of our food scientists, who is a mother, came up with the insight that if you slice apples and skin them, they look like french fries.

When Burger King first began serving the fries, they were hand cut. We were hedging our bet we could make the machine that would do this. We were successful, and after packaging them in the FRY-POD®, we knew immediately they would be a hit. We put them in the FRYPOD® and the minute Russ Klein, president of global marketing strategy and innovation for BK, saw them, he said, "This is it!"

▶

Did you have any challenges to overcome in developing the product?

Syracuse: Once we had the concept, we went through our rigorous protocol for developing new products. We had to determine where to source the apples, what the shelf life of the product was and how to cut them. We had to build the supply chain and the infrastructure. This development went pretty fast; we are in the fast-food business, and we like to move quickly. Summer is the height season with people in the cars and traveling, so we were aggressive in targeting a summer launch.

Tell us about your launch program.

Syracuse: We launched the new BK® Kids Meal, which included the BK® Fresh Apple Fries, with Pokémon trading cards and toys. We also had a sampling program in 15 major cities. We had various activities like building sandcastles and relays to create awareness and reach families where they are in the summer—outside enjoying the weather.

About two months before the launch, we signed an agreement to sponsor the Jonas Brothers summer tour and added sampling in all 48 cities in the tour. When we actually planned BK® Fresh Apple Fries, the Jonas Brothers weren't part of the mix, but we realized the concerts would offer a great opportunity to target moms and kids. That was a last minute add-on and created incredible awareness for us in every city.

The concerts were outdoors; the weather was hot and we were handing out cool BK® Fresh Apple Fries. We had activities like picture booths; it was a blast. While we had national television advertising support, getting our product in the hands of moms and proving that kids liked them really worked. That's why we signed up again for the Jonas Brothers tour the following year.

What did you learn from the launch?

Syracuse: One of the surprising, residual effects of the launch was that healthy, better-for-you products do create news. When you're a brand like BK, people tend to think only Whoppers and other big burgers create news. We had almost 200 million media ▶

impressions between the two announcements of BK® Fresh Apple Fries. You can change things as long as it's based on a consumer insight. At the end of the day moms have to like it and kids have to eat it so they're not throwing away their money. If it's something consumers want, they'll give you their money and they'll come back. In the first two weeks, we sold a million orders of BK® Fresh Apple Fries— a million people ate apples instead of french fries! •

TIP 4 | Have a thoroughly articulated launch strategy... and put it in writing.

Going hand in hand with the need to use a multidisciplinary approach to launch is the need for a detailed written plan that explains your launch strategy and tactics and addresses critical issues such as timing and budget. Don't try to wing it. Plan ahead and implement meticulously. Make room for changes along the way when something doesn't work as well as you hoped or when something works great and you decide to do more of it.

When we first started doing research on launch, we were astonished to find that 45 percent of the companies we studied that were launching completely new products (as opposed to line extensions) conducted their launches without having a written plan. This makes as much sense as trying to sail from Boston to Buenos Aires without the aid of navigational charts or a GPS device. You may eventually get to your chosen destination, but the trip will be far from pleasant and worry free if you don't have a route planned.

TIP 5 | Set a separate budget for launch.

Just as not having a written launch plan is a recipe for disaster, so is the lack of a separate budget. If you don't have a launch budget, ask management how important this product is

to long-term corporate success. Without a clearly defined launch budget, a high probability exists that your product will fail. A separate budget is that important.

Not setting aside funds that are dedicated to launch activities means the budget cannot be linked to specific goals and deliverables. If the budget is ad hoc, rest assured the launch results will be too. If you fail to define the budget in advance, you will have even more difficulty obtaining money to support your launch initiatives as time goes on and you will be put in the position of borrowing from other budgets.

The discipline of creating a detailed launch budget forces you to tie your launch initiatives to goals. The value of budgeting launch separately from other marketing and sales activities is that it forces strategic spending and builds launch success. In addition, it pays to develop metrics that prove that the money you've spent is performing against your business goals. Later in the book, we talk more about metrics and why you need to have different types of benchmarks to prove launch success.

Launch on a Budget

What if you can't afford to buy trend reports from the leading futurists? Thankfully, the Internet gives you access to scads of free information that can help identify trends that are pertinent to your new product. All it will cost you is time.

Also, here are three no-cost tips from well-known futurist Faith Popcorn on how to stay abreast of trends:

"Read everything. The next time you're stuck in the airport, purchase three magazines that you would normally never read.

"Observe, and whenever you see something unexpected or interesting, ask yourself, 'What does that mean?'

"Go up to strangers and ask 'Are you happy?' and ask them why or why not. It's not just about trying the latest restaurants; it's about capturing how people feel, what people need in the moment."[4] ●

TIP 6 **Be sure your launch plan is flexible.**

Launching a new product is a complex undertaking. It is almost inevitable that changing circumstances will dictate that you need to make changes to your original launch plan. For example, production delays of all sorts can pop up, especially if the product you're launching features a major technical innovation. What if you're launching a seasonal product and you miss the ship date? How does that affect the launch? Conversely, competitive pressures may result in a need to speed things up. If your competitor is rumored to be announcing a new product similar to the one you have planned, you may want to accelerate your launch and move up the date to trump the competition.

So while we firmly believe in the wisdom of having a written launch plan, don't carve that plan in stone. We often see launch plans marked "final." There is no such thing as a final launch plan because it needs to be reviewed and revised continuously. You need to be flexible in terms of timing, budget and strategies to take advantage of positive events that occur in the market—and the ever-changing media—that could favor your launch. At the same time, you need to be able to react quickly and effectively to any unexpected negative developments that may come your way.

What about opportunistic media, a new partnership opportunity, a cause you want to support, or a new distribution channel? All these situations require a change in the plan. It's okay to change the plan, as the goal is to always look for incremental improvement.

TIP 7 **Listen to the customer and build a customer-centric launch.**

Now more than ever, new product launches need to be customer centric. As we mentioned earlier, the "build it and they will come" era of launches is over. To succeed now, new products need to be closely connected to what the consumer wants, not just to what the company can offer. Similarly, launch strategies that don't align closely to what consumers think, how they behave, and what they need in their hectic lives aren't going to work. We'll talk more about this later when we describe the importance of messaging. We'll also discuss virtual and real-world strategies and tactics, but for now, suffice it to say that listening to the consumer—really listening—is the key to launch success.

TIP 8 **Never try to pawn off a product re-launch as a new product introduction.**

If you're going to re-launch a product, find a new twist. Reporters are a savvy and skeptical group and if you rehab a product and call it brand new without major changes, your new product will either be ignored or receive negative reviews. Of course, it's possible to bring attention to a product without it being new, but don't try to pull the wool over anyone's eyes and say something is new when it's not. You'll be discovered, especially now that information about past launches lives on the Web in perpetuity.

When we met with the trade editors at BNP Media, one of the nation's leading business-to-business media companies, their number-one pet peeve was companies who re-issue press releases about the same old product. Editors asked us: Don't companies think we read what they send? Why would we run the same thing twice? Where are the new features/benefits/news that make me want to run this again?

If you are going to re-launch a new product, make sure you add a new twist that makes the campaign newsworthy. Adding a cause-related or charity component to a campaign breathes new life into an existing product. Consumers respond to corporate social responsibility and want to buy products from companies that do good things for the community or the environment. There is no better way to add sizzle to a re-launch than to feature a cause-related marketing component that links to the product and has an emotional tie with consumers.

TIP 9 **Don't give short shrift to your launch.**

In a business climate where speed is everything, it is tempting to want your launch to be implemented immediately. "As soon as the product is done…or even if it isn't done, let's just get it out there. Time is of the essence." We've heard this over and over, and in some cases, it *is* critical to launch the product right now. In others, companies completely miss the importance of context and timing when launching a new product. What time of year is best? Can we tie this to a moment in time? Where is the best place to launch this product? What is the best methodology to explain its features? Where in the country will our product best be received? Should we tie into an existing event, holiday or cause that makes sense for our product? These types of considerations need to be figured into the launch equation.

Also, give your launch adequate time to work. To ensure your initial success is sustained, extend launch activities beyond what you would normally consider the introductory period. Refine the tactics that are working and recalibrate those that aren't. Then redeploy your proven tactics, improved tactics and even some new tactics to keep consumers and the media interested and engaged with your product.

TIP 10 **Avoid premature launches.**

Don't start launch activities until your product is up to standard and your launch is well planned and ready to execute. We're always surprised at how many consumer product companies—including some major brands—make the mistake of ginning up media attention for a product that is still being tinkered with by R&D, has not been consumer tested or does not have national distribution. Don't get your consumers excited about something until you are reasonably sure you can keep your delivery date and brand promise.

Of course, as Google has proven, there are exceptions to this rule. If you're an Internet company, you can get away with not being perfect right out of the gate and go the "beta launch" route. Techies expect things to be a work in progress and love to participate in perfecting the product.

While launching beta versions of new products often works in technology, when it comes to other types of consumer products, the public is not as forgiving. You market it, they buy it, and they expect the product to be perfect. Of course, launching "limited time offers" (LTOs) to quickly push a product out the door is one highly effective strategy for lower price-point seasonal goods. Consumers will buy a new Valentine's Day candy or a new suntan lotion and if they don't like it, they'll buy something else next year—even from the same company. They aren't expecting wonders; they're looking for something new.

The good thing about selling on the Internet is that it provides instant national (and global) distribution. When you're pitching the consumer media a new product, the first question is always: "Is this product available nationally?" If the product is available only in selected stores and not offered on the Web, you may find it difficult to get reporters and bloggers to cover the launch, as it will be hard for consumers to buy the product. (Note: If you can't get national distribution, make sure you can sell your products on your Web site...or on another Web site.)

TIP 11 Don't forget the tried and true while you pursue the trendy and new.

Right now, everyone's a-flutter about Facebook, Twitter, YouTube and all manner of social media, mobile applications like texting, ads to your phone, and information being pushed to your iPhone based on GPS data and special offers—not to mention the world of iPhone "apps." As the world changes and new technologies emerge, which they will at breakneck speed, we want to remind marketers that every launch should have some tried-and-true

initiatives that have worked for your company or product category in the past, as well as brand new strategies that are emerging each day.

We look at these new technologies as channels, not as strategies. Facebook and Twitter are one more distribution channel for our new product messages. Mobile devices are a way to push messages or allow consumers to interact with your brand through texting at retail or by receiving coupons as they walk by a store. These are hot today; who knows what will be hot tomorrow? The bottom line is that your company harbors a huge repository of historical knowledge in the experience of brand and marketing managers who know what has worked, what *is* working and what they think will work in the future. Talk to them, listen to their successes and failures, and adopt successful tactics that might work for your launch. Also, expand beyond your circle of colleagues and consultants and talk to the social media measurement people, the mobile phone experts, and the public relations professionals about new distribution methods as a result of the decline of newspapers. Dror Liwer, principal of the digital agency Zemoga, believes this is only the beginning for mobile marketing. "The iPhone set the bar so high for what a mobile experience should be; now everyone will have to catch up to that," said Liwer. "Competitors, who launched the Palm Pre and the BlackBerry Storm, are trying hard but they don't have the 'cool factor.' The bar for the mobile experience has been set so high, with the speed and ability of connectivity, plus the interactivity of the whole experience."

TIP 12 Be able to prove your product claims, and if you can't, don't make them.

Nothing—and we mean *nothing*—will doom a launch to failure faster than making claims for your new product that you can't substantiate. In a 24/7 Twitterized world, there is nowhere to hide if word starts to spread that your new gizmo does not actually do what it should.

TIP 13 Be transparent in all that you do.

Far more than just the corporate buzzword of the minute, transparency in all aspects of your operation has become essential to building and maintaining consumer trust. Wall Street greed that caused the worst recession in decades, the increase in food safety issues, the near-collapse of the American auto industry, and the constant parade of political corruption scandals are just a few of the major events that have caused consumers to be cynical about almost everything. Even the green movement has left some people skeptical about corporate honesty. "In a Mintel survey, three in five respondents said they were skeptical over many companies' green marketing claims," said Joan Holleran, Mintel's research director. "Green manufacturers need to clarify their environmental efforts and communicate their eco-effects, so shoppers can trust that they're truly benefiting the environment."[5]

When the consulting giant McKinsey & Co. recently looked at the issue of corporate trust, they concluded that "reputations are built on a foundation not only of communications but also of deeds; stakeholders can see through PR that isn't supported by real and consistent business activity. Consumers, our research indicates, feel that companies rely too much on lobbying and PR unsupported by action. They also fault companies for not sharing enough information about critical business issues— for manufacturers, say, the content of their products, their manufacturing processes, and their treatment of production employees. Transparency in such matters is crucial."[6]

When you launch a new product, you must be prepared to answer questions about how the product is made, where it is made and by whom. Also, every aspect of your launch campaign has to be transparent, from whether someone is being paid to be your spokesperson to exactly how much is being donated to a charity for each purchase made of your new product.

In our wired world, it is all too easy for bloggers and Twitterites to publicly question your every action when you're launching a new campaign. For example, Ford Motor Co. caught flak from skeptical bloggers by not being 100 percent clear about how the people who were chosen as the 100 Ford Fiesta "agents" would be compensated. In this innovative program, which was created to tout the 2010 introduction of the European-built Fiesta to the United States, people submitted videos for a chance to win a Fiesta to drive for six months and then create social media content about their experience with the car. The agents were awarded points for their social media activity and the points could be redeemed for gifts. Since the types of gifts were not disclosed, consumers were left to wonder just how much these "enthusiasts" were being paid to promote the new car and how much that might influence what they said about the Fiesta as they talked it up within their social networks.

As one blogger wrote about the promotion: "Where it gets messy for me is when people do and say things to their networks that they wouldn't otherwise because of the reward involved. Maybe for most people this is a non-starter, but I think it does raise the possibility of social networks getting flooded with brand-related spam, coming from compensated advocates."[7]

In this instance, Ford probably should have revealed up front what types of compensation the Fiesta agents were to receive. The issue of blogging for pay is an extremely touchy one, and rightly so (See Chapter 10 regarding the recent FTC ruling on blogger product reviews). But it's just one of dozens of areas of your launch where you have to make sure you're being as transparent as possible. While many companies are not yet used to being under the microscope, the call for transparency is sure to only get stronger in the years ahead. So be prepared and act wisely when it comes to planning each element of your launch campaign.

TIP 14 **Use After Action Reviews to improve your launch success rate.**

After Action Reviews (AARs) are a tool used by the U.S. Army to effect instant improvement and iterative learning about maneuvers in the field. Each day, soldiers come back to the base and review what happened, what they learned and how performance could be improved tomorrow. Businesses are adopting this "daily/weekly review" strategy to learn what is happening with their new products, who is talking about them, how sales are doing and what small tweaks or major changes can be made to tune up the marketing.

The chart on the next page shows the numerous differences between an AAR and the typical postmortem activity conducted at the end of many launches or other marketing campaigns. Using this tool throughout your launch will help you react to the realities of the marketplace and media more effectively and quickly and will provide you with input on where changes need to be made in strategies or tactics.

KEY DIFFERENCES BETWEEN
A POSTMORTEM AND 'LIVING LEARNING' PRACTICES

A typical retrospective:	A living AAR practice:
▶ "Learning" happens at the end of the project.	▶ Learning happens throughout the project.
▶ Called for after failure or high stress.	▶ Planned for any project that is core to business goals.
▶ The meeting is planned after the project or event.	▶ The meeting is planned before the project or event.
▶ One meeting with all participants in one room.	▶ Meetings with smaller, task-focused groups.
▶ Reviews the entire process.	▶ Focuses on key issues relevant to going forward.
▶ Produces a detailed report leading to recommendations.	▶ Produces an action plan participants will implement.
▶ Focuses more on dissecting past performance.	▶ Focuses more on planning for future success.

CHAPTER 4:

Matching Launch Strategies to Product Newness

The more innovation a new product brings to market, the better its chances of standing out and surviving in today's crowded marketplace. Everything we've learned from our annual Most Memorable New Product Launch Survey (MMNPLS) confirms that the bedrock of a successful launch is real innovation. Many of the products consumers have ranked as "Most Memorable" represent totally new choices—from the iPhone and the Nintendo Wii to alli® weight-loss capsules and the Clorox® Bleach Pen®.

In addition, what we learned from our in-depth study of consumer launches, in conjunction with Boston University in 2001, continues to be true today:

Nintendo Wii
addicts?

Products that are innovative and represent technological breakthroughs are more likely to succeed than "me too" products that mimic something other companies have already brought to market. In our Boston University study, 20 percent of successful products represented breakthroughs, while only 5 percent of less successful products fell into this category.

If you aren't building a high level of innovation into each new product, it's a gamble to expect the launch campaign to generate enough excitement to make a big success out of a less-than-innovative product. While clever advertising and public relations can bring attention to any new product— and can even convince some people to try the product once—if the product doesn't deliver on the launch campaign promise of innovation, people won't purchase it again and follow-on sales will not materialize.

No matter what you're launching, there's one very important lesson we've learned from seven years of conducting the Most Memorable New Product Launch Surveys and 30 years of launch experience: **Different launch strategies and tactics are required based on your product's degree of newness.**

It is important to match the type of launch to the product's level of innovation. A tool we use is the Product Innovation Spectrum. This tool applies to consumer products and as the graphic shows, the launch message, brand voice and launch tactics change as a product moves across the innovation spectrum.

While we encourage as much innovation as possible, it's important to acknowledge that there is still money to be made from meaningful line extensions. Products that are new to your company but not necessarily new to the world can add to your bottom line. They may include more features and benefits as well as added value that competitors can't match, or they may be existing products for which you've identified a new use or a new target market.

Another way to revitalize your brand is to re-launch iconic products with a new twist. Coca-Cola, for instance, has made it onto our Top 10 Most Memorable New Product Launch list with five different line extension products. The Campbell Soup Company launched two different versions of soup-to-go, Campbell's Soup at Hand in 2002 and Campbell's Chunky and Select M'm! M'm! Good! 'To-Go' in 2003, which made it onto our Top 10 list in successive years.

Here's how your launch needs to change as your product ages:

Revolutionary Product: With a truly breakthrough product, all you need to do is tell the world about its exciting attributes, fascinating research and development process and amazing benefits. At this stage, early adopters who want to be the first to have the latest gizmo, gadget or phone make excellent messengers; they often become almost evangelical in their zeal to tell others about the great new product they've found. Cultivating these apostles so that they can create buzz and set the stage for others to consider your product's merits is key. Early adopters are worth their weight in gold, and you need to create launch strategies and tactics that educate and activate their enthusiasm. According to the Retail Customer Dissatisfaction Study 2006 conducted by the Jay H. Baker Retailing Initiative at the University of Pennsylvania's Wharton School of Business and the Verde Group, a Toronto consulting firm, only 6 percent of shoppers who experienced a problem with a retailer contacted the company, but 31 percent told friends, family or colleagues what had happened. Of those, 8 percent told one person, another 8 percent told two people, but 6 percent told six or more people.[1] Whether your product is reviewed on a blog, on a product site or on your own Web site, consumers have access to lots of information about your product prior to purchasing it. Harnessing the power of consumers online to promote your product is an art and a science, which we will discuss in Chapter 9.

Evolutionary Product: You've still got a solid product with strong benefits, but it's no longer totally new, and in fact, your competitors are now offering something similar. Talking about what makes your product different is no longer sufficient because others may have copied it and added more features at a cheaper cost. With an evolutionary product, you need to add interest to the product by understanding how it fits into the world. This often involves using third-party spokespeople who can lend their credibility to your message.

If it's a health product, is there a prominent physician in the field who has conducted research that validates the efficacy of your product? If it's a food product, is there a chef who can add cachet to your product? By understanding how and where the product fits into your consumer's world, it's possible to borrow interest from experts and continue to generate buzz about your product.

Line Extension Product: Now that you've built a customer base, it's critical to ensure that consumers continue to embrace your product as part of their lifestyle. At this point, introducing line extensions is critical to keeping your product in the consumer's consciousness. To break through the clutter, you'll need to create a strong lifestyle message that shows how your product fits into the broader context of societal issues and trends.

Cause-related marketing is a way to emotionally connect your product with a worthy organization that consumers value. Sponsorships with nonprofits are a great way to reach a more broad-based audience, give back to society and align your product with a meaningful cause. Does your product solve a problem that matches with a nonprofit's mission? Is your product "green" enough to align with an organization that is devoted to the environment? Matching your product to the appropriate cause-related marketing opportunity adds new interest and value to an evolutionary product and should not be overlooked.

Celebrities are another way to lend credibility and excitement to

New York Yankees shortstop Derek Jeter stands in front of the Gatorade G2 backdrop at a media event in Herald Square to preview the Gatorade 2008 G2 Super Bowl ad that launched the low-calorie sports drink.

Indianapolis Colts quarterback Peyton Manning takes a drink of new Gatorade G2 before competing with media in a charity bowling match at the G2 Lounge in the Super Bowl XLII media center to help launch the new low-calorie sports drink.

your launch. If your target audience is moms, is there a celebrity mom who embodies the attributes of your product? Would a sports figure speak to the target audience? If the product is geared toward teens, what celebrity teen is popular with that age group? If you are a nonprofit, is there a newscaster or a political figure who can embrace your organization and add news value?

Susan Viamari, the times and trends editor at IRI, discussed one of our 2008 Most Memorable New Product Launch finalists: "The number one new CPG food product launch in 2008 was G2, by Gatorade. The launch of G2 was supported by a substantial integrated marketing campaign, which included television and print advertising, digital, retail, sampling, and cause-marketing efforts [for example, by supporting the United Way]. G2 has been highly touted as a low-calorie lifestyle beverage, which, of course, fulfills an important consumer need. Gatorade did a lot of things right with this launch," said Viamari.

"Most importantly, there was a true need for this type of beverage: consumers [athletes and non-athletes] have been clamoring for low-calorie hydration options. Gatorade clearly communicates this key product attribute across marketing efforts, and supports the value of the product with celebrity product endorsements," she continued. "Print, television and digital media communicate to shoppers in the

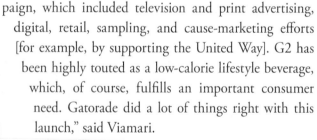

G2 20-ounce bottle

home, while sampling and in-store merchandising efforts have been heavy, reinforcing key messages at the point of purchase."

With cause-related and celebrity campaigns, be sure to price out these program components as part of your ongoing launch campaign, as donations and appearance fees add significant costs to the bottom line.

USO Case Study

Stephen Colbert, host of *The Colbert Report* on Comedy Central and a political writer, satirist and comedian, decided to visit the troops in Iraq to boost morale as a United Service Organizations (USO) volunteer. To entertain the troops, he had a business suit custom made by Brooks Brothers from camouflage materials and shaved his head on live television to show solidarity with the troops. The appearance, broadcast live from Baghdad, not only boosted troop morale, it increased donations and volunteers for the USO. The following, provided by Mark Phillips, vice president of communications for the USO, is a case study that reflects what a celebrity did for their cause.

Gen. Ray Odierno, commanding general, Multi-National Force-Iraq, pretends to give actor/comedian Stephen Colbert of Comedy Central's *The Colbert Report* a haircut during Colbert's performance for U.S. military personnel at Al Faw Palace in Baghdad on June 7, 2009. Colbert participated in a USO/Armed Forces Entertainment tour to the Persian Gulf region June 5-11, 2009.

How did this campaign support a launch for the USO?

Phillips: To coincide with the tour launch and increase surrounding publicity, *The Colbert Report* teased out the tour on air for several weeks and built a special Web presence for the tour duration. We also built a dedicated landing page (www.MrUSO.com) that the main USO page redirected to during the tour. Our "Mr. USO" page was intended to generate even more interest in the ▶

tour and drive people to the *Colbert Report* and USO sites. To do this, we built a spoof site with the idea that Colbert's character is a spoof of network on-air "news" personalities; we were spoofing the spoofer. This was done with the show's cooperation and Stephen even taped several public service announcements (PSAs) to run on our spoof site. We also promoted the site via social media, including Facebook, Twitter and the USO community on Ning.

What were the goals you set for Stephen Colbert's visit to Iraq?

Phillips: As with all of our celebrity entertainment tours, the primary goal was to provide the maximum entertainment value to the troops. This is in keeping with the USO's mission to lift the spirits of the

USO PHOTOS BY STEVE MANUEL

Actor/comedian Stephen Colbert of Comedy Central's *The Colbert Report* performs for U.S. military personnel at Al Faw Palace in Baghdad on June 9, 2009.

troops and their families, wherever they serve. We worked with Colbert's staff for several months planning the trip and negotiating between the U.S. Department of Defense, the military leadership in Iraq and Colbert's producers; everyone essentially wanted the same things, but had different ways to go about it.

A secondary goal, for both the USO and for *The Colbert Report*, was to maximize the media exposure created by the tour. Comedy Central generates revenue by selling advertising space (both on air and online). Increased viewers equals higher ad rates. Because the USO is a nonprofit, we rely on donations. For us, the logic is essentially: More media coverage of our

Lt. Gen. Charles H. Jacoby Jr. (right), commanding general, Multi-National Corps-Iraq, was a guest on *The Colbert Report* on June 10, 2009, at Al Faw Palace in Baghdad.

▶

operations increases the number of potential donors who understand who we are, what we do and why it's important. If the coverage is positive and accurately describes our mission and the benefits we deliver to our customers, potential donors viewing the coverage will be more likely to respond positively to a request for support.

Tertiary benefits include greater awareness of USO operations among employees and volunteers, which should result in increased retention; increased stature in the public sphere, which should result in more (or more valuable) corporate partnerships, and so forth.

Tell us about the impact the Stephen Colbert visit had on the troops.

Phillips: The Colbert trip, like all USO operations, lifted troops' spirits. Each year we produce between 60 and 75 entertainment tours around the world. These tours represent just 20 percent of the USO's operations and the other ways we deliver "goodness" to the troops and their families. These ways include USO centers in airports and on military bases, USO care packages for deploying troops, free Internet access and free phone calls home, the United

Actor/comedian Stephen Colbert of Comedy Central's *The Colbert Report* poses with U.S. military personnel assigned to the 3d Airlift Squadron aboard a U.S. Air Force C17.

Through Reading Military Program (in which military parents record themselves reading stories to their children; the DVDs and story-books are then sent home to the kids, who can enjoy story time with Mom or Dad even when they're separated by thousands of miles), and many other programs.

USO entertainment tours tend to be the most top-of-mind of our operations for several reasons. First, a common perception of the USO comes from the Bob Hope network specials that once broadcast during holiday seasons from former war fronts in Vietnam, Korea and other hot spots. Second, each tour comes with significant star power. For example, when Scarlett Johansson, Robin Williams or Toby Keith goes on tour with us, the media and the public are automatically interested. Third, each of these celebrities has a publicity machine behind them, which will help to tell the story; other USO programs don't have this advantage. Fourth, with the advent of social media, celebrities have legions of fans that help further distribute the stories as they share and comment on photos and news clippings, effectively multiplying the reach of traditional media.

Thus, we see USO entertainment tours as a great way to deliver entertainment value to the troops and their families, and also as a platform to tell about other parts of the USO's mission.

Did you recruit him to go or did he volunteer?

Phillips: Colbert volunteered, but we have an active, ongoing celebrity recruiting effort. Of the entertainment tours we do each year, there is a nice mix of celebrities that we recruited and those who came to us with tour ideas. One really interesting phenomenon we've noticed is that once someone has gone on tour with us, frequently a deep personal connection is made and the artist and their management become advocates and recruiters for the USO. Because of this, we see artists and management coming back to do multiple tours and also bringing their friends.

Whose idea was it to make the suit? Did the USO make it? The Army?

Phillips: During the brainstorming phase, we kicked around a lot of ideas. Stephen's team is incredibly talented and creative. They thought up the suit and Brooks Brothers made it using Army camouflage material; it was brilliant! We went through a lot of back and forth with things like the set design and props to ensure everything in the production was appropriate, doable (we were doing this production in a combat zone, after all) and provided high-quality entertainment for the troops. We also worked very hard to help the producers deliver a broadcast-quality show every day of the tour.

▶

How did you orchestrate shaving his head on air? Did you handle the media coverage and stream it live to U.S. stations?

Phillips: We did an advance trip to Iraq to scout locations. During the trip, we met with General Odierno, commander of Multi-National Force–Iraq. We asked to use his headquarters as the studio for a week and for him to appear on the show. The producers walked him through the head-shaving skit, which he thought would be very funny, and he agreed to do it. We knew that our request was a huge imposition; he and his staff were incredibly gracious and supportive. This project would have been impossible without their approval, cooperation and assistance. His two requests were that we portray the military with dignity and that we provide good entertainment value for the troops. This was completely in line with our mission.

Was Colbert's visit more successful than the visits of other major celebrities?

Phillips: Many USO tours create a lot of buzz, particularly within an artist's particular genre and online community. When it's an entire television show going on tour, that automatically comes with increased visibility, because there is a built-in audience, both on air and online. Although we had restrictions on the specific tour details that we could release beforehand, the show did a wonderful job of promoting the tour and building interest by actually using the pre-tour secrecy as a comedic device.

As for measuring success of a particular tour, there are several things we look at. One is the numbers of troops to whom we're able to deliver "goodness." Another is the anecdotal feedback we get from troops, both in the moment and later via e-mails and letters from them and their families. •

On the B2B Side

Our business-to-business clients asked us if the Product Innovation Spectrum applied to launching business-to-business products. Because we thought the question was relevant, we teamed up with Babson College's Innovation and Corporate Entrepreneurship Research Center to conduct a study to determine if B2B launches had similar characteristics to B2C launches.

Using the Babson database, we surveyed 10 companies by phone and 90 companies via survey and found that products or services launched by B2B companies fell into three distinct innovation categories that were different from the consumer categories discussed previously.

Despite the fact that the categories differed, there are some important lessons to learn from the research for both B2B and B2C companies. It's critical to understand if your product really is revolutionary, or just an incremental improvement from previous generation products. Developing a launch plan for a revolutionary new product is totally different from developing a plan for a "better mousetrap" product because each requires a different type of introductory strategy, budget and implementation plan. While most launches in our Babson study were for better mousetrap products, we learned it takes far longer to sell chasm and supply shock products than to market incremental improvements to products customers already understand.

Let's look further into these three types of launches we found from interviewing B2B companies:

Better Mousetrap: This involves making one or more incremental improvements to your product. Launching a better mousetrap requires using educational strategies to communicate new features and benefits to current and future customers. Always sell to current customers first. You can expect quick adoption on mousetrap products because people understand what they do—and as a result, you can see a rapid return on your launch investment if you articulate how the new features and benefits are true product improvements. If customers liked the old version, they're going to love the new one.

Companies need to be painfully honest when deciding if a product is a better mousetrap or a revolutionary new product. Saying your product is revolutionary when it's just a better mousetrap will hurt launch success.

For instance, if the product is a better mousetrap, it will be hard to secure major news coverage on incremental product improvements. With better mousetrap products, companies need to place advertisements or borrow interest from experts or other partnerships to generate enthusiasm and media coverage.

Chasm: These are new-to-the-world products that Geoffrey A. Moore wrote about in his classic marketing book, *Crossing the Chasm*. The challenge with a chasm product is to move it "across the chasm" that lies between a market made up only of enthusiastic early adopters and one in which you have just enough customers to make the product viable.[2]

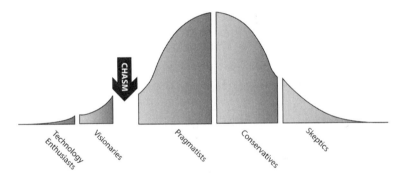

Educating stakeholders and influencers about the product is the key to developing early sales. Finding a respected industry leader, a university or a third party to advocate for or test your product is a way to speed adoption. While your company believes that this is the best new product created in the past decade, it is more important to find a third party who can corroborate that fact.

Word-of-mouth campaigns and consumer-generated media can also prove very effective in engaging potential customers. Also, it is critical to learn why early adopters purchased the product so you can replicate and build on that success.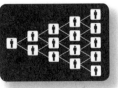

Don't expect record sales in the first year with a chasm product since educating the target market takes time—and money. Plan for and budget launch and marketing activities over a two-year period. It's best to under promise and over deliver when it comes to launching chasm products. Manage expectations, because it isn't easy to sell something that is really new. The old adage that buying something proven is a lot less risky than buying something better still pervades the corporate and consumer mindset. Conserve cash, and don't spend everything in year one because you're going to need it in year two. Launching a chasm product is often a marathon, not a sprint, so be prepared for the long-haul theory of product adoption and sales.

Supply Shock: In this category, products are developed because innovation is a requirement for customers, not a choice. This is innovation that is driven by a change in the environment that compels customers to buy something new. This environmental change can come from any one of a number of external factors, including new government regulations, supply disruptions, new competitors, new technologies, disasters or health threats.

A supply shock product may be a breakthrough, but the market doesn't necessarily perceive the need until a shock wave goes through the environment that makes the product absolutely necessary to them. So if you're launching in advance of this wave of change, you need to find a way to make your product relevant by hooking it to a trend or aligning it with breaking news. One way to drive sales is to identify an organization that has a complementary agenda to help "push" the use of your product. Use research, lobbying and publicity to establish credibility. Use third-party endorsement and testing to prove efficacy.

In this category, think seat belts, vaccinations for the human papillomavirus (HPV), treatments for flu epidemics—products that respond to legislation, health crises or other disastrous events that lead to product introductions.

3M's N95 Respirator/Flu Mask, designed for the construction industry, is a great example of a B2B product now widely coveted in the consumer world. When the N1H1 virus, commonly known as "swine flu," first struck and initial forecasts of a global pandemic were made public, the 3M mask suddenly became the one seen on television as the mask to have to prevent airborne illness.

When budgeting to launch a supply shock product, realize that adoption may be very slow. You need to conserve cash and plan for at least two to three years of launch and marketing spending while you're establishing credibility for your new product…and hope that there is an "event" that paves the way for product adoption.

Keep in mind that how you evaluate a product may not be how your customers perceive the product. So it's important to get feedback from customers—in advance of your launch—to understand where your target audience thinks the product fits. Will customers embrace it quickly because it's so new, or will they want to take a "wait and see" attitude because it is so new? Depending on what you learn, you'll have to adjust your launch timetable and sales projections, as it may take longer for adoption than originally planned. We'll talk about techniques for doing this in Chapter 12.

R&D Phase Insights

In addition to determining what type of launch is required based on the product's level of newness, here are more insights into choices to make and things to do during the R&D phase that will affect your chances of a successful launch:

TIP 15 Look for consumer opportunities; make sure there's an actual need for your product.

Don't get stuck in the "if we build it, they will come" mentality. Just because you can develop a product doesn't mean you should introduce it. With the cost of launching a new product going up each year, the cost of failure also goes up dramatically.

Carefully research whether there is an actual need for the product, whether the market size is adequate enough to justify the R&D and launch costs, and whether the purchase price required matches the price people would be willing to pay.

"The #1 mistake is 'testing the wrong thing,'" according to Lynda Gordon, marketing metrics maven and co-founder of Decision Metrics. "For example, sometimes the focus is so intent on 'taking market share' that firms forget to test the potential for cannibalization of their current product with the new product launch. Companies are always asking if you like the product, but liking the product and buying it are two different things. New Coke is a good example of testing the wrong thing," said Gordon. "Sergio Zyman, former chief marketing officer for Coca-Cola, shared his perspective on the launch as being totally focused on taste comparisons between old Coke, new Coke and Pepsi. Pepsi drinkers preferred new Coke to old Coke. However, this alone did not mean that Pepsi drinkers would abandon Pepsi for new Coke. More importantly, it did not mean that old-Coke drinkers would gladly give up their old Coke for new Coke."

TIP 16 **Have consumers taste/test your product. We know you like it, but will they?**

Once you've determined there is an actual need for your product, you will still require additional consumer research to test the actual product. After you've got a prototype, you have to make sure your idea of a great new product matches that of consumers. One of the biggest mistakes we see in new product launch is assuming that just because management likes the product they've developed, consumers will as well. But what if they don't like the taste? Or the color? Or the packaging? Or the pricing?

Don't get locked into company or group mentality; encourage colleagues to speak up and voice their true opinions about the product, whether they're positive or negative. Sure, doing taste tests or other types of research with real consumers adds costs and can be time consuming, but launching a product that doesn't delight consumers' taste buds or appeal to them visually—or have whatever other key product attributes they require—is the most costly mistake of all.

"People are always willing to try new candy, but you can't ever assume you know everything your consumer wants. You have to ask them, talk  to them," explained the New England Confectionery Company's [NECCO] vice president of marketing, Jackie Hague. "There are now so many ways to talk to consumers, it's great. I don't have to sit here and wait for IRI data, I can engage with consumers on Twitter. I can talk to them on blogs."

Consumers will not only tell you if they like the product, they'll tell you how to make it better so they will buy it—and often they'll do it for free. Make sure to consumer test your product before you manufacture and market it, because this important step will pay off not only in sales but in developing a product that is based on consumer reality. "You have to understand the consumer," said Michael Guggenheimer, vice president of business development at Radiator Specialty Company. "You can't change consumer behavior in a recession if the outcome you are trying to deliver is dependent on coming out of the recession."

Bud Light Lime is a great example of how to get things right by involving consumers in product development. This product took the third spot in our 2008 Most Memorable New Product Launch Survey by essentially co-creating the product with consumers. Learn more in the interview with Pat McGauley, vice president of innovation at Anheuser-Busch, at the end of this chapter.

Of course, the ultimate in bringing consumers into your new product development process comes when you ask them to actually develop the product for you. That's what Dunkin' Donuts (DD) did when it launched a campaign to revive donut sales by having a contest in which consumers were asked to create the next new donut that would then be offered at Dunkin' Donuts stores for a limited time. A dozen finalists were chosen and the grand prize winner received $12,000 (a dozen thousand dollars, which tied in with a typical purchase of a dozen donuts). The finalists participated in a bake-off at Dunkin' Donuts University, the worldwide training center for the company, in Braintree, Massachusetts, complete with celebrity judges, and the winner was announced on National Donut Day.

Bud Light Lime ranked #3 in the MMNPL Survey in 2008

The Twitter spokesperson for the Dunkin' Donuts Brand, Dunkin' Dave, also known as David Puner, whose day job is communications manager at Dunkin' Brands, shared the highlights about the contest with us:

"We wanted to build a loyal following online for DD because DD has a loyal following already. Coffee as a ritual is conducive to Twitter. You can follow Dunkin' Donuts and it remains a part of your day—fast, fun and delicious. The contest was launched using Facebook and Twitter and we had 130,000 entries for donut flavors," said Puner. "People built them on dd.com, could post their creations on Facebook as a status update, and all the while we were gauging the pulse of what people think about the contest on Twitter and using it to generate discussion: *What is your favorite donut? Tweet about it!* (with a hash tag for tracking of #favdonut). We got far more submissions than we expected after launching the contest. At the end of the contest, we went to the winner's home in Birmingham, Alabama and produced a video for YouTube."

Ben & Jerry's has a history of taking customer ideas and turning them into winning products. Some of the company's most iconic flavors, including Chunky Monkey, Cookie Dough and Cherry Garcia, came from the imaginations of Ben & Jerry's fans. To capture this creativity in a more official way, they now run several flavor contests.

Their 2009 contest was called "Do the World a Flavor," in which they asked people from 17 countries to develop flavors using a number of base flavors and mix-ins listed on special Web sites that were set up for each country. Or, people could participate through the Ben & Jerry's corporate Facebook page. The grand prize winner's ice cream is being launched as the 2010 global flavor.

Of course, the degree to which you can involve consumers in the actual product development varies significantly by industry, but in the consumer products realm, there is great opportunity to make customers part of your process. With the advent of social media, there are numerous ways to invite consumers to share their input on a new product prior to its launch. As more and more companies move toward open innovation, new ways are being developed all the time for finding inspiration from the marketplace. If you haven't tried something like this before, find out what other companies are doing and start thinking about how you can use social media and other online consumer input methodologies to receive cost effective, genuine consumer input. We believe social media is going to play a huge role in launching new products. (For more information about social media, turn to Chapter 10.)

"We're in a society where people have lots to say. To capture the sweet things consumers are saying, we created the My Sweethearts contest,  where customers were asked to submit great new ideas for the Valentine's Day expressions on Sweethearts candies," said NECCO's Hague. "How silly of us to think we know the best way to say 'I love you.' It's such a personal thing. We learned there are traditional ways to say 'I Love You' and there are fun ways to manipulate words and phrases. English is being modified and language is evolving. There are new words, symbols, abbreviations, shapes, emoticons—there are different ways to express all kinds of things. But the one thing that remains the same is when you have something sweet to say, say it with Sweethearts."

KFC Goes Big with Famous Bowls and Earns Top Spot on the MMNPL List

Sitting in first place atop the Top 10 Most Memorable New Product Launches in 2006 was KFC's Famous Bowls, a new fast-food product that put KFC's favorite flavors into one convenient bowl. Mashed potatoes, sweet corn and bite-sized crispy chicken, drizzled with signature home-style gravy and topped off with a three-cheese blend, were layered into a one-bowl meal. In the first 10 months after the May 2006 launch, nearly 81 million Famous Bowls were sold, and sales have continued strong since then. Here's the story behind this highly successful new product launch, as told to us by KFC's Charles StClair, senior director of marketing, and Rick Maynard, manager of public relations.

KFC's Famous Bowls earned the top spot in the 2006 MMNPL Survey

How was the idea for KFC Famous Bowls developed?

StClair: We have a proprietary innovation process; it's an innovation model that starts with the consumer. We source ideas from everywhere: suppliers, our franchisees, from wherever. This particular item was an internal idea that was developed when some of our leadership team was doing an innovation session in our test kitchen.

Our process at that stage was to do some very early prototypes. It is easy to make food that tastes great, but it is really the consumer insight that drives the success of the product. So we did some qualitative work with the consumers, and some quantitative work at the contact level with consumers.

PHOTO COURTESY OF KFC CORPORATION

The interesting thing about the Famous Bowls is that everyone here [who] tried it, loved it, but what we found almost immediately with consumers in both the quantitative and qualitative research was this idea was very polarizing. There are people who really liked their food touching and there are people who do not like their food to touch. If you are one of those people that like things separated, Famous Bowls were not for you. If you are one of those people that likes casseroles, this is like heaven.

In the normal process, if you find a product that is polarizing, it won't always score like a winner in the tests. When some people love it and some people don't, it averages out to maybe it's an average idea. But there is so much passion internally and with the early consumers who we talked to about the product—the people who loved the product absolutely loved it! So we took a step that was new for us at the time—and that we have now incorporated into our process—of actually taking this product and putting it into some stores to see how some consumers are going to react to it prior to going through all the additional work we usually do. We put it into a handful of stores, and, lo and behold, it sold really well with no advertising and a little bit of in-store merchandising. That gave us the heart really to push forward with it.

From there we went through a whole set of quantitative and qualitative tests with consumers where we worked to optimize the product [and] get the right amount of gravy, the right amount of corn, the right kind of corn, the right amount of chicken and so forth—to optimize that product. Then we moved to a test market. We tested the Famous Bowls in two different markets, Phoenix, Arizona, and Columbus, Ohio. We tested advertising the product with or without a price point. What we found and what we used to launch was going without the price because the product itself was strong enough to garner consumers' interest. They did not need to have the value price point associated. Since it's over a pound of food, it's a great value for consumers.

The test went very, very well and we knew we had a big winner on our hands, so we moved it to a national launch really quickly. It was just six months from the time we tested it to the time we launched nationally.

▶

What's your normal turnaround?

Maynard: Normally, from test market to national launch is about a year.

We know this product was considered memorable by consumers because it topped our list in our survey that year, with 24 percent of the people we surveyed naming it as the most memorable new product launch. But did that translate into sales? How successful was this launch for you?

StClair: At the time, Famous Bowls set one-week and one-month sales records, and it really started a trend in bowls. Bowls weren't a new idea; there were some places out there that had them, but they weren't really mainstream yet. But a lot of people followed us into bowls. You saw breakfast bowls and you saw other chains doing that. Even today you still see bowls in pop culture; comedians will talk about that bowl! It has some sort of cult-like following in the marketplace, even now three years later; it is an important layer in our business.

After three years, what are the sales looking like? The bowls have become a staple of the stores, have they not?

StClair: Sales have stabilized. We promoted it pretty heavily in 2006, and we came back with a line extension in the Biscuit Bowl in 2007. We did a special two-week promotion in March 2009 and it did very well. It is a mainstream item for us, and a staple of the menu.

What were some of the tactics you used for the launch and which ones do you think were most successful?

StClair: From a launch standpoint, this was a big promotion for us. We hit our normal media mix of TV and radio, and, of course, the PR team did a fabulous job. We had a lot more Internet presence with this promotion than when we do a typical promotion; we were trying to get that marketing integration. We also did a lot of billboards.

The TV ad was pretty memorable. The advertisement was a guy who came into a store interacting with a team member saying, "What's new here?" and the lady describes the bowl and the guy counts on his fingers the layers of flavor because it is all his favorites ▶

stacked up one on top of another. It was something people picked up and walked into stores and mimicked because the ad resonated with them; they got it. "Why would I love it? Well, I love mashed potatoes and corn and chicken and gravy; it's all the stuff I love and you put it all in one convenient bowl for me." So it was a memorable insight that really resonated with the consumers. So that hand signal became shorthand for the bowl itself.

What were some of the PR initiatives in the launch?

Maynard: One insight we used on the PR side was just to tap into the fact that America's work force is having a more difficult time leaving their desk for lunch. About 50 percent of workers only have 30 minutes for lunch. So the thought was you can have a full wholesome meal and get it delivered quickly and it's portable. And so you can enjoy the Famous Bowl as opposed to trying to squeeze something that is less satisfying into your 30 minutes for lunch.

We always pitch the morning shows and all of the food media. This was a product that was immediately resonating with people and there was a lot of buzz about it because it was so different than what you could get at another fast-food restaurant or anything else on our menu.

Tell us about your buzz marketing initiatives.

Maynard: We have a team, the buzz team that meets once a week; it's a cross-functional team, a PR team; it's commercial marketing and finance and every other group around KFC. We look for creative people who are passionate about some topic; we have sports fans, entertainment fans and people who are interested in politics and we get together and talk about what is going on in the world and then look for opportunities for how KFC might be a part of it.

At the time Sanjaya was very hot on *American Idol* and, as you remember, not so much because of his musical talent but because of his ever-changing hair style and the fact that he kept surviving week to week. So we made the offer that if Sanjaya would cut his hair in the shape of a bowl, a bowl haircut for KFC Famous Bowls, then we would give him his first recording contract. We were going to invite him to participate in our KFC radio commercial, and it created a tremendous amount of buzz. You know Sanjaya was all over the news anyway, so to give people an additional reason to talk about Sanjaya and to inject the KFC message in there was very effective.

What was the most positive thing you learned from the launch and what might you do differently next time?
StClair: There are three things that stuck out in my mind; this was ac-tually an eye opener for us within our innovation process. I don't think we ever stumbled on a product that was polarizing to this degree.

Now, if we come up with something that intuitively seems like a big idea and we are starting to get average results, we dive into it a little bit further to see if we have a significant portion that is a big fan of it or is it really a mediocre idea.

A second learning experience for us was the speed to market. We moved from test to nationals, which showed us that was possible. As a result, I think some of the things we did helped to shorten our time to market with everything going forward.

The third lesson is when we have ideas of this magnitude, we have to unleash everything in terms of marketing. We have to really go big! ●

TIP 17 Stick to your company's core values when developing new products.

In today's tough launch environment, companies need to go back to their core values, contended Joan Holleran, research director of Mintel. "What are you trying to accomplish with this new product?" she asked. "Are you trying to demonstrate that you have a solution for consumers in this tough economy? Can you help them simplify their lives or address their shrink-ing wallets? Are you speaking to the consumers' desire for customizable, multi-functional products that are not wasteful? Will people buy it…and then buy it again?"

As Holleran points out, the days when companies could get by introduc-ing quick-fix line extension after line extension are gone. "People need to be more thoughtful about the launch process and the new product," she said. "The companies that will succeed in today's tough launch environment are those that are committed to sticking with their core values and are focused on consumer needs and how to best address them. This means not watering things down and not letting people slip in their pet projects."

TIP 18 Develop new products with multiple uses.

One way to tie your new product to the new consumer consciousness about value is to create products that have multiple uses. "This makes new products risk free and flexible," continued Holleran. "Everything needs to have multiple uses. Condiments are a perfect example; you can have a salad dressing that works great as a marinade. Or dryer sheets which have dozens of uses; they remove lint and odors, they repel insects. Give consumers lots of ways to use your product. Think about all the cleaning products; there is one for surfaces, one for wood, one for windows, and one for stainless. Is that really necessary? They're all hard surfaces. Why can't one thing do it all? Consumers are hoping they can find a product that can do many things."

TIP 19 Don't overestimate the life of your new product.

Make sure you have a steady stream of innovations in the pipeline because the amount of time your product remains "new" in the minds of the media and consumers is shorter than ever before. Consumer trends are short lived and consumers move quickly from one product to another. So you need to identify a trend, develop a product that fits into that trend, and get it out there *fast*.

For example, NECCO has produced Sweethearts Conversation Hearts since 1847. NECCO was purchased by American Capital and the new management team decided to breathe new life into this important icon product. Known for sayings like "Marry Me," "Kiss Me," and "Hug Me," NECCO decided to team with Summit Productions and launch a line of heart-shaped Sweethearts to be released in conjunction with the DVD for *Twilight*, the book and movie sensation that has taken teen hearts by storm. The candy, which features phrases like "Bite Me," shows how a 163-year-old company can "hip it up" and get with the times.

"We knew Sweethearts needed to do something innovative. We knew the brand was targeted to older moms and grandmoms but yet had the functionality to be relevant to teen girls who were IM'ing, on Facebook and Twitter. We needed to find a fresh way to put messages out there and *Twilight*, which is about forbidden love, seemed perfect," said NECCO's Hague.

"The stories in Stephenie Meyer's books worked perfectly for the franchise because both Sweethearts and *Twilight* are about expressions of love. Creating our new Sweethearts line of Twilight candies was about saying something sweet with messages that were relevant to kids and teens and acceptable to moms," continued Hague.

"[The candy] incorporated expressions between the two main characters, Edward and Bella. The wisdom that came out of the *Twilight* community which we are incorporating into the candies now is we can say what the fans are talking about, not just what the characters are saying. Phrases like 'True Love,' 'Always,' 'Scratch Me,' and 'Imprint Me' appear on our Twilight candies and illustrate the audience's connection to the franchise."

TIP 20   Don't overextend your brand.

Understanding what your brand stands for is an excellent guidepost when it comes to expanding it into new categories. While it is tempting to extend your brand into new product areas, make certain these product extensions make sense for the brand. If extending the brand causes it to lose meaning and connection with core customers, you may end up tarnishing the brand's reputation instead of expanding it to new customers. If you are thinking of moving from food to clothing to some other unrelated field, think again. Is this really what your customers want and expect from you? Do you have the expertise to be successful in a whole different line of business? If you license the brand to another company, are there checks and balances in place to ensure they are being true to the brand's ethos and personality? Diluting your brand to the point where it's meaningless is a big gamble and it might not be one you should take. Again, rather than guessing if brand extensions will appeal to consumers, do market research to test their reactions. There's only an upside to understanding whether consumers will embrace your new ideas for extending the brand.

A company we admire that's a genius at brand extension is Harley-Davidson. From a merchandising point of view, they understand that their customers will buy anything of quality at a fair price with a Harley logo on it. They have successfully extended their brand from motorcycles, gear and bike parts, and accessories and clothing, to furniture, housewares, and now even coffee.

TIP 21 Co-brand.

Sometimes one plus one equals three. By co-branding a new product with another company that can bring name recognition to the table, you can often create something that will really grab consumer attention. A perfect example is Domino's Oreo Dessert Pizza, which earned the number-four spot on the Top 10 Most Memorable New Product Launch list in 2007.

Domino's Partners with Kraft Foods to Hit a Home Run

Domino's Pizza and Kraft Foods introduced the Oreo Dessert Pizza for a limited-time offer of six months in 2007. The product was the first nationally available dessert pizza in Domino's 47-year history. The Oreo Dessert Pizza was a new dessert-style thin crust that was layered with vanilla sauce and covered with Oreo cookie crumbles.

"The idea was part of an annual recipe contest we hold called Pie In the Sky," said Dana Harville, a spokeswoman for Domino's. "We put it through a test market and found the customers really liked the pizza."

Interestingly, this promotion defied the major overall trend of fast-food companies providing healthier options on their menus. High-profile launches like this and Wendy's® Baconator, launched during the same year, show that fast-food brands don't need to completely shy away from unabashedly unhealthy offerings.

Marketing Mix

An ad campaign directed by the Perlorian Brothers was put in heavy rotation nationally and garnered substantial attention online. In the ad, a dad and his teenage son discuss their respective Oreo Dessert Pizza mustaches. The dad's cookie mustache, which continues to grow during the ad, is so full it would make Groucho Marx jealous. This led to a totally unplanned but highly serendipitous happening for the product, as people uploaded videos of their own attempts to create an Oreo Pizza beard and mustache. Domino's also posted a viral video on YouTube that featured Nate Robinson of the New York Knicks hosting the debut of the pizza at St. Jude Children's Research Hospital. According to Domino's, the launch generated 66 million media ▶

impressions, including articles in the *Houston Chronicle, Detroit Free Press*, and *Los Angeles Times*, as well as mentions on *The Tonight Show with Jay Leno*, *The Daily Show with Jon Stewart* and several other high-profile shows. ●

TIP 22 **Use packaging as a differentiator and capture people's imagination.**

Today, packaging plays a more important role than ever before as you can recast your product as totally new with packaging innovation. With so much competition for consumer attention, every aspect of your new product should stand out, and that includes how your packaging helps you grab consumer attention when your product's on the shelf.

Here's a good example of how focusing on packaging can make a difference. Heinz Tomato Ketchup Easy Squeeze ranked fourth on our Most Memorable New Product Launch Survey Top 10 list in 2002. While it was the same Heinz Tomato Ketchup everyone loves, it was delivered in a new bottle that made it easier to pour ketchup on burgers, making it feel like an entirely new product.

Heinz Tomato Ketchup Easy Squeeze ranked #4 in the 2002 MMNPL Survey

Having a great graphic look to your packaging is essential. Thanks to the Internet and other graphic influences, consumers are increasingly more visually sophisticated, so you can't afford to skimp on delivering something that is eye appealing. Also, make sure your packaging easily conveys the essence of the product to busy, distracted shoppers who are moving down store aisles talking on their cell phones and possibly trying to manage a child or two.

When you're thinking about packaging, consider other factors beyond how it looks. Can you design packaging that is more convenient for consumers to use? Or just easier to open? Or more environmentally friendly and resealable or reusable so that it appeals to consumers who are part of the green movement?

Some companies just tweak the look of their packaging without making changes in how the packaging actually works. A new look can give an old product a lift, but be careful. As Pepsi learned when it tried to radically change the look of its beloved Tropicana orange juice line, loyal customers can resist change in a big way. When the orange with the straw that had represented the brand for eons disappeared and was replaced with a design that people said made the product look like a cheaper store brand, consumers spouted off in droves on blogs and other online forums. As a result, Pepsi was forced to retreat from its multimillion-dollar makeover. So tread lightly on this path and make sure you check in with your loyalists before wandering too far from your tried and true brand image.

Bringing the Customer into the Product Development Process

Bud Light Lime earned the number-three spot on the Most Memorable New Product Launch Survey in 2008. Pat McGauley, vice president of innovation at Anheuser-Busch, was responsible for ushering the product from development through launch. He attributed customer involvement as one of the key ingredients in the creation and launch of this highly successful new beer. Supported by a $35 million marketing campaign, Bud Light Lime became the number-one seller in the convenience category in terms of dollars during its first year on the shelf.

Tell us about Budweiser's approach to new product development.

McGauley: We are very consumer centric in our approach to innovation but this was not always the case prior to five years ago. Since then, we've made a concerted effort to put consumers as "the boss" in the center of the universe. A lot of companies spend time creating products they need but not necessarily creating products consumers need. Now we consciously identify consumer needs.

In the case of Bud Light Lime, we identified a sweeter palate for consumers; 29 percent of consumers have a sweeter palate. So delivering on this need to consumers was our first goal. Another goal was to deliver the product within the Bud Light brand. Our intention was that this brand had a different feel from Bud Light, but was complementary to it. We packaged it differently and we priced it differently. (Ed. Note: Bud Light Lime comes in a clear bottle ▶

and is priced $1 to $1.50 higher than other six-packs.)

The development process included a number of focus groups and some ethnographies and sessions to speak one-on-one to core consumers. We first worked with consumers on the overall concept until we really zeroed in on what was important. It was all about the real lime flavor and hint of lime, not a lot of lime—this is beer with a hint of lime and not a lot of lime.

We developed 26 different prototypes and then narrowed down that number with internal taste panels. Then we went out to consumer sessions. It was a very collaborative effort.

Why was this product such a big win for Bud Light?

McGauley: We expanded the category of beer with Bud Light Lime; that was the real win for us. Within our segmentation study there is a category called Trendsetters; they like this style of beer. Also, there is an ethnic market for this beer. Not every Bud Light drinker is going to like a lime-flavored beer, but we definitely stretched where we can take the brand.

How long was this new product in development?

McGauley: We began with product development in 2006 and then kept it on the shelf for most of '06 and started working on it in mid-2007 when we refined and optimized the final concept. Then we selected the launch date, which was April 28, 2008.

What we found with the launch plan was the longer the lead time, the more success we had. We announced the product to the system in January and were able to give retailers and wholesalers time to prepare and identify shelf space. The new product was not located next to Bud Light but instead was in the micro-specialty area. We also had adequate time to provide selling tools, so retailers could hit the ground running. At the same time, we announced the product in the media. We do these two steps simultaneously to be sure we don't get in trouble with our retailers if the press learns about new products before they do.

We've gotten much better working with national retail sales account folks and bringing them into the loop. Months out we sat with ▶

our distribution chain account folks and talked about how this launch was going to impact all elements of the retailers. Our salespeople went in with all the appropriate information to sell the product in. We had messages about the customer we were targeting and why we were launching this specific product. We got tremendous distribution right off the bat; we really used the power of our system and the power of the brand with everything hitting at the same time.

What were the key elements of your launch campaign?

McGauley: We ran a tremendous amount of teaser campaign ads, 15-second ads where the Bud Light bottle was displayed and then a lime peel peeled away and the clear bottle was revealed.

These were run about three weeks out before the launch. We tracked all the chatter the ads were creating with our call center; people started calling and asking where they could find the new product.

We did not do an official launch event; we've done them in the past and instead encouraged our wholesalers to host events in their regions. I don't think launch events are bad, but we were spending a lot

of money on them and we thought it was better if the local markets hosted their own events. Also, each local market had activities they were required to do during the summer.

We did a lot of sampling because we knew if people tried Bud Light Lime, they would like it.

We provided a full list of summer-related point of purchase materials, like key chains, hats, t-shirts and other promotional things of that nature. Wholesalers hosted Bud Light Lime parties on an evening, put the beer in people's hands and hosted contests to win t-shirts, etc.

We had a viral campaign with a character called Limey, which was a lime with human arms and legs. When we were working with our agencies on TV advertising, one agency brought forward Limey. It was quirky, it was out there, and was something you wouldn't run on TV but we used it on YouTube.

I don't think we'll do this on every single brand but it fit with the summer launch for this particular product.

As far as publicity, on the consumer side, there was a significant media wave when we launched the brand.

In the last three to five years we've continually improved our launches. We launched five beers last year. Our system is getting better, and we have gotten much better as far as timing, integration, and having the tools to be successful. The more we can provide data about the product, the more input we have to talk to retailers in the up front to really pave the way, the more we are seeing greater success in the marketplace.

What trends are you seeing in product development? Are companies condensing new product development time?

McGauley: I think most companies probably have a new product cycle and I would guess there is acceleration to that cycle because most companies are looking for more organic growth. I think if you skip steps in your process, there are big mistakes to be made. So we're trying to go as quickly as possible but are doing all the homework to make sure we don't fail. One of the things we learned is we don't launch with as many SKUs as in the past. A narrower line gives us greater focus.

Do you hold postmortems with brand managers?

McGauley: Absolutely. We bring in most all of senior management and review what's working and what isn't. One of the things that has improved is that our innovation is much more collaborative. Brand teams worked with us all along the way. We keep getting better and better and more collaborative. We try to work with wholesalers and retailers so they're on board, too.

The fun thing in this product line is after you've done all this work, suddenly you drive down the highway and see the first billboard or the first ad. It's high excitement. It's what you live for when it hits the market and you see the sales figures; those are the things that drive us here. ●

CHAPTER 5:

Navigating the Selling Environment

Developing an exciting new product that matches a consumer need—preferably one that's growing in demand—is the first major hurdle required for launch success. The next big challenge is to get your product on the shelf. These days, the "shelf" can be in a brick-and-mortar store or in a warehouse where your product awaits incoming orders from your Web site, Amazon.com or other Web aggregator sites.

On the brick-and-mortar side, you have an industry that is undergoing massive changes. Being a retailer is tough these days. Just reflect for a moment on the big-name stores that disappeared from sight during the recession (Circuit City, Tweeter, Steve & Barry's and Linens 'n Things, to name just a few). To survive in this new climate, where "shop 'til you drop" is no longer every consumer's motto, retailers must keep a razor-sharp focus on providing value to their customers. And while retailers understand the need to offer consumers something new, at the same time buyers are more risk averse than ever before.

As retailers struggle with the new normal, they are demanding that manufacturers offer them price concessions that they can pass on to consumers. In addition, they are even encouraging manufacturers to suggest promotions and other offers that will drive traffic and repeat sales.

"There is a huge amount of deal constructing going on," said Thom Blischok, president of consulting and innovation for IRI, which provides enterprise market information solutions and services for the consumer packaged goods (CPG), retail and healthcare industries. "Every day of the week manufacturers are being asked by retailers to make concessions to stimulate traffic growth. A retailer fundamentally says, 'I want to feature this product in a buy one/get one free or a buy five for $10 offer.' It's not like it is that negotiable."

To break through with your new product in this environment, you have to do two things: First, convince retailers that you have an innovative product that is really worthy of their valuable shelf space because it will drive traffic and sales. Second, have a plan for grabbing customer interest so that your product flies off the shelves. If it doesn't sell, rest assured it will be yanked off the shelf by the retailer before the next shelf set, making way for another product that offers better returns.

On the e-tail side, after taking a recession hit like all other types of retail, online shopping is projected to move back to double-digit growth rates by 2011, reaching $203.5 billion by 2013.[1] Some online retailers are using innovative strategies to strengthen their relationships with outside vendors. For example,  Amazon is offering manufacturers and publishers the opportunity to have their new products reviewed by a select group of Amazon's customer reviewers on, or just prior to, the item's release date. Through the program, called Amazon Vine™, Amazon provides Vine members with free copies of the products that have been submitted to the program by vendors, who pay Amazon a fee for this service. The reviewers, called Amazon Vine™ Voices, receive a list of items to review twice each month. Products include books, movies, electronics, food items and other consumer products. This program is a great way to generate advance buzz in the marketplace.

While such developments are exciting and certainly worthy of consideration, online sales are projected to still represent only 9 percent of all retail sales by 2011. So, the vast majority of products will still be launched through brick-and-mortar stores.

Here are some tactics that are helpful in meeting distribution and retail challenges:

TIP 23 **Study your target retailers and align your product with their ethos and policies.**

Just as it's important to know as much about your customers as possible, understanding the retailers you hope to sell through is also essential. Fortunately, the information you need is readily available online via company Web sites and, if they are public companies, through their annual reports and press releases.

"If you start a conversation about a platform that is important to the retailer, it is easier for them to see you as aligned with what they are doing," said Eric Baty, a consultant in the consumer packaged goods industry. "Retailers are interested in the alignment a manufacturer can provide with the strategies the retailer is striving to achieve."

What are they talking about in their investor relations materials? How are they positioning themselves against the competition? Are they focused on sustainability? What social initiatives are they supporting? Are they stressing health and wellness through on-shelf signage and other tactics? What is their positioning, vis-à-vis key shoppers' interests, such as value, quality and variety? Each retailer is different. You will benefit from doing your homework prior to meeting with them to find out how to tailor your pitch specifically to each outlet.

If you are talking to Walmart, a company committed to sustainability, you might want to stress efficient packaging, shipping and the recyclable nature of your product. If you are talking to a major supermarket chain, many of which are committed to helping their customers make healthier choices, stress the health aspects of your product and demonstrate how it fits into their nutrition positioning and labeling campaigns.

TIP 24 **Get referrals that will open doors for you at retailers.**

Retail buyers defer to people they trust, just like the rest of us do when we use our friends as valued sources of information about new products. When it comes to talking your way into a buyer's office, having a reference from someone a buyer already knows and trusts, or retaining a broker that is already involved with other products at a particular retailer, is worth its weight in gold. "The world of referral and introduction is more important than ever before," said Baty. "While this is obviously not the case if you're from Procter & Gamble, it is true for the tens of thousands of smaller companies. These companies have the likelihood of being more innovative and having more inventive products, but they have no name recognition. So the question becomes, can they be trusted? If you're an unknown manufacturer, you need to find access into a targeted retailer. Who would that be? It could be a broker, a strategic partner who sells into the category, or someone at a high level in the organization who knows someone you want to meet."

TIP 25 **Take your agencies to retailer pitches; they can help you sell in.**

The time you have with retailers is precious. Having someone from one of your creative agencies at your side to answer questions about your launch campaign can be very helpful in terms of maximizing the value and shelf space you gain from a meeting.

"When you're able to get time with a merchant, it might only be 15 minutes while you're pitching your new product and going over your plans for POP [point of purchase] materials or a promotion," said Jeff Falkowski, account manager with R solutions, LLC, a Cleveland, Ohio, firm that provides sales promotion, partnerships and integrated marketing services for manufacturers and retailers. "It's not the easiest thing to get back in front of the retailer down the road, so if you can close them on the spot and allay any concerns they have and answer all their questions, that's the best case scenario. If you have to say, 'Let me get back to you with an answer,' you've already lost their attention. Often manufacturers can't answer questions right on the spot about things like POP or promotions, so having an agency person there who can seal the deal is a strategic advantage."

TIP 26 Avoid embarrassment and increase your success rate by knowing a retailer's regulations regarding such things as POP and pallet size before you make your pitch.

The proliferation of clean store policies means retailers are placing ever-stricter and more-encompassing controls on the number, size and characteristics of displays, according to Blischok of IRI. In its *CPG Merchandising Trends 2007*, IRI reported a 10 percent drop in the number of grocery store displays, with 60 percent of categories experiencing declines in overall merchandising activity.[2] Since each retailer sets up its own rules, it is critical to know in advance what clean store guidelines the retailer you are pitching has in place.

"When it comes to the visual merchandising standards of the big box retailers and others, it's important to get a grip on what the standards are or align yourself with an agency that understands the guidelines," advised Falkowski. "It will save you time, money and embarrassment, if you have appropriate materials that fit their merchandising standards and will be accepted in the store. It's important to go into retailer pitches with innovative ideas that will not get turned down."

Some of the specifications you run into might be surprisingly comprehensive. For example, Costco requires that when a pallet comes into one of its facilities, employees only have to take the sleeve off and stack it. All pallets must be the exact same size and height, and merchandising has to be built into the display. This seems straightforward enough, but things can get complicated when you realize that every warehouse club store has its own unique set of requirements.

For example, Sam's Club wants the 40" dimension of the pallet to be the selling face, while Costco wants the 48" side to face shoppers. But pallets for BJ's can be only 50 percent of the height of pallets at Sam's or Costco to conform efficiently to BJ's smaller stores.[3] One way to traverse this complex maze of requirements is to hire a co-packer that specializes in helping manufacturers meet them.

| TIP 27 | Have a finished product ready to show retailers.

How do you convince wary retailer buyers that you've got your act together enough to be worthy of their consideration? "Nothing is as good as walking in with a finished product that is ready to go," said Baty. "One simple way to prove you're ready to go to market is to bring the new product to the meeting."

This is especially important if you're a small company. If you're a big established company, you can walk in with digital images and they will trust you. For smaller companies bringing your first product to market, nothing beats having the real thing ready to present.

| TIP 28 | Educate consumers *and* store personnel with your POP.

According to Rob Adelstein, a partner with R solutions, the trend in point of purchase materials is to make them educational. "Retailers are grasping for consumer education," said Adelstein. "They want POP that keeps the consumer in a department for a longer time, so things like flat screen display monitors where the customer can go up and learn about the product and at the same time be incentivized to buy are very effective."

"One of the important things about educational POP is that it really needs to serve a dual purpose in retail, not only in educating the consumer but also in educating store personnel," added Falkowski. "At Lowe's or Home Depot, for example, not everyone who works in the store is an expert on all the thousands of products sold there, so the more accessible product information is to store associates, the better."

Handy tools for training store associates in environments such as Home Depot or Lowe's are apron cards that can be shipped to store department heads for distribution to floor personnel to put into their pockets. "Apron cards let you put the information about your product right in their hands," said Adelstein. "Keep in mind that sales associates are not necessarily advocates for your product, so if you can provide educational information on the POP where the consumer can find it themselves, or in a place where sales associates can easily find it to provide the information to the consumer, you'll be ahead of the game."

TIP 29 **Make sure your POP materials actually get used; provide retailers with support at the store level if necessary.**

Retailers are running lean and mean in terms of staff, so you can't always count on your POP marketing materials being in place in time to take advantage of other launch campaign elements such as coupons, TV ads or your public relations campaign. You're spending a lot of money on POP, so having it sit unopened in the back of the store two weeks into a promotion is a disaster. Don't let this happen.

Fortunately, there is a solution in the form of in-store merchandising organizations that service specific categories. "These companies have taken over some of the traditional retailer responsibilities to assemble displays and stock shelves to make sure things get done," said Randy Golenberg, a partner with R solutions. "Retailers are asking manufacturers to pay for part of this, often through co-op dollars."

"More often than not, if there is something that is going to cause us a problem both at the beginning and the end of a promotion, it's usually a communication breakdown somewhere in the store regarding making a change to the store's new planogram," added Falkowski. "One of the most important things we do is to give specific and simple instructions for in-store merchandising to help store personnel place the POP correctly. We recommend labeling the outside of boxes clearly and addressing the boxes to the department manager."

Falkowski continued: "That way you have a person to call if there is a problem with the delivery or product setup. If all else fails with a specific retailer, talk to a service group about helping you with setup to ensure displays are put together as planned."

TIP 30 **Don't immediately rush to the latest and greatest in-store gadget.**

High-tech POP solutions such as in-store videos have come a long way, but they still can present operational challenges for retailers, and hence, for you. Consider whether old-fashioned solutions such as pamphlets and booklets might work just as well with far less maintenance required; all someone has to do is keep the brochure holder stocked. These "no-tech" solutions also give customers something tangible to take with them, so the sales process can continue even after customers leave the store and head for home.

TIP 31 | **Make smaller and local chains your new best friends.**

Sometimes you just have to accept reality. Mass retailers and big box stores may not be the best place to launch your new product. There could be any number of reasons your product is not attractive to major retailers, making big box stores a poor fit with your sales strategy. You may not be willing (or able) to pay slotting fees. You may not be willing to produce enough units of the new product (or well-financed enough to meet the baseline numbers required by multi-unit stores). Or, you may not be able to offer a generous enough promotional campaign to secure shelf space. More important, you may not want to discount your product initially to meet the price at which mass retailers want to stock it.

But that doesn't mean you should give up. If knocking on doors of major retailers produces lackluster results, refocus your strategy and instead of thinking big, think small.

You may be welcomed by smaller, local chains rather than Target or Walmart. To differentiate themselves from the mass market retail giants, smaller retailers often focus on providing customers with something new and innovative. For this reason, smaller retailers may be more willing to give your product a go. Their slotting fees may be more manageable or non-existent, and their requirements regarding packaging and other promotional requirements less rigorous. Also, with the movement to "buy local," if your product is produced in the area, that is another impetus to put it on the shelf.

Some companies have succeeded by building their entire retail strategy around smaller chains. For example, Stihl Incorporated offers its high-quality power tools only through a dedicated network of small retailers. "You can't find their products at Home Depot or Lowe's," said Baty. "Their message is they want to be sold by specialists."

Don't forget that your distribution strategy should match the message you want to convey about your product. Is it a high-end product? If so, the worst thing that could happen to you is to receive a big order from Walmart, because its shopper demographic doesn't match the target consumer demographic you are seeking.

TIP 32 | **Sell on the Internet if you can't get retail distribution quickly.**

Selling online can help build a track record of sales that you can then leverage to interest brick-and-mortar retailers about your new product. Keep in mind that if you're going to sell online, two things are essential:

a great Web site and an effective back office system to speed products quickly and safely to customers. Some young companies get so caught up in designing the Web site that they don't focus as much attention as they

should on the e-commerce and fulfillment part of the process. And as we all know, the dangerous thing about the Internet is that just a few dissatisfied customers can quickly do severe damage to your product, brand and online reputation.

TIP 33 **Start by selling direct with infomercials if retailers aren't willing to give you shelf space.**

Selling your product through infomercials is another way of getting it into the hands of consumers, especially if you're running into roadblocks with retailers. Once you're a success with direct sales generated through infomercials, you have a solid story to tell retailers that can greatly increase your chances of securing precious shelf space.

"An infomercial is a paid television program, 30 minutes long, that explains to someone why they want to purchase a product. It takes that long to educate a consumer about a more expensive product, and get them to pick up the phone," explained Dan Danielson, co-chairman of the board of directors and co-founder of Mercury Media, a media placement firm for direct response TV products. "Infomercials can be produced for $60,000 all the way up to $250,000 if you are using celebrity talent."

66% watch TV while surfing the Web, with 85% searching for something they just saw

The good thing about infomercials is that you buy the time, so you know when they are going to run and you can quickly measure their effectiveness. The goal, according to Danielson, is to get a two-to-one return on the infomercial investment. "If you spend $200,000 a week in media, your hope is to get $400,000 in sales," he said. "Certain categories like greed (real estate), sex, vanity, self-improvement, health and fitness, technology and religion are all good categories for infomercials."

Long-form advertising airs only on certain networks and during specific time periods like overnight, Saturdays, Sundays and early mornings. "Infomercials are a great way to sell features, benefits, problems and solutions, and demonstrate reasons why the product is needed," said Dany Sfeir, of DS & Associates. "In long form, you can do a great deal of selling; in short form, the selling is done via telemarketing or the information you send to the consumer after the call."

TIP 34 **If you can't afford infomercials, try direct television.**

Another effective and more affordable alternative to promote your product on television is direct response advertising—fondly known as "yell and sell" advertising, according to Beth Vendice, president of Mercury Media. These short-form infomercials, which come in 30-, 60- and 90-second versions, are designed to make the phone ring. They offer the product and a special incentive like free shipping, a product upgrade or a promotional item, if you call *now*. And unlike long-form infomercials, you can air them during any part of the day and on any network.

The good news is you can test a short-form infomercial for about $20,000 for production and $20,000 for time, and generate immediate orders. "It's much cheaper than doing focus groups and at the end of the day, you get orders, not just data. Short-form infomercials give people who see the spot an incentive to buy, and it allows the manufacturer to track results," said Vendice. "If your spot pulls, you can see results within 15 minutes after it airs. Everything is tracked; there are separate 800 numbers for every ad, every station. We can tell you exactly which spots produced the most revenue and give real-time feedback about the effectiveness of the ads."

TIP 35 **After infomercials, sell into *As Seen On TV* sections of retailers.**

One of the fastest-growing sections in drugstore and specialty chains is the As Seen On TV section. *"As Seen On TV* is a good approach for seasonal or fad products," said Sfeir. "Most of these products came in with a big hoopla, were promoted on air through direct response for two years, and then disappeared. Companies that introduce these products are not about building a long-term product or brand; the products are hot and then they die down. If they were introduced at $50, you ultimately see them in club stores for $20 and then the products go away. But it is a great way to extend the life of a short-term product before it sinks into the sunset."

TIP 36 Partner up.

"There's a trend toward cross aisle promotion where you say, buy this product and get this companion product for a reduced price or some similar offer," said R solutions' Adelstein. "You might do this with a shelf talker or a wobbler or an on-package sticker."

"We try to bring two companies together that are complementary to each other," added R solutions' Golenberg. "For example, we brought a milk manufacturer and a muffin company together during December, which is a big baking month. If people bought two gallons of milk, they also received a free sample size box of muffin mix. The muffin mix was displayed in the dairy aisle. This was a good example of what we do with these partnerships," he continued.

"We find a partner with brand awareness that helps elevate our customer's brand as well. We brought a national partner to the table to give us free product in exchange for the awareness they would receive in the milk aisle during an important selling season for them. You are the company you keep, so finding a partner with brand awareness helps increase visibility for your customer's brand as well."

For a younger company with little or no brand recognition, this type of promotional program can be particularly powerful. We urge marketers to merchandise items outside their usual aisle to capture impulse and incremental sales.

TIP 37 Forget the industry trade show and consider attending direct-to-consumer venues.

Industry trade shows just aren't what they used to be. Attendance figures at many shows began to sag even before the recession hit, making the significant financial investment—not to mention staff time—entailed in hosting a booth of questionable value.

"Retail consolidation has made these shows less important for domestic suppliers," said Ken Braaten, vice president of sales at Radiator Specialty Company, which manufactures products for the automotive aftermarket, as well as the plumbing, hardware and appliance industries. "Fewer customers are coming to the shows and the ones who do attend are people we see regularly anyway. Over the years we've found that most important business is handled prior to the show."

Braaten added: "On the international side, it's a different story. The international customers who travel to shows come to do business. Our international representative at the automotive show is the busiest guy in the booth from the opening to the closing bell. So that makes some of these trade shows still worthwhile."

Direct-to-consumer venues like health fairs, bridal shows, home expos and farmers markets make sense as launch tactics, especially if you're having a difficult time convincing retailers to commit shelf space for your new product. In fact, having several success stories to share with retailers about how well your product sells can bolster your pitch.

Food products and other locally manufactured goods lend themselves to this type of strategy, and there is no shortage of venues for displaying your wares directly to consumers, thanks at least in part to the increased interest in buying local. The U.S. Department of Agriculture reports that direct-to-consumer food marketing at places such as farmers markets rose by 104.7 percent from 1997 to 2007.[4]

TIP 38   **Consider giving a retailer an exclusive.**

With retailers struggling to stand out from the competition, you may find them willing to take on your new product if you offer it to them as an exclusive, or if you provide an exclusive promotion. "We always consider giving a big chain an exclusive if the retailer is going to give us something over and above what they normally do, such as good placement for a few SKUs, and if their objectives match ours," said Braaten. "Sometimes the exclusive is for six months, or a year or longer, depending on individual situations. We don't do it very often but it is something we would entertain. Some retailers are gung-ho on having a unique product offering versus the competition. Lowe's is one of them. They want to have a different assortment from Home Depot."

Be aware, though, that giving a retailer an exclusive on your new product has minuses as well as pluses, according to IRI's Blischok. "You can get some degree of backlash from shoppers today who are being told they can only buy a single product at a single store," he said. "It can be a bit of an irritant."

Account-specific promotions can also help persuade retailers to take on your new product. "You can only reduce your price to a certain level, but each merchant is looking for what else you can do for them besides pricing," said Falkowski. "The price is the price, but 'What other kinds of dollars can you put behind this product from a merchandising or promotional standpoint that is going to increase my turns?' they'll ask. So at the end of the day, retailers make money based on volume. It's about giving the retailer a warm and fuzzy feeling that you're doing something special for them."

TIP 39 Understand the realities of today's co-op marketing.

While it is certainly worth a shot to ask retailers about the possibility of co-op marketing for your new product, don't be surprised if they want to know more about what you can do for them as opposed to what they can do for you. In fact, some retailers tend to think of co-op dollars as profit centers. While many manufacturers try to influence where their co-op money is going to be spent, it frequently doesn't work that way. If you can align your co-op marketing ideas with a retailer's key objectives, you have a far better chance of getting the positive response you seek. For example, when Home Depot set its sights on being designated as the ENERGY STAR® partner of the year, they were eager to jump on board with co-op marketing that was focused on green initiatives.

TIP 40 Align with a larger firm to distribute your products.

Companies of all sizes are looking for ways to wring out costs from their operations. "People are more open today to alliances," said Baty. "For example, for a decade Frito-Lay distributed Oberto Beef Jerky. Frito-Lay

had trucks rolling with their dry snacks and a distribution partnership with Frito-Lay was more efficient for Oberto than to distribute on their own. Although they have ended the relationship, it is still a good example of a company like Oberto that had a competitive product, but not the ability to reach all the retail touch points. As a larger company with incredible clout, Frito-Lay could speed distribution by delivering beef jerky to shelves at multiple doors."

Baty acknowledged it's important to understand that these types of alliances typically originate much higher up in companies than at the brand manager level. They are designed to meet broad corporate objectives such as gaining more cost efficiencies from resource allocation. Of course, creative product and distribution ideas are also generated at the brand manager level and brought to the attention of higher-ups. So if you've got a good idea for an alliance that might benefit your new product, package it up and take it to both senior and brand management.

CHAPTER 6:

Honing an Effective Launch Message

Of the many critical questions that need to be answered before a new product launch, there are two we find pivotal: Why did you create this product? And why would someone want to buy it? Answering these questions with compelling messaging is central to your success.

But finding the right messages is a challenging task. By and large, today's consumers are a cynical lot. They've heard and seen it all before. They are also leading ridiculously busy lives in which they are constantly bombarded by marketing messages. No wonder the percentage of consumers who can recall—without being prompted— even one new product launched during the year keeps plummeting.

What can you say that will grab the attention of your target customers to make them try your new product? This chapter covers ways to ensure you can meet this ultimate launch challenge.

As you read these insights, keep in mind that the sooner you tackle this portion of launch planning, the better. Launch messaging development needs to be done early in the process and requires time. We recommend creating messaging as soon as the product receives a "go" directive from management. Developing the messages about your product provides a road map for all future written and produced materials. It enables everyone to

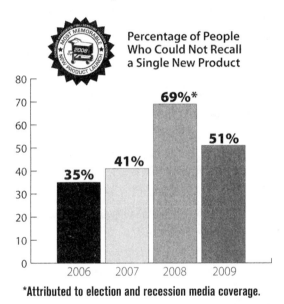

Percentage of People Who Could Not Recall a Single New Product

*Attributed to election and recession media coverage.

speak in one voice about the product so that management, sales reps and agencies can talk and write about it in the same way. By providing common messaging you will avoid the pitfalls of people making up their own versions of the product's attributes, features and benefits.

Getting Started

TIP 41 Create key messages.

If you put together messages without a framework, you will probably be mired in wordsmithing before you know it. Instead, begin by working logically from questions to answers. Assemble key individuals who will be involved in your launch, such as the brand manager, thought leaders from your public relations and advertising agencies, internal personnel with marketing savvy, and consumers. Ask each individual to write down any questions they think might be asked about the product, from the global to the specific. How does this work? What's new about it? How much will it cost? How long will it last? Where can I buy it? Why would I buy this when the competition already has a better product on the market? Who tested the product to prove its efficacy? At this point, all questions are important to consider and none should be disregarded as irrelevant.

Working with a trained facilitator (from your PR agency or a resource within the company), write all the questions on a flip chart or whiteboard so the group can see them. Review the queries to learn what the group thinks about them. Then ask the participants—working either alone or in teams of two or three—to group all of the questions into buckets. These will most likely address the product's benefit to the consumer and what is new and different about it. We suggest having two or three buckets, one for each subject.

Now comes the hard part: The facilitator needs to keep a relatively tight rein on the participants. Break people into groups and ask each team to formulate one sentence with the dominant answer or statement about the subject matter addressed in each bucket. Compare the input from the groups. You will find that the answers are usually very similar and will give you the essence of your key messages. Test each message you formulate by asking this question: If people hear, understand, believe and act on each key message, will it drive sales of the product and make the launch a success? If the answer is yes, you have likely formulated effective key messages.

Be sure to take a break at various intervals, as messaging requires time and perspective that can be gained only through discussions about each message and its meaning.

We've also found there is more to messaging than key messages. After you have your dominant or key message formulated, you need to develop more content around it. We do this by drawing a pyramid and dividing it horizontally into three sections to create a Key Message Pyramid.

The top section of the pyramid is devoted to the key message. This is where you articulate the best words to use when describing the product. The information needs to be concise and memorable because if it isn't, people will not be able to remember or articulate the most important information about your product.

The middle section holds factual proof points that support and expand on the key message. It should contain a series of facts that explain and validate the key message. In this section are the reasons to believe why this new product is great—you need to provide the factual proof to back it up.

The bottom section of the pyramid holds what we call the "make me care" messages. These can be anecdotes about the product, analogies that will help explain how the product is used, pithy sound bites that drive home the value of the product, a memorable statistic, or other points that will add interest to the messages.

KEY MESSAGE PYRAMID

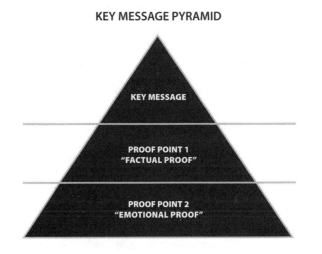

KEY MESSAGE

PROOF POINT 1
"FACTUAL PROOF"

PROOF POINT 2
"EMOTIONAL PROOF"

DEVELOPED BY LOUISA HART AND SCHNEIDER ASSOCIATES

An example: For a recent product launch, we formulated the following key message about the product using our Key Message Pyramid: "The Zeo™ Personal Sleep Coach is the first science-based product and educational program that allows you to track your personal sleep patterns and reveal lifestyle habits and behaviors that may be helping or hindering your sleep." A consumer hearing this message might be intrigued but would want to know more in the form of additional proof. So the middle section of the Zeo pyramid—the "prove it" level—contained specific information about the four components of the product (a headband worn at night to monitor sleep patterns, a bedside display that shows the result of that monitoring, a Web site that gives additional information about personal sleep patterns, and a personal sleep coaching plan). We also included extensive information about the scientific basis of Zeo, as well as the involvement of a highly credentialed scientific advisory board. All of this information was designed to educate consumers so they could believe in the value of the product.

The third or bottom layer of the pyramid was designed to make people care and get them excited about Zeo. Here we put in sound bites such as "This is like working with a personal trainer to get in shape, or with a nutritionist to lose weight." Another "make me care" sound bite said, "Zeo helps unlock the black box of sleep," and we showed consumers how variables such as caffeine intake, activities just before bedtime, and even pets sleeping in the bedroom can impact the quality of their sleep.

When you finish filling in this pyramid, you should have a good draft of not only your key message or messages, but also important and persuasive supporting points. Remember, the media need to be able to tell a good story about your new product. While you want them to include your key message (because it will drive sales), you also need to supply the press with convincing facts and/or quotable remarks. Those elements of the story, more often than not, come from the lower levels of the pyramid. Don't confuse a key message with a good sound bite. You—and the media—need them both, but they are usually very different from each other and contain very different types of information.

TIP 42 Know consumer trends and how your new product fits into them.

Notice we said "trends," not "fads." It's important to know the difference. Trends represent the direction mainstream society is taking over a long period of time. Trends have momentum and durability.

Fads, in contrast, are short lived. "In the first half of the 20th century, when mass-communication technologies like radio were new and novel, consumers were far more likely to simultaneously hear about and adopt the same styles and products," journalist Miriam Marcus wrote for Forbes.com.[1] Now, in the 21st century, while some fads go national, most are localized due to the fractionalization of the marketplace. "Every generation, region or socio-economic group has its own cool, hot fad," wrote Marcus.[2]

Hooking your launch message to a fad may generate great initial results for your product, but those results may drop off precipitously as the fad inevitably fades. In contrast, connecting your launch messages to one or more trends can produce long-term success, especially if you're catching the trend early.

Keeping current on trends is essential to launch success. What are your target customers thinking about? What do they care about? How are they feeling? How is their behavior changing? What are they missing that your product might provide? What is happening with the economy? Are world events impacting their lives? These are all questions that require answers prior to creating launch messages.

Trends versus Fads: Do You Know the Difference?

Lynn Dornblaser, Mintel International Group's leading new products expert, provided us with a helpful guide to identifying which market movements are trends and which are fads.

It's a fad when:

1. The products that fulfill the fad appear in a very limited number of countries.

2. The product types appear in a very limited number of categories (unless the fad/trend is applicable to only specific categories, e.g., gluten-free).

3. Product introductions skyrocket in a very short period of time, far in excess of normal new product introduction growth.

4. The consumer press tends to take a sensationalist view of the fad.

It's a trend when:

1. The products that fulfill the trend appear in a number of countries, often at or near the same time (although depending on the trends, they sometimes take quite a bit longer to move from Asia to the West, for example).

2. The products appear across a wide range of categories (unless the trend is applicable to only a few categories). ▶

3. Product introduction growth is slower than that for a fad, although usually still greater than overall new product introduction growth.

4. Nutritionists, marketers, retailers and the press take a more balanced view of the trend.

To put these guidelines to the test, consider these two trends/fads of recent years: low-carbohydrate food and whole grains. On the face of it, these two areas may seem very similar. Both have their genesis in the U.S. marketplace. Low-carb products were designed to aid weight loss, to help regulate insulin levels in the blood and to promote good health in general. The same statements also apply to whole-grain products. Looking solely at new product introduction figures, it is clear that while low carb was a fad, it could very well be that whole grain is a trend that is here to stay. Additionally, low carb was centered only on the U.S. market, while whole grain is more evenly spread globally. When we examined these introductions, low carb showed a steep rise followed by a steep fall, while whole grain has demonstrated a steady growth in the marketplace.

When a fad becomes popular, many companies jump in with new product activity. The products appear in categories in which the fad makes sense (low-carb products in the bakery category, for example). But as the fad progresses, new products begin to appear in less likely categories, or products that really do not fit with the fad are labeled as being part of it (e.g., products that always have been low carb bearing a "low carb" sticker on pack). Companies that do not de-list their products before the fad begins to fade will often pay a price with declining sales and de-listed products. •

TIP 43 **Make sure your WIIFM message is clear and on target.**

Consumers want to know, what's in it for me, also known as WIIFM, especially when they buy a new product. This is particularly true when the product represents new-to-market technology or is creating a new category. Then your WIIFM message has to be especially well thought out and clear because while "new" sells, "new" also takes some convincing, especially if there's a high price tag attached to it.

Having a well-defined value proposition is essential. This statement of value should grow out of what consumers say about your product, not just what management believes the value to be. Brainstorming about why consumers will want your product is not the same as going out and asking them what they think about the product. To get the real skinny on the value consumers see in your new product, you have to go right to the source.

"People want to get back to basics with simple, multi-functional solutions," said Joan Holleran, research director of Mintel. "There are still a lot of 'my way' and 'for me' attitudes in the marketplace because if a consumer is scrimping and saving in one area, they will spend in another."

TIP 44   Prepare messages for different demographic groups.

Once you have your main WIIFM message set, consider how it will play with different demographic groups. You cannot afford to overlook the rapid growth projected for minority populations in the United States over the next few decades. According to the U.S. Census Bureau, by 2050, the Hispanic population is projected to nearly triple from 2008, from 46.7 million to 132.8 million; this means one in three U.S. residents will be Hispanic. The African American population is projected to increase from 41.1 million, or 14 percent of the population in 2008, to 65.7 million,  or 15 percent in 2050. The Asian population will climb from 15.5 million to 40.6 million, moving its share of the population from 5.1 percent to 9.2 percent.[3] Each of these groups needs a version of your WIIFM message that is tailored to their particular needs and concerns.

TIP 45   Give 'em reasons to spend their hard-earned money.

In today's economy, consumers are not participating in mindless shopping. The recession has forced just about everyone to shift their spending habits. "Cutting back, trading down, shopping in less expensive stores, putting less on credit cards is now a way of life," said Wendy Liebmann, chief executive of WSL Strategic Retail.[4] WSL's data shows that this trend actually started long before the recession. In fact, they track it back eight years ago to when gas prices first jumped above $2 a gallon. Consumers have gone back to basics and now realize they can live with less. Getting them to return to a free-spending mentality will take time. Matching how your product fits into the new frugal mentality and pared-down lifestyle embraced by consumers is critical to product success. What makes your new product relevant to today's consumer? What are the key product benefits and how can they be communicated in a crystal-clear way to help consumers understand why they need this product? If you're doing a cause-marketing tie-in, does the campaign speak to your core consumers?

"Consumers relate to the company and make a connection beyond the product through the causes your company supports. If I am a breast cancer survivor, I am probably going to go for Yoplait because it supports breast cancer. Even if I can't give to Susan G. Komen [for the Cure] directly, I am giving by purchasing these products," continued Holleran. "That makes the consumer feel they are participating in doing something about breast cancer, while helping the company that they support.

"As a consumer, you want the good guys to win. Don't you love the retailer that is selling things that are locally produced and grown? Who doesn't want to support the guy down the street?" she said.

Consumers are more skeptical than ever before and can spot hype a mile away. The recession, financial bailouts and massive layoffs have made people doubt the credibility of corporate America. While consumers are not necessarily painting every company with this broad brush, you still need honesty and genuineness as your watchwords in this new environment.

TIP 46 Find a campaign theme that has legs across all disciplines.
As we stressed in Chapter 3, your launch needs to include strategies and tactics that will work across all marketing disciplines. This means your overall launch theme needs to be something that is readily adaptable to both traditional and online settings. This requires more up-front planning, but it pays off in the end by resulting in a stronger campaign that speaks to consumers with one voice.

Having your agencies ideate together to create a launch theme is extremely helpful. Allowing everyone to offer input at the outset is far better than announcing a theme as a *fait accompli*. Don't tell the ad agency, public relations firm, Web company and point of purchase agency to "make it work" with a theme, tag line and product name that they don't believe in. That's a recipe for not getting the best work from your creative partners.

Having a consistent theme also makes it easier to break through the media clutter to become one of the few new products that consumers will actually recall. Since it's often difficult to reach consumers, hammering your theme home multiple times using a variety of marketing techniques is vital. In addition, since consumers seek multiple sources of information about new products, you need to provide information in a variety of places while staying faithful to your product messages.

TIP 47 | Deliver launch campaign ideas that match your brand's promise and personality, and the product's attributes.

The essence of your brand should be at the heart of everything you do during launch. From the overall campaign theme down to the smallest detail of each launch component, make sure you stay true to the spirit of the brand and to the nature of the new product. Cling tenaciously to your brand and what it stands for with your customers. Put launch ideas through a filter that tests whether they are true to the brand.

While this advice may sound obvious, we all know how easy it is to get carried away by a sensational idea during a brainstorming session, only to realize later that it is not a good fit for your brand. It's one thing if this realization hits you after sleeping on the idea overnight. It's quite another if you don't see the problem until you've actually invested time and resources in the idea and perhaps even made it a key part of your launch plan... or worse yet, you've actually gone public with it and are getting negative feedback from consumers.

TIP 48 | Test your campaign theme and marketing messages— and not just with your colleagues.

We've all seen far too many launch campaigns based on ideas that should never have made it out of the conference room. It's too easy to get caught up in groupthink and ignore possible problems with a campaign theme or messaging. The panic that results from starting launch planning far too late in the process often leads to snap judgments that may soon be regretted. And let's face it—it's never easy to voice concerns about an idea that could create problems once the entire group has agreed to pursue the concept. Corporate politics sometimes makes it difficult for people with doubts to have their voices heard.

That's why it is absolutely essential to test your campaign theme and marketing messages outside the corporate or agency bubble—among real, live consumers. These are the people whose opinions you really need to hear. What resonates with them? Do they understand what you are saying about the product? What isn't clear about what you're trying to tell them? Would your campaign theme intrigue them enough to buy the product? At what price point? Do your launch messages help differentiate your new product from others on the market? The answers to these and similar questions regarding consumers are worth their weight in gold when it comes to helping avoid potentially fatal choices.

| **TIP 49** | **Remember: Words matter, especially trend words.** |

Now that you know what your launch messages should be, you can move on to the challenge of crafting ads, Web copy, press releases, packaging, point of purchase materials, and all other forms of communication that will help connect your product with consumers.

Bear in mind that words that resonated with consumers last year may have lost their cachet this year. It's important to know what words are speaking to customers *today*.

Many trends head to America from Europe, particularly from the United Kingdom. For example, Holleran reported that the U.K. is now focused

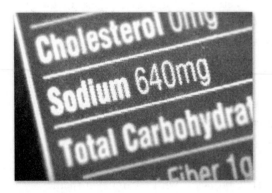

on eliminating salt. "Salt is the new trans fat," she said. "In the U.K., they are mandating sodium limits on products. We tend to take our cues from the U.K., so there have been rumblings about this here in the U.S. Companies need to be ready for 'no-salt' to become a trend word here."

There are many ways to say the same thing. Your job is to find the language that will work for your new product right now. Be careful not to go overboard with trendiness in your choice of words. Although the cool young copywriter at your ad agency may know all the latest lingo, the moms you are counting on to buy your product may not. There is such a thing as being too cutting edge, just as there is such a thing as being too unhip, especially when the product is being marketed to tweens or teens. Finding the right words is important.

Tone also matters. How do you want to talk to your customers? Should your tone be formal or more relaxed? Will humor work for your product? If so, what type of humor—sarcasm, silliness, parody? Not everybody shares the same funny bone, as many, many companies have learned to their dismay. Studies of the use of humor in advertising have found both positives and negatives. "On the one hand, humor has been credited with calling attention to an advertisement, increasing comprehension of the ad, contributing to the positive attitude toward the ad, and enhancing the positive attitude toward the advertised product," wrote Gail Tom, a professor of marketing at California State University, Sacramento. "On the other hand, the use of humor may not be suitable for certain products or services, is thought to lead to faster advertising 'wear out,' may offend some members of the audience, and may result in the so-called 'vampire effect,' where the humor sucks attention away from the advertised product/message."[5]

> **54% were influenced by the absence of trans-fats, 42% by high-fructose corn syrup and 34% by low-salt content**

TIP 50 **Make your point quickly.**

In a world where attention spans have been reduced to Twitter's 140-character limit, shorter is better when it comes to launch messages (see sample tweet below). Edit, edit and then edit again. There's almost always a shorter way to say something. And while it's tempting to wax eloquent about your new product and how it will absolutely, positively change lives, avoid that temptation.

What's happening?   140

Check out some of the innovative new product launches being considered for the Most Memorable New Product Launch survey at: www.mmnpl.com

Latest:

update

(sample tweet)

This advice may be particularly difficult to follow for those at start-up companies. If you've spent years developing an exciting new product and are finally about to bring it to market, it's tempting to want to gush about the value and importance of this new device. Just stop and realize that nobody is listening much past your first sentence. Seriously. They're not.

TIP 51 **Bring your product to life with real consumer stories and testimonials.**

People relate to real people. As we'll discuss later, celebrities have a role to play in launches, but nothing is more effective in bringing the value of your product to life than stories from real consumers about how they are using your product and why they love it. In fact, if you don't have consumers who have used your product, please find some! Reporters will not write about a new product if you can't produce human beings who have tried it. In addition to commissioning independent testing of your product that proves its efficacy, try out your product with consumers prior to launch. By doing this, you will have people ready, willing and able to share their opinions about the product.

Dan Danielson, co-chairman of the board of directors and co-founder of Mercury Media, is an expert at long form infomercials. He stands by testimonials as a tried-and-true selling method. "Testimonials on how the product has changed customers' lives and made a big impact are important buyer influencers," he said. "Testimonials can be found by the client or the producer, or you can sample the product with 100 people and choose the people who most loved your product and are good on camera."

TIP 52 **Create stunning product visuals.**

Strong visuals are the bedrock of a launch campaign. For the portion of the population with a visually oriented cognitive style, the chief way they're going to absorb information about your new product is through compelling visuals. And even for those who aren't visually oriented, having strong visuals helps to tell the product's story.

We live in a world where people are exposed to stunning images every day through the Internet and other media. You simply can't afford to have bland packaging, blah print ads or a so-so Web site. Your visuals need to be crisp, compelling and eye appealing.

TIP 53   **Keep your messages consistent across all platforms.**

Besides having a campaign theme that works across multiple disciplines, make sure the people working within those disciplines are bringing that theme to life with consistent messaging. Be wary of messaging drift that can occur when people working in the various launch disciplines are left to their own devices. After all, you're dealing with creative people who, not surprisingly, can sometimes get a little too creative.

Frequent and thorough team communication can help avoid such problems. Keep reminding team members of the need for consistency. But don't stifle creativity altogether. If someone comes up with a new, interesting approach to one of your launch messages, give it due consideration, and if it appears workable, make sure other team members know about it so they can incorporate it into their own thinking. The end result should be consumers receiving the same message about your new product whether they visit your Web site, read a magazine ad, see a TV commercial, or attend an event you've sponsored.

TIP 54   **Respect your company's heritage.**

What is your company's history? Has it been around for decades and have consumers built up a fairly rigid view of what your company is all about? Or do you have a history of morphing to serve the times? Is the new product you're launching a natural extension of the company's history or will people be surprised by the type of product you're launching? If you're headed in a new and unexpected direction, be aware of how hard it will be to retool the image of a company with a long and well-known history. It won't happen overnight.

Also, think carefully before you walk too far away from the company's heritage. Companies with long histories have lasted a long time for a reason. They have managed to establish an emotional connection with consumers and the importance of this connection should not be overlooked when you're developing your launch theme and messaging. Don't try to make the company into something it is not. Leverage the power of the past instead of ignoring it.

CHAPTER 7:

Generating Buzz through Media Coverage

There's no doubt that social media—Facebook, YouTube, blogs, Twitter—is the hip new kid on the block. But media relations targeted to traditional outlets (newspapers, network and cable TV, magazines and trade publications) is still one of the most important tools for spreading the word about a new product. Think about it: Even on a "bad" night, the network newscasts combined reach almost 20 million people, while *The New York Times* reaches approximately a million people every day and almost half that many on Sunday. In our Most Memorable New Product Launch Survey, year after year, consumers have told us that new products mentioned on TV or in articles, or product reviews in magazines and newspapers, are among their top sources of new product information.

In our most recent survey, seeing a new product talked about on TV was mentioned by 49 percent of respondents as a way that they learned about a new product, while 18 percent said they saw new products mentioned in print articles or product reviews. These numbers may fluctuate each year but have not changed dramatically since we conducted our first survey in 2002. Media coverage is still a powerful driver of launch messages and deserves your attention as you plan and execute your new product introduction.

In the Internet age, the job of generating publicity has taken on a few new twists, but the basics of creating sound public relations strategies have not changed. You still need to conduct research to identify the right media contacts (whether they are TV news producers, newspaper or magazine editors, bloggers, online editors, partner Web sites or prominent Twitterites who may be interested in your story). If you're pursuing traditional media or online media, understanding the person and outlet you are pitching is still essential. Just as you would read a newspaper or magazine to see a reporter's past articles before you pitch a story, the same holds true for online media. And, of course, good writing prevails no matter what media you target.

In 2009, 81% cited TV commercials as where they learned about new products versus 72% in 2008

If you have a tight launch budget, media relations can be your best friend. Publicity campaigns are relatively cost effective compared with other launch tools such as TV advertising, Web site advertising and hosting special events. The credibility of traditional media (and their online news sites) also provides powerful return on investment. Some companies rely totally on media relations and social media campaigns to build their brand and serve as the launch pads for new products.

Each year, Baskin-Robbins hosts 31 Cent Scoop Night to kick off the spring ice cream season, introduce a new product (like Soft Serve), and thank local firefighters for their contributions to the communities they serve. In conjunction with a national fire-related charity, such as the National Volunteer Fire Council or the National Fallen Firefighters Foundation, Baskin-Robbins donates $100,000 and offers 31-cent scoops to consumers. The only systemwide promotion that Baskin-Robbins executes each year, 31 Cent Scoop Night is the perfect blend of cause-related marketing, traffic-building promotion and local media relations. To build momentum for the brand in the important time frame leading up to summer, 31 Cent Scoop Night depends solely on print Free Standing Insert (FSI) coupons, online promotions and social media to drive traffic to stores for this one-day offer. The campaign, which is not supported by advertising, instead uses outreach to mommy bloggers, deal sites and blogs, the company Facebook fan page, Twitter microblogging, Flickr photo sharing and the Baskin-Robbins Birthday Club.

By engaging in multiple forms of Internet communication and social media, Baskin-Robbins has created incredible buzz and goodwill as a result of this campaign. The media results from a carefully planned strategy of old and new tactics were exceptional: Print media coverage included 550 placements in publications such as the *Chicago Sun-Times* and *The Washington Post*; broadcast accounted for 232 segments; online impressions reached 190 million, and the event had more than 150,000 confirmed Facebook guests in 2008.

According to Nicole Murra, brand manager for PR and promotions at Baskin-Robbins, 31 Cent Scoop Night is a perfect example of not needing advertising to have an impact on retail sales.

"The event drives hundreds, and in some areas thousands, to the store on one night. The entire event is primarily driven through PR efforts with social media playing a big part in spreading word of mouth," said Murra. "The campaign works because it is something consumers care about, or rather, are passionate about—ice cream. Mixed with the worthy cause of honoring and fostering goodwill toward firefighters, it is something every person can get excited about in all our local markets.

"Events like 31 Cent Scoop Night are ideal for Facebook and Twitter because it isn't about just sharing a marketing message or saying 'try our new product.' It's about a timely event and an offer that is compelling to the consumer," added Murra. "We just put the event out there and it's the people who do the rest.

"In real time you can see what people think of the event. Whether it is a mommy blogger spreading the word to her readers, or on Twitter, or just comments left by teens on our Facebook wall, we can see what people think of the event and see the excitement spread as people invite friends. When the event is over, we use these same channels to see whether we lived up to consumer expectations, and make improvements for the following year."

Other companies use a combination of paid and earned media for major product introductions. As Al Reis, author of *The Fall of Advertising and the Rise of PR,* said, "Public relations builds the brand and advertising sustains it." We too advise using an integrated launch campaign—including advertising—to launch new products whenever possible.

No matter what the medium, once you've distributed press materials and/or a pitch letter, you have to relentlessly follow up to ensure your story is not overlooked in the avalanche of e-mails and snail mail that bombards traditional and social media people each day. We are now sending information via fax and FedEx because editors' e-mail boxes are filled with online pitches, so we're taking a counter-cyclical approach and returning to traditional methods of distribution. Whatever way you contact a reporter, keep a record of the communication method he or she prefers. Reporters are quirky and if you know what they like, you've got a leg up on competitors who don't take time to research such details.

Justin Esch and Dave Lefkow, who co-founded Bacon Salt, a gourmet seasoning blend with the taste of real bacon without the meat, fat or calories, said they didn't know anything about public relations when they launched their product. "We really didn't understand it wasn't cool to call editors a hundred times until one of them actually picked up the phone to talk to us," said Esch. "We figured it was like sales; you keep calling until you finally get someone on the phone. We weren't hindered by protocol and thus were able to convince a producer at Oprah that we had a good story and [we] appeared as guests on the show. It was great."

At a time when newsrooms all over the country are being downsized dramatically, the remaining reporters, editors and broadcasters are now busier than ever. Not only are they worried about their own jobs, but they are now covering more than one beat. This means reporters are extremely stretched for time and even more selective about what stories they tackle, as the pressure is on to produce twice as many stories in the same amount of time.

In this atmosphere, the smart approach is to help harried media members as much as possible by providing all the necessary information in an easily decipherable form. Given the choice between a story that practically writes itself and one that requires substantial research, fact finding, and extensive interviews, a time-squeezed editor, producer, reporter or blogger is much more likely to choose a story that is "packaged" and ready for consideration.

A primary objective in media relations is to make sure your story is newsworthy. Make it easy for the reporter to dive into the topic, determine what makes it newsworthy, and understand the value of the story to the outlet's audience. Having key sources (including consumers who have tried the product and researchers who have tested the product) readily available and willing to talk may be the difference between a reporter covering your story or telling you, "I'm not interested."

Here are steps to conduct a media relations campaign that will generate the buzz you'll need to get your new product off the launching pad:

TIP 55 | Make a media list and check it twice.

Create a media list by following key news outlets and identifying specific reporters, or by using a media database like Media Map, Cision, Vocus or Media ContactsPro. It's good to create a media list well in advance of your launch to be sure you've included all the people you want to reach. Just prior to launch, call to make sure those reporters are still at the publication or check online to see if they are still writing. There's nothing worse than sending critical new product information to the wrong reporter or to someone who is no longer with the media outlet. Google is another great resource for checking to see who has covered an issue, as are data services like Dow Jones or LexisNexis. Use Technorati or Google Blog Search to find relevant blogs. Do a search on Twitter to identify influencers and enthusiasts who may be critical to your product's adoption. Never rely on one source to create a media list—use all the data services available to ensure your list is complete.

While the best way to structure a media list is to use a variety of sources, in the case of Bacon Salt, a few targeted social media options fueled their launch. Esch and Lefkow launched their product on a small budget using social media as the primary piece of their media strategy. "We tried to figure out who the key influencers were around bacon—people who are crazy about bacon, write about it, blog about it and eat a lot of it," said Esch. "We reached out to them in a variety of ways, including Twitter and Facebook. We made them feel part of it, but we had no real idea of what was going to happen when we launched. Believe it or not, 3,000 jars sold out in nine days. We had 800 orders from 25 states and four different countries and from the minute we launched, it was insanity."

TIP 56 **Avoid mass mailings and e-mail blasts to reporters and bloggers.**

Disseminate your story to reporters who cover your field and/or write about new products. Abandon the shotgun approach and pursue a more focused strategy to identify

and pitch media. "The days of mass pitches to 100 staff reporters are over," explained John McIndoe, vice president of global media & analyst relations at Information Resources, Inc. "You really have to understand what reporters are writing about in terms of their focus area, what they're interested in and what they're currently writing about. And then you have to communicate with them via the vehicle they request. Some reporters still prefer to receive faxes. Some prefer phone pitches and others like e-mail." The same holds true for bloggers. "Listen" to what's being said on blogs— both by bloggers and their followers—before jumping in to pitch a story. The fastest way to get shut down is to intrude. Be sure what you are pitching is relevant and fits in with the content and context of the medium.

TIP 57 **Create lasting relationships with reporters.**

Reporters have always been a mobile group, but as a result of media consolidation, they're moving even more frequently. Make sure you create, cultivate and cherish your relationships with key members of the media.

If you are lucky, you will cross paths with the same media many times throughout your career. Reporters value people who bring them news, particularly breaking news, so think carefully about how you select the reporter or media outlet that will break your story. The same is true with bloggers and people on Twitter. Don't be a one-story wonder.

If you are going to join the conversation, bloggers and Twitterites expect you to be part of the community. Katie Paine, founder and CEO of KDPaine & Partners, helps define the nature of the relationship: "In social media, if you talk to me because I am an influential blogger, and at the end of six months you no longer give me exclusives and product, I am going to start dissing you," she said. "It's different from traditional media where reporters don't want to talk to you unless you have news. With social media, you have a personal relationship with the bloggers and their communities and are expected to remain in contact."

TIP 58 Build relationships with the media *before* you need them to cover a story.

The time to get to know a reporter or blogger is before you need him or her to cover your launch story. Regularly read reporters and bloggers who cover your industry or new product news. If you have a tech product, read Walter Mossberg of *The Wall Street Journal,* David Pogue of *The New York Times* or Michael Arrington from *TechCrunch*; they're the current authoritative sources on what's hot in technology.

When possible, provide reporters with information they might find useful even if it is unlikely to lead to a story about your company or new product. Reporters appreciate it when you supply valuable information, and may be more disposed to telling your story when the time comes. For instance, if you see an interesting article in a competing publication on a topic that a reporter on your target list has written about in the past, send it along. It may spur an idea for a follow-up story. Or if you see a reporter seeking industry data on Twitter, on Profnet (a paid service that journalists use to find sources or background information), or on Help a Reporter Out (a free service where reporters can post queries for sources), be willing to do some legwork for him or her. This type of kindness frequently pays dividends.

"Show you understand their world," said McIndoe. "We have an automated proprietary program that identifies the right media person and then tracks our interactions with them. Coming to reporters with relevant information is the best way to build relationships. The last thing you want to do is call up a reporter and say, 'I'm Bill Smith and I don't know anything about what you're covering, but I have a story about XYZ that I'd like to talk to you about.'"

Pleasing Reporters 101

For our first book on launching new products, we talked to a group of trade publication editors and asked them to tell us what mistakes companies made when sending them press materials about new products. Seven years later, we went back and posed the same question to a different group of editors, and we're sad to report that the same mistakes are still being made. Because of their importance, here again are media relations sins to avoid in your quest to interest an editor or reporter in your launch story:

- **Not knowing what the publication covers.** Pitching a story that is completely off the publication's subject area should never occur, yet editors tell us this happens all the time! It is a huge waste of everyone's time to pitch the wrong story to the wrong publication. Do your homework and avoid this major mistake.

- **Ignoring editorial calendars.** Most publications post their editorial calendars online. If your story doesn't line up with the "Ed Cal," it becomes more difficult to sell. When you pitch a story a month after the publication ran a special issue on the topic, you instantly lose all credibility.

- **Sending in sloppy, error-filled press releases.** While editors will rewrite what you send in, they don't appreciate getting press materials that are filled with typos or other mistakes. Make sure your materials are professional in every way. The editors told us they've received releases with Track Changes showing. Don't embarrass yourself or your company with these kinds of mistakes.

▶

- **Omitting key details, such as pricing, size of item, weight and other pertinent facts.** Editors hate when you omit important details that describe the new product. If it is a food product, editors are interested in the nutritional information as well. Always ask yourself, "If I were writing this story, what information would I need?" Once you think about what facts are necessary, press releases write themselves. And always include the cost of the product: It makes editors crazy when they have to follow up to find out a simple fact like manufacturer's suggested retail price.

- **Not returning editor calls or not having someone available for interviews.** If the goal of the press release is to secure coverage, editors cannot understand why company representatives do not  return their calls and sometimes are unwilling to provide sources to talk about the new product. If you are lucky enough to generate media interest, call the editor back promptly and offer a spokesperson to talk about the new product. Giving editors what they want—plus additional information—often results in larger new product stories.

- **Failing to include contact information.** Believe it or not, some people actually forget to include a contact name and information in their releases ... or they put it in such an obscure spot that editors have a hard time finding it. Contact information should be prominently displayed at the top of your releases and should include the contact person's title, phone number and e-mail address. Don't make it hard for the media to reach out to you if they want to set up an interview or need additional information. If you can't be bothered to include something as basic as contact information, why should an editor bother to track you down to cover the story? •

TIP 59 Personalize your pitch; reporters want to feel special.

Journalists and bloggers are experts at sniffing out a generic pitch. Avoid the bad impression this creates by taking time to personalize the beginning of your pitches. This is where familiarity with what the reporter has been writing about lately comes in very handy. Any reporter would be grateful to receive an e-mail praising a story that he or she produced a few days earlier. This is an important part of the relationship-building process and will go a long way toward assuring that your pitch actually gets read. The same holds true for Twitter. Avoid blasting out tweets; be strategic in what you say in those important 140 characters.

TIP 60 Develop key media messages and make sure everyone is speaking in the same voice.

Don't consider launching a new product without creating a Media Message Guide (MMG) to serve as a handbook for preparing all press materials and training spokespeople. See the sidebar below for what to include in this important tool.

Your Media Message Guide is a living document. Over the course of time, what you've written may need to change. Be sure to re-read and revise it frequently. As you launch the product, you'll learn which themes resonate with consumers and the media. Be sure to update your MMG and its Frequently Asked Questions (FAQ) section so that what you are saying is in line with the current situation. We've also been adding a social media section to our MMG where we identify short form messages that can be relayed via this medium.

The Contents of a Media Message Guide

Here are the elements of a Media Message Guide. We have noted some sections that are optional depending on what type of product you're launching.

- **A Single Overriding Communications Message (SOCM):**
  This should consist of one or two sentences that sum up the major points you want to communicate about the product.

In other words, what is the one message you'd be thrilled to see in every story about your product? This is the statement you want everyone to memorize and always use when talking about the product.

Here's the SOCM we developed for the launch of Baskin-Robbins' BRight Choices:

"Baskin-Robbins, America's favorite neighborhood ice cream shop, is introducing BRight Choices, a lineup of frozen treats that respond to growing consumer interest in better-for-you options. Available nationwide, the BRight Choices options include new Premium Churned Light Ice Cream, which offers the same great creamy taste of traditional Baskin-Robbins ice cream but with 50 percent less fat and 20 percent fewer calories."

Your SOCM should be able to pass this test: "If my potential customers hear this message, understand it, believe it and act on it, will it help drive my business?" If the answer is no, you need to do some clear-headed thinking and revise your message.

- **Supporting Messages:** These messages should support or reinforce the overriding message and provide additional information or proof points to solidify product and company credibility. When combined with the single overriding communications message, these facts relay the "short story" you want to consistently tell about the product. These supporting messages should help answer the question that every consumer asks on some level: What's in it for me? The BRight Choices message tells me that I can enjoy a specific flavor of ice cream without the usual fat and calories.

- **Key Words:** This list should include 10 touchstone words used in the messages. By memorizing this short list, spokespeople and those pitching the media can incorporate these key words and phrases when talking about the product. When creating this list, be sure to include key words from the product positioning, such as the adjectives that bring the product to life and express the emotions you're trying to evoke. For example, the list of key words we developed for the launch of Baskin-Robbins' BRight Choices included, among others, "healthier options," "better-for-you," "fewer calories," "less fat," "delicious," and "irresistible."

- **"Do Not Use" Words (optional):** If there are words that are often mistakenly applied to your product, your brand or your company, include them on the "Do Not Use" list so your spokespeople stay clear of these red-light words. In addition, you may want to include words to avoid when speaking about your target market. For instance, in promoting a luxury retirement community, management preferred the words "active adults" and wanted to avoid referring to its residents as "senior citizens" or "elders."

- **Key Messages:** Key messages are often broken into sections. For example, you might create a section about product and brand messages, a section on corporate messages and a section about event/program messages. You may also want to include messages about your launch event and related programs such as contests or partnerships with nonprofits. Each section should contain no more than six to 10 messages that are concise and make ample use of the key words. Remember, all key messages should support the SOCM.

    Make sure the messages are user friendly and not written in stilted language. Avoid industry or business lingo at all costs. The messages must be easy and comfortable to deliver and understandable to people who are not in your industry. Key messages should be conversational and should be read aloud prior to presenting to management to ensure they are usable sound bites and not too lengthy or onerous for a spokesperson to use in conversation.

    "If spokespersons are not comfortable with key messages, they won't use them easily and frequently in interviews. Your media messages will be garbled and your customers won't receive good information about your wonderful new product," said ▶

Louisa Hart, Schneider Associates' media relations coach, who spent 15 years as a broadcast news producer.

- **FAQ:** This section should focus on commonly asked questions, including those you hope reporters never ask. The FAQ section of the MMG is one of the most important components of this document. By providing answers to all questions a reporter may ask, this road map gives everyone in the company answers to all the different types of questions that may come their way.

We recommend creating two different versions of the FAQ—one that gets included in the press kit and is featured on the Web site and a second one for internal use only. The second FAQ document should list the challenging or probing questions a reporter or consumer might ask that you may not want to answer, but need to be prepared to answer.

By anticipating the tough questions prior to launch, you can prepare management, your spokespeople and agencies to handle any topic—even the ones they dread. Make sure the "ugly" questions are developed by someone outside the management team. The use of objectivity is key to crafting tough questions. If you truly want to be prepared for difficult questions, they need to be created outside the inner circle to ensure objectivity.

Ask your public relations team, media trainer, outside research consultant—people you trust—to articulate what keeps them up at night and you'll get the kind of difficult questions we're describing.

"The marketing team may think they have identified and dealt with all the questions and problems. But when reporters and consumers hear the information, the facts about the product may still not be clear," said Hart. "That's why it is imperative to test messages outside your inner circle. What seems perfectly evident to people who have developed a product may be perfectly unclear to your target market."

We always say that if you get through our media training ▶

boot camp, the actual launch interviews will be a breeze. The goal is to get all the tough questions out into the open prior to launch when there's still time to tighten up product messaging, or tweak an element of the campaign.

- **First/Milestones:** If your product is breakthrough, or is creating a new category, or is accomplishing some other first/significant milestone that supports your new product message or leadership positioning, include this information here.

- **Analogies (optional):** If your product is technical, complicated or difficult to understand, provide useful analogies that can be offered to help support key messages. Anecdotes that bring the product story to life are appreciated by the media and consumers. The more you can support key messages with interesting, personal stories about the founders and how the product was developed, the more believable your launch story will be. If your new product does not have a story, we suggest making sure you create one prior to launch.

- **Myths & Misconceptions (optional):** Always Google your product category, key words and other topics prior to launch. Certain words, numbers and ideas may have negative connotations or have received negative press.

Rather than deal with a negative at launch, do your research prior to launch to determine that there are no skeletons in the closet about your product category, product name or other details relating to launch. In the myths and misconceptions section of your MMG, describe potential myths and provide accurate information to dispel them. There's nothing worse than learning your launch campaign has some pivotal detail that activates negative feedback from consumers and the media.

▶

- **Third-Party Endorsements:** Third-party credibility is critical to supporting key messages. Members of the media often require individuals outside the company to comment on the efficacy of the product or the emerging trend into which the product fits. This section can contain brief (two to three sentences) third-party testimonials regarding the product or your company. Or it can include a list of third-party contacts (with phone numbers) that can validate the product and provide comments and data to the media. This list comes in handy during media interviews as a source sheet of experts that you can suggest to the media as ballast for the story.

- **Industry/Trend Overview/Statistics:** This is the type of information that reporters love. Keep it brief and provide no more than six to 10 pertinent facts that are relevant to your product. Offer insightful and, whenever possible, "new-to-the-world" information. While the goal is not to inundate your spokespeople with reams of data, it's critically important they remember key facts and figures, and are conversant with the product's features, benefits and attributes. If a reporter is a data junkie, remember you can always e-mail or snail mail additional research, facts and customer data. Since you should always follow up after an interview, providing additional pertinent facts is an excellent way to keep the dialogue going.

- **Major Competitors (optional):** In this section, try to anticipate questions about the competitive environment your new product is entering. These messages should offer responses to inquiries about the category and the overall market without dwelling on the competition. The goal here is for your spokespeople to fit the product and its launch quickly into context and then bring the focus back to your product and key messages—not to educate the reporter about your competitors and why their products are inferior to yours. Bashing the competition is bad form and has no benefit. Avoid the temptation to dwell on competitive product pitfalls.

▶

- **Glossary of Terms (optional):** If your product is highly technical, a glossary of terms can be helpful in bringing your spokespeople and the media quickly up to speed. Remind your spokesperson to use everyday language and to avoid technical jargon that consumers and the media might not understand. Clear, simple language is the best way to explain something new. •

TIP 61 Avoid foot-in-the-mouth moments; get media trained.

The Media Message Guide serves as the training manual for everyone who will be speaking to the media about your new product. All spokespeople should attend media training to assure they are familiar with the launch messages and are comfortable handling difficult questions.

When we say that "everyone" should go through media training, we mean *everyone*. Don't let higher-ups off the hook when they say they're too busy to fit the session into their schedules or when they claim to know the product so thoroughly that they don't need media training.

"There are two purposes for media training," said Louisa Hart, Schneider Associates' media relations coach. "The first is to give spokespeople practice with using the key messages and dealing with difficult questions. The second, which is just as important, is to get final feedback on the key messages and make sure that spokespeople can comfortably and effectively use them. It's a two-way process and if all the important folks are not involved, the messages may not be totally on target and the media outreach will not be as effective."

Even people who have gone through media training at other companies can often use a tune-up on how to deal effectively with reporters. Since no two product launches are exactly the same, the information will be different every time, thus requiring new ways to talk about a product and category. The best way to convince executives who think they don't need media training is to ask them some of the ugly questions you've created and see how they answer them. If they stumble, perhaps it's a good time to suggest that they, too, attend media training.

Hiring an excellent media trainer is money well spent as it prepares spokespeople to be more confident, knowledgeable and believable. It also helps them avoid making misstatements or other faux pas because they are nervous when dealing with the press or appearing on camera.

Here's an interesting new development that can help with media training: Some reporters are willing to provide questions in advance of an interview. "In the increasing age of demands for accuracy and also due to reduced deadline cycles, many reporters will provide questions prior to an interview via e-mail," said McIndoe. "We have begun to ask for these on a regular basis and we're finding people are responding."

Don't expect all reporters to respond positively to such a request, but for those who are willing to play ball, the preparation benefit is obvious. We've found the trade press to be more willing than the business press to provide advance questions. That being said, we suggest asking all reporters for questions: The worst they can say is no.

Tips for Mastering Interviews

Here are a few pointers to consider when talking with the media:

- **Avoid saying "no comment" at all costs.** It's difficult when a reporter asks a question you do not know how or want to answer. There are some good options for dodging dangerous bullets that you'll want your spokespersons to become adept at before granting interviews. This is where key messages can save the day.

  In the first instance, if you've done your homework, you'll have answers prepared to virtually every question. If you are asked a negative question, you'll need to bridge to one of your key messages to provide a credible answer. We use bridging phrases all the time in our daily conversation: "on the other hand," "you also need to realize," or "much more important" are samples of the hundreds of bridging phrases that we can use to move from what the reporter asks to what you really want to say. You can also tell reporters they are asking about proprietary information that you are not at liberty to reveal. But don't stop there. Follow this with, "What I can tell you is ... " ▸

"Always keep in mind that reporters are looking for a good story," said Louisa Hart, Schneider Associates' media relations coach. "If you can't give them exactly what they are asking for, give them something else that is just as interesting and supports your business goals. Chances are the information you provide will work just as well for them, and make it into their story."

- **It's okay to say, "I will get back to you."** When you don't know the answer to a question, it is fine to say, "I don't know the answer but I am happy to look into it and get back to you." It's better to be honest, especially with sales figures, statistics or other data points, than to make things up. Reporters appreciate when you are genuine and follow through with accurate data.

- **Find a way to take charge.** If a reporter calls you unexpectedly for an interview, say that you are in a meeting and will call him or her back in half an hour. Ask about the topic of the interview and the deadline. This puts you, instead of the reporter, in charge when you call back.

- **Never say anything to a reporter that you wouldn't want to read in the paper or see on the Internet.** Don't assume the interview is over once a reporter closes his or her notebook, turns off the camera or stops typing during a "phoner." Never let down your guard or assume a reporter is your friend just because you've dealt with the person before and she or he seems like a nice person. We always say, there is no such thing as "off the record." Even when a reporter tells you that what you are saying is not being recorded, be circumspect and again remember, don't say anything you would not want to see in print.

- **Don't answer questions you find offensive.** Instead, redirect the reporter to one of your key messages with a statement that begins with something like, "I prefer to focus on … " •

TIP 62 Understand media deadlines.

Be mindful that it takes five months to get an article placed in most long-lead magazines and less than five minutes to post a story on the Internet. The instant nature of the Web and the 24/7 news cycle is a far cry from the timeline of a popular women's or men's monthly magazine. Most glossy publications close three to five months in advance of their publication dates, Sunday newspaper magazines close two to three months in advance, and major newspapers like *The Wall Street Journal* often require a month to do the research on a major story. The big three morning television shows (*The Today Show, Good Morning America* and *The CBS Early Show*) schedule segments with a slightly shorter lead time, booking guests within a week of pitching.

Keep in mind that major television segments planned for seasonal events (Christmas, Easter, back to school, summer) are often booked at least a month ahead, if not longer. Competition is fierce so it's best to pitch your story with lots of time to spare. That way, if the angle you are pitching gets rejected, you have time to go back to the producers with other story ideas.

If you are looking for instant coverage, a news syndicate such as the Associated Press is a valuable resource. The Associated Press has the power to place your story in newspapers throughout the country within one day. And while broadcast television and daily newspaper deadlines have shorter lead times, there's nothing like the Internet for lightning-speed coverage. Take advantage of the immediacy that Twitter, blogs and the Web provide to break major news stories.

TIP 63 Educate reporters.

One of the downsides of the shrinking newsroom is that many seasoned editors and reporters have taken buyouts and left the news business, leaving behind young and eager but relatively inexperienced journalists. No longer can you automatically expect to find a reporter who has been covering your industry for years, let alone decades. Now you're just as apt to get a new journalism school graduate or even a newsroom intern who knows relatively little, if anything, about your topic.

This presents you with a great opportunity to educate reporters and bloggers—you can be the one who makes their jobs easier by giving them a tutorial on your industry and new product. This is a great way to build the types of relationships with reporters that we discussed earlier. Conduct media research and outreach early so you can begin talking to the major reporters prior to your launch date. Get on the phone now (or start e-mailing) to help new reporters learn the ropes of the beats they're covering. They will show their gratitude when it comes time to report on your new product.

TIP 64 | Volunteer to fact check articles.

Whether you're dealing with a veteran reporter or one who has been covering the beat for a week, it is extremely important to offer to fact check articles. Reporters don't always offer this opportunity, but volunteering never hurts and, if they agree, it helps eliminate factual errors. Simply say, "I realize I've inundated you with so many data points about the industry, and facts about our new product and the research we conducted. I would be happy to fact check the article to be sure all the technical information is correct." Some reporters will take you up on the offer, but many publications have specific policies against showing information to sources before an article is published.

TIP 65 | Find an expert who does not work at the company to validate your product.

The only expert the media are going to believe when they're told your product is revolutionary is one who's not on your payroll. Identify an academic or influencer who has done research in the field or is a devotee of your product who can provide independent third-party endorsement. Brief the expert in advance so he or she is able to accurately provide background information about the industry and your new product. Once you establish credibility, feel free to hire a paid spokesperson.

TIP 66 | Use a spokesperson to spread the story.

Someone articulate and knowledgeable should serve as the face and voice of your company when you're launching a new product. Whether it's your CEO, president, general manager, celebrity or industry expert, the person you select must be able to deal with the media effectively and convey credible, accurate information in an animated way.

If you have a revolutionary new product that is a game changer, you may want to have more than one spokesperson on hand. Along with the

CEO, consider having an academic, an industry expert or a customer who has used the product and is available to comment on its efficacy and importance.

If the new product is simply a line extension, assigning a product manager or a general manager to deal with the media may be adequate. Remember, even line extensions need a new twist to be media worthy, so we often like to tap the research and development people to talk about how the product was developed and why the company added this new SKU to its line.

Generally speaking, we recommend that marketing and sales executives not serve as spokespeople, unless they have off-the-wall titles. If an executive's title is "Director of Brand Excitement," "Idea Director" or "Brand Evangelist," the media might be impressed by such a creative moniker and speak to the executive out of curiosity. But no matter how well prepared and articulate the vice president of marketing or the public relations director might be, journalists don't value or trust the credibility of people who are totally engaged in promoting the company. The media want to talk to decision makers—the people they believe are in charge of launching the new product and those who are responsible to shareholders.

TIP 67 | Use celebrity spokespeople when it makes sense.

Celebrity spokespeople can be expensive, so use them judiciously when the nature of your launch requires this tactic. A line extension that otherwise might be greeted with a yawn can benefit from the extra buzz a celebrity spokesperson brings.

No matter how famous the personality, be sure to conduct due diligence prior to hiring a celebrity spokesperson. Know the person's background as well as what your target market values.

Research the celebrity's Q Score, which is a measurement of his or her familiarity and appeal. The higher the Q Score, the better known and more highly regarded the person is.

Make sure your spokesperson aligns with your brand's values and personality and that there is a legitimate tie-in between the celebrity and your product. Naturally, you want to avoid celebrities who have become overexposed by promoting too many products, particularly if they are not relevant to your brand and may confuse consumers.

Questions to ask when considering celebrities include:

- **What is the celebrity's Q Score?**
- **Is this person relevant to our brand?**
- **Will this person be believable when it comes to talking about our product?**
- **Does his or her experience relate to what we are launching?**
- **Has he or she done media before?**
- **Will people in our target age group relate to this person?**
- **What products/companies has this person represented and what do we know about these endorsements?**
- **Based on the talent's other endorsements, what limitations does he or she have in terms of appearing on television? For instance, if a celebrity is a regular guest on** *The Today Show***, he or she may be prohibited from going on it to promote a product for which he or she is being paid as a spokesperson. If a celebrity has a show on one network, he or she may be prohibited from appearing on competitive shows airing on other networks.**

Doing a background check on a potential celebrity spokesperson is a must. Avoid stars who are controversial unless you have an unusual product that might benefit from controversy. Negotiate a contract that protects you as much as possible from any potential bad behavior by the spokesperson. Make sure you include a "morals" clause in the contract so that if the person does something that is anathema to your brand, you can cancel the contract.

Would it be a problem if your celebrity was arrested for drunk driving? Carrying arms? If your celebrity gained weight (if you are a weight-loss product)? Altered her body (if you are a bra company and the celebrity has breast reduction surgery) or was involved in any other situation that could hinder sales?

If you are a family brand—cereal, candy, soft drinks, cookies—does the celebrity have the type of image that moms respect? Is your product geared to football fans, DIY-ers, foodies or motorcycle enthusiasts? Who best speaks to each group?

Finally, be sure to train the celebrity on how to stay on message about your product during appearances. The media will inevitably question the "star" about his or her latest movie or current projects; the goal here is to talk about your product, not the star's career. Always work to get the show producers to write into the script, "So what interesting things are you doing right now?" That provides an opening for the celebrity to talk about your product and the campaign.

Learning how to bridge away from personal questions and onto talking about your product takes practice. Don't let the agent tell you the spokesperson is a pro and media training isn't necessary. Write into the contract that a media training session is required. If the agent and talent aren't willing to agree to the session, chances are they aren't going to be adept at conveying your product messages.

| TIP 68 | Offer an exclusive story to snag a bigger media story.

As you develop your media relations plan, the subject of whether to offer a journalist an "exclusive" should be discussed. More and more, journalists require an exclusive to break an important story. Approaching a reporter at *The Wall Street Journal*, *The New York Times*, *BusinessWeek* or *The Today Show* can yield huge benefits but can also have its risks.

While you can often negotiate exclusives in the four media categories (newspaper, weekly magazines, broadcast and online), you run the risk that an enterprising reporter will take the story and run with it on the Internet or not respect the embargo and run it prior to the official launch date. Then what?

The prospect of a well-known journalist at a high-profile media outlet breaking the story about your new product can be very enticing. It is often—although not always—possible to leverage an offer of an exclusive into a bigger or more prominent placement. In fact, we always say "media begets media." All newsrooms read feeds from other print and broadcast outlets. If you go into the newsroom of your local television station at 9 on any morning, the assignment desk editors will have the local papers open to look at what was covered by their competitors. They will also check out the AP wire, the Internet and other aggregated news sources to see what's happening around the country and the world. In addition, they will watch the news and feature coverage on their network feed. These are stories that happened overnight and the previous day that local affiliates put up on the satellite; news editors can use them to augment the local newscast.

If there are high-profile reporters who are the thought leaders in your industry, it makes sense to offer them an exclusive since once they cover your new offering, others are sure to follow. Similarly, persuading one of the network morning news programs to agree to cover your new product in exchange for an exclusive might be your springboard to print coverage.

Then there's the Oprah factor. There's no doubt that if you can get Oprah interested in your story, exposure on her television show can lead to massive media. The challenge of having your product appear on *The Oprah Show* is not demand, it's supply. If Oprah fans fall in love with your product, do you have enough manufactured to meet the demand? How long will it take to fill back orders generated by Oprah's viewers? Can your customer service handle this kind of onslaught? With Oprah retiring from *The Oprah Show* after 25 years and moving to the Oprah Winfrey Network (OWN), it will be interesting to see who replaces her as the Queen of Daytime TV.

It's important when reviewing launch scenarios that you list the pros and cons of each strategy—including an exclusive strategy.

The trade-off you make when you offer an exclusive is that you are "betting the farm" that this media outlet will run your story in a timely manner. Not only does this delay coverage from other media outlets, it may preclude you from placing stories in competitive media. If you are on *The Today Show*, other morning shows won't touch your product. If you are in *The Wall Street Journal*, chances are *The New York Times* or *USA Today* won't run your story—unless you offer them a different angle. If it breaks on Twitter, you may have the opportunity to encourage all types of reporters to cover it—or maybe none at all.

Media relations is always both an art and a science. But media coverage is never guaranteed. Journalists, editors and producers have been known to change their minds or have their minds changed for them by unforeseen circumstances—such as a late-breaking news story or a better story—that kicks yours to the curb. Avoid telling management that a major story is going to run until the day it is going to appear (and you've confirmed with the reporter or blogger) because there are no guarantees. Nothing gets management more upset than thinking the new product is going to run in a prestigious publication or online site, only to find that your product story has been trumped by something else.

TIP 69   Use consumer surveys as a news platform.

The media love to write about consumer surveys. Fielding a survey that produces newsworthy results, like interesting consumer insights or fun, provocative facts, can provide a great hook for your launch. This strategy is particularly helpful if you're launching a product that in and of itself is not that newsworthy, such as a product extension. But even breakthrough products can benefit from the cachet and news value of fresh consumer data.

If your budget doesn't provide for your own proprietary research, check to see if other organizations have recently released consumer survey results on a topic related to your new product. For example, we cited consumer survey data from the nonprofit National Sleep Foundation in the launch press release for the Zeo Personal Sleep Coach. Not only did it add interest to the release, it also provided third-party credibility to the company's mission of helping consumers understand the importance of getting a good night's rest.

TIP 70   Optimize your press releases, video and photos for search engine optimization (SEO) and for social media.

The online visibility of press releases about your new product will be greatly enhanced by optimizing them so search engines can easily crawl the content. Use Google Analytics to find the words consumers use to research your product's category as well as the product. "Google Analytics is the platform of choice for most companies because it ties into search engine marketing programs," said Chris Pape of Genuine Interactive, a Boston-based agency that creates award-winning Web sites and online marketing campaigns. "Google Analytics helps you quantify the key metrics you want to measure, like visits to the site, bounce rate, and conversion to sales, among others. Bounce rate is an important number to measure. It tells you what percentage leaves immediately after looking at the home page. From this number, one can deduce how effective the home page or landing pages are, and if the traffic you are driving to the site is the proper target audience." The bounce rate will also show you if you are converting visitors from interest in the product to buying the product—which is a good indicator of whether the product is priced properly. If your conversion rates are poor, rethink your homepage and pricing.

TIP 71 | **Make sure the press area of your Web site is user friendly.**
Journalists have come to rely on the press areas of corporate Web sites for quick facts, information and contacts. Yet when Web guru Jakob Nielsen conducted a user study of 42 Web sites with 40 journalists from around the world, the results showed that many of the press areas did not meet user needs. Many Web sites failed to enable the journalists to do the top five most important things:

- Locate a PR contact (name and telephone number)
- Find basic facts about the company, such as titles, location of headquarters, the spelling of an executive's name, and other corporate information
- Learn a company's spin on a recent event
- Check financial information
- Download images to illustrate stories[1]

Check your own site's press area. Is it easy for reporters to find this information? If not, some reworking of the site is needed.

TIP 72 | **Don't launch a new product by issuing a press release on Business Wire®, PR Newswire or any other mass distribution technique as the first entry into the market.**
In our opinion, it's like throwing away your most treasured possession—the news value of the product you've created. We counsel our clients to have a written media strategy that considers different tiers of media that would be best for launching the product into the marketplace. There's a time and a place for using mass distribution wire services—for instance, if you are a publicly traded company—but wire service distribution is not always the best vehicle to use when introducing new products.

Clients ask us why we resist using news services to launch new products since they have such incredible mass distribution. That's just the point—since everyone gets the news at the same time, unless it is earth-shattering product news, no one cares about it. The story is not tailored to their publications. We are not talking the iPhone here. We're talking about putting the new product in a context that the media and the public can understand. Most new products require an explanation, plus information about the company releasing the product, in order to make them relevant and newsworthy. Sure, if you are launching a product that is going to cure cancer and you have the clinical trials to back it up, by all means use a wire service to tell the world. But even in that situation, it might make sense to give the story as an exclusive to the most prestigious media outlet that will forward the business ball for the product. For instance, if you are trying to raise money for the drug you are announcing, it might make sense to give the story as an exclusive to *The Wall Street Journal*, as it is a bible for investors, venture capitalists and bankers.

We favor creating an "exclusive" media strategy where you determine which media outlets, in order of importance, would drive product sales, or raise money, or get distribution—or do whatever the stated goal is for the media. The categories we use are:

- **Top Tier Publications:** National business press like *The Wall Street Journal*, *The New York Times*, the *Financial Times*, *USA Today*, *BusinessWeek*, *TIME*, *Newsweek*, *Forbes* and *Fortune*, and their Internet sites, plus influential bloggers in the particular product space.

- **Mid Tier Media:** Regional media such as daily newspapers, regional city magazines, and popular consumer press (*Martha Stewart Living*, *Real Simple*, *People*, *Glamour*, *O, The Oprah Magazine*) that would be interested in the story.

- **Top Tier Broadcast:** Such programs as the three network morning shows: ABC's *Good Morning America*, NBC's *The Today Show*, and CBS's *The Early Show*.

- **Mid Tier Broadcast:** Local broadcast stations in specific markets, plus shows that speak to the audience, including local morning news and talk shows. If it is a home improvement product, any of the HGTV shows; if it's a food product, try *The Martha Stewart Show* or *Unwrapped* on the Food Network.

- **Specialized Press:** Every hobby has a publication geared toward enthusiasts. How does your product fit into these publications? There are hundreds of offerings on beauty, health, home improvement, decorating, motorcycles, cars—you name it, there's a publication that covers it. The goal here is to find how your new product fits into these different lifestyle and hobbyist publications.

- **Trade Press:** Not to be overlooked is the trade press. While many companies are reluctant to send news to the trade press, it does help generate distribution for new products. We always hear, "We don't want to give away our trade secrets to the competition," but then again, if you don't tell the industry trade press you have a new product, how are buyers going to know they should stock it? One thing we know: Buyers may or may not read *The Wall Street Journal,* but they all read the trade publications covering their industry. If you are marketing candy, you want an article in *Candy Industry* or *Candy Business.* "Almost all publicity, be it trade or consumer, is good publicity for a manufacturer," said Deborah Cassell, executive editor of *Candy Industry* and *Retail Confectioner,* published by BNP Media. "The goal should be to get the word out about what you have to offer to everyone within an industry. Trade magazines are powerful in that they fill such a niche, they're invaluable to the reader, and they have a great pass-along effect, reaching far more people than their circulations imply."

When we create media lists, we "bracket" the different media to fit into the categories just highlighted. Next, we determine in a very surgical way which editors at each publication we are going to contact. We talk to editors one-on-one, offer them the story, provide the background and then work to interest them in an interview. If it looks like they are going to pass, we move to the next publication on our list in order of importance.

TIP 73   **Use proven wire services to distribute media materials.**

Once you complete the initial launch and are seeking additional ways to secure coverage, consider using a wire service. For example, if you're conducting a seasonal or holiday pitch, the wire services can help you quickly reach almost every media outlet in the country.

We know what you're thinking: Services like Business Wire and PR Newswire are pricey. It's true, they are. But we think they're worth it, especially now that they offer numerous ways to optimize your release, with embedded photos, video clips, slide shows, and other attention-getting multimedia options.

According to Laura Sturaitis, senior vice president of new media at Business Wire, enhanced press releases can improve product launch. "If you are writing the press release with links and multimedia, people can use

that to get more information. You can write a shorter press release, incorporate more links and visuals, embed your video and photos of your product, and of course brand the content with your logo." She added: "The press release goes to search engines, online news sites and social media sites. All of this can be tracked, which is great because measurement is such a huge component. To be able to see how your release moves and what search terms are used to go to the Web site is instructional. We can track the ROI from the press release and see it on Google Analytics. The press release will drive people to optimized landing pages for the product. Here at Business Wire, we can create a handshake to the Web site from the press release that is really effective."

There are lower-cost options, such as PRWeb and even some services that distribute a basic release (without any SEO bells and whistles) for free. But as with everything else in business, you get what you pay for. If your new product launch is really important to your company, the investment in one of the larger, more proven distribution service providers is justified and safer. In addition to superior outreach capabilities, these services also provide measurement and monitoring reports that help you know whether you're meeting the goals and parameters you set for your campaign. And who's to say you shouldn't use both kinds of services?

TIP 74 | **Expand your media reach with tools such as radio media tours, satellite media tours, video news releases, and mat releases.**

If you're doing a national launch, these are all great ways to reach media outlets in as many parts of the country as possible. Radio media tours allow your spokesperson to make highly efficient use of his or her time by being interviewed by multiple radio stations or networks within a few hours. Video news releases (VNRs), which are in essence video versions of your launch press release, can be edited and tailored by TV stations to fit their local markets. VNRs are popular with the media because many TV stations have fewer resources at their disposal than in the past, yet still have lots of airtime to fill with newsworthy, informative and entertaining content.

With a satellite media tour, your spokesperson is able to interact live with reporters on local TV news or with personalities on local talk shows. If a solo satellite media tour is out of your budget, consider participating in a more affordable co-op media tour to lower your costs. With a co-op tour, one expert talks about products from several companies that all fit into a common theme. For example, seasonal stories such as *It's Time for Spring Cleaning* or *What's New for Halloween* could feature products from various companies, all described by one spokesperson. All these "pay-to-play" methodologies extend the reach and frequency of your campaign and make you less dependent on "earned" media for coverage.

Mat releases, which provide features to newspapers with camera-ready artwork already typeset, have been around for decades and are a proven communication tool. North American Precis Syndicate, a partner of Business Wire, is the industry leader with a reach that covers more than 10,000 newspapers in the United States with more than 225 million in cumulative circulation. They also cover online publications. If you're conducting a national launch, you should definitely consider doing one or more mat releases over the course of the launch. Since the articles need be only 400 to 500 words long and can include a product photo, the effort you expend to write the story and identify a photo is minimal, and the return can be fantastic. Mat releases are often organized around seasons or lifestyle issues. If your new product launch fits into their themed format, it can yield hundreds of articles that boost the impressions numbers substantially.

TIP 75 | Make sure you can describe how your new product works; use visuals.

Don't take it for granted that reporters will automatically understand how your product operates. Be ready to clearly and easily articulate its intricacies, and have visuals ready to show how it works and to support key messages. Some types of products cry out for visuals that show them in action. In a YouTube world, the video showing how your product works can do double duty by first educating the media and then serving as a direct-to-consumer online offering that can be a tremendous buzz generator.

"Using video to simply articulate a brand's differentiators or a product message is a macro trend that is going to continue to grow," Genuine Interactive's Pape explained. "As the convergence of TV and the Internet continues to push forward, video will be an important element of a solid 360-degree online communications plan."

Unless your product is serious in nature, like a lifesaving medical device or a drug, remember what we said earlier about having a sense of humor and having fun with online product visuals. The last thing you want to post on YouTube is a boring video that is a snoozefest.

TIP 76 Offer reporters a plant tour.

Journalists love to get a behind-the-scenes look at "how the sausage is made." Taking reporters on a tour requires that the plant be spotless and meet all Occupational Safety and Health Administration (OSHA) requirements.

Make sure everything is shipshape and employees get advance notice that reporters are coming on site so they can wear clean uniforms, be properly groomed, demonstrate the correct safety equipment, and be willing to be photographed. If plant tours are not a regular part of your company's repertoire, be sure to take the plant tour yourself and rehearse the entire tour several times with the management team to make sure everything goes smoothly when the press arrives.

Here are more plant tour pointers:

- Always work with operations, research and development, and marketing to organize plant tours.

- Have someone who understands production and marketing lead the tour, and have someone on hand who can answer technical questions.

- Most plants are really loud; don't expect to get much talking done on the tour. Meet with the reporter prior to the tour to explain the product's features and benefits.

- Safety gear (think hard hats and hairnets) is not an attractive look for executives, so try not to take executive photos on tour.

- Be sure the places on the tour are obvious to the reporter. The media love seeing the product being assembled or coming off the assembly belt; they also like to see the finished product. Everything else is probably too much information.

- Make sure the workers are wearing clean clothes and have gloves on (if appropriate) and that their production areas are spotless. Also make sure they are citizens, as the last thing you want is a worker declining to be photographed because of green card issues.

- If you are planning a number of tours, make signs for the different areas so it's clear what is happening, or provide a map so reporters can get oriented.

- If your factory is older and not photogenic, hire a videographer and take your own B-roll footage to distribute to the media. Many manufacturers are limiting access to their production facilities for safety reasons. Keep in mind, if your goal is to place a Food Network story on a show like *Unwrapped*, denying access to film the production line most likely is a deal killer.

Of course, there are cases where the revelations of the manufacturing plant can be damaging to the brand in some way. "I don't think people need to see the plant," declared New England Confectionery Company's [NECCO] vice president of marketing, Jackie Hague. "In the candy industry, when people think about a plant tour, they think they are going into Willy Wonka's world, when in reality, they are walking into a manufacturing facility focused on food safety, quality control and people safety. It's a cold dose of reality. I would rather people keep thinking about Willy Wonka and looking for the golden ticket, and skip the plant tour entirely."

TIP 77 Don't hold a press conference unless you have earth-shattering news to announce.

OK, maybe earth-shattering is a bit of an exaggeration, but not by much. If you hold a press conference, you'd better have some real news to announce. It's hard to know which is worse: taking the time and effort to organize a press conference only to have just one or two reporters attend, or finding yourself

looking at a standing-room-only crowd of reporters who expect to hear about breaking news but instead are treated to a ho-hum announcement. Either way, your credibility is shot.

There are ways to craft newsworthy product launch events without calling them press conferences. Instead, we call these gatherings "editor briefings" or "editor events." The modus operandi of these types of special events is to select a snazzy venue, especially when launching in New York City, so that editors will come to see the place—and your new product.

With newsroom staffs slashed, it's harder than ever to get people to attend news conferences and media events. You definitely have to make it worthwhile for a journalist by creating an event that generates an actual story. Make sure you have all the ingredients on hand to make your special event a one-stop shop for securing background information to write a great story. "It starts with the product—an interesting, innovative product always attracts more interest than a line extension for an existing product," said Olivier Cheng of Olivier Catering and Events, a New York firm that works with such clients as Louis Vuitton, Hermes, and Bulgari. "If you are launching a product that is from a company that already has high cachet, it is easier to make editors feel compelled to attend your event if the product is something they actually want or aspire to own."

Press Event Basics

Here are guidelines for creating a press event that will deliver what the media want and need:

- **Create a theme that intrigues the media.**

- **Identify a place that is hip, trendy and appropriate for your product—the newer the place, the better—so that reporters will want to go there.**

- **Make sure the event is conveniently located.** If it is a news event, make sure the television trucks and the media have a place to park close to the venue.

▶

- **Provide transportation to make it easy for editors to attend.** Pick them up at work or at home; do whatever you have to do to get them to the briefing.

- **Distribute clever and informative invitations to lure people to the event.** Make sure the invitations include all the information people need to find the event, including an emergency phone number that is operable that day.

- **Have a draw.** Your chances of dramatically improving attendance increase if you can present a famous spokesperson, an important physician, or a researcher who developed the product. Send out a media alert the day before the event to remind reporters and editors to attend.

- **Don't rely on e-mail or snail mail.** Be sure you personally call everyone on the list several times to encourage them to attend, and then confirm their attendance.

- **Be prepared to have 30 to 40 percent of the people you invite not show up.** Be sure to ask enough people to the event so that if half of them decline or are no-shows, you still have a quorum.

- **Engage your own photographer and videographer in case media cannot attend due to a late-breaking story.** That way you can send footage and photos following the event to media outlets that weren't there. (Note: Some stations cannot accept video and/or photos if they are union shops.)

- **To save on costs, television stations are using "pool cameras," which means one camera shoots an event and provides the footage to all the participating stations.** Be sure you know which station is the pool camera for your event.

▶

- **If a TV station sends a cameraperson without a reporter, be sure to send the cameraperson back to the newsroom with a press release and the names and titles of the people who were filmed so he or she can hand this information to the reporter writing the story.** The same holds true for newspaper photographers. Make it easy: Provide all the facts, figures, names, titles and contact information so a news desk person can easily write the story or call for more information.

- **Organize interesting photo vignettes at the event.** Offer photos of people who have agreed in advance to be photographed. Provide signed photo releases to the media with the person's name, title, company and hometown on the sheet to make things easier for the photo desk.

- **Tell reporters, videographers and photographers that they can call you directly for any reason at any time.** Be sure to have a supply of business cards on hand. Also make sure other team members have their business cards to distribute, as this will cut down on errors in names and titles. Also, it never hurts to offer your cell or home phone number, particularly if the event is taking place after business hours. You never know when a reporter will need to check a fact.

- **Create a "Time and Action Plan" that outlines exactly what needs to be done, when it needs to be done and by whom to make the event a success.** This type of action plan enables each team member to stay on task and lets management know exactly what everyone is responsible for, both before and on launch day.

- **Conduct a "Before Action Review."** Gather those working on the event and pick apart each section of the launch to see where there may be holes in launch planning. Since most launch plans have an event, suggested questions to ask at a Before Action Review could include:

▶

- What are your concerns as they relate to the physical event venue?
- What can go wrong with the audiovisual equipment? Who will be on site to fix it?
- When will the editor gifts be available? What if they don't arrive? Do you have a contingency plan?
- The spokespeople are coming in the night before the event—what if their planes are late? What is the backup transportation?
- What signage was ordered? Did you walk the route the people will take to be sure the signage is sufficient?
- Did someone leave instructions at the front desk of the venue about where we want our guests to go? Does the listing of the day's events include our event?
- Did you meet personally with the food and beverage director to be sure everything is exactly as ordered?
- What time is the rehearsal for the presentation? How are we going to train the people who are arriving after the presentation prep?
- Who is staying late to go over the presentation and technical equipment for the late arrivals? What time are the guests arriving?
- What time is the team going to be in the room to re-check all details before the guests arrive?
- Do we need security for the event?

Identify someone on the team or even outside the team—with a great deal of special-event experience and who is not serving as the day-to-day person managing the account—to dissect the Time and Action Plan and ask "what if" questions. The event logistics team is usually too focused on planning the event to consider all the things that could happen to derail it. The goal here is not to be negative but to positively plan for all eventualities so that no matter what happens, the event people are in control and have already thought of a solution. The old adage, "An ounce of prevention is worth a pound of cure," certainly applies when it comes to event planning. •

TIP 78 Create drama to attract busy reporters and to make the events memorable.

"I always try to create something interactive," said Cheng. "I try not to have everything static—just product displays and the client telling the story of the product—that is like Product Launch 101. For example, we recently designed the launch for a brand extension of a deodorant line of body mists which had floral notes. It took place at Dylan's Candy Bar and one of the event elements was a flower bar where editors each got the opportunity to have a custom floral bouquet made for them that had the floral notes in it. They loved it and could not stop talking about it." This is an example of creating something memorable that helps editors remember the product. Think of this type of event as "subconscious imprinting."

"Generally, I think launch events, if well done, are a very important part of getting your product's message out," said Cheng. "If you host a great event, editors will remember your product and still talk about it six months later."

When it comes to budgeting for a press event, Cheng advised focusing on the things that matter most. "If you can't do it all, don't!" he said. "I honestly think if you are tight on money, you should do the least amount of food and beverage you can get away with, for example (and I'm a caterer)!" Also, be sure when designing your event that you carefully tie in with the brand culture of the product. "But don't overdo it," he cautioned. "Over-branding can start looking tacky and all the editors know where they are; you don't have to constantly remind them."

Sweet Dreams with Zeo – at the Standard Hotel in NYC

When we launched Zeo, the world's first consumer sleep monitoring device designed to help people improve the quality of their sleep,

our mandate from Zeo President and CEO David Dickinson was to "do something bold." ▶

When hosting a launch event, don't forget to have fun.

Since Zeo was not only a new product but was also creating a new category of personal sleep devices, the Schneider Associates/Zeo team believed we had to think big and create a launch event that would not only provide the opportunity to try Zeo but also drive consumer editors to cover Zeo, post event. At the Idea Camp[SM], one idea emerged that seemed totally right for the brand: Invite editors to sleep over at a trendy New York hotel to try Zeo and host a "Night Cap" briefing once they checked into the hotel to illustrate how Zeo works.

The plan called for providing 24-hour coaching the night of the event followed by a breakfast briefing the morning after to explain the technology, decode their ZQ scores (the score Zeo produces that tracks the quantity and quality of sleep) and answer questions. Some of the nation's most renowned sleep experts were on hand including Kenneth Wright, Ph.D., director of the Sleep and Chronobiology Lab at the University of Colorado, Boulder; Michael Breus, Ph.D., aka "The Sleep Doctor," author and sleep wellness coach for WebMD and AOL; and Charles Czeisler, M.D., Ph.D., professor of sleep medicine and director of the Division of Sleep Medicine, Harvard Medical School, all of whom serve on the Zeo Advisory Board.

Of the 50 editors we invited, 36 attended the event. The media coverage that resulted included placements in publications such as *The Wall Street Journal*, *The New York Times*, *USA Today*, and on television shows like *Regis & Kelly*, *Fox & Friends* and *The Today Show*.

Editors learn why the Zeo is exciting.

Why was this event so successful? It had a number of things that made it cool in addition to the product being new and different:

- The invitation for the event was sent in an empty Zeo box, enticing editors to come to the event to try Zeo firsthand.
- The hotel we selected, the Standard in New York, was one of the city's newest hot spots. Located above the historic High Line (a section of the former elevated freight line that is now greenway) within the stylish Meatpacking District, our overnight venue

▶

became a lure that editors couldn't resist. Additionally, we extended our overnight experience to their partners to spend the night as well, a perk not often offered to the media.

- Zeo's colors are black and yellow, so everything associated with the event featured these colors, from the invitation to the attire of staffers who worked the event.
- The "Night Cap" featured special Zeo cocktails created by Sasha Petraske, proprietor of Milk & Honey, one of New York's choicest cocktail bars.
- A 24-hour sleep concierge service was offered to editors. A Zeo staff member was on call, ready to help answer any questions during the night to make their first night with Zeo flawless.
- The breakfast briefing was a multimedia presentation featuring some of the nation's foremost sleep experts. After the briefing, editors could interview the experts in a "stay and play" area where they could learn more about how to get the most out of Zeo and their sleep.
- Editors got to take their Zeos home, use them for two weeks, and purchase them if desired at a "friends and family" rate.
- All editors were given a black-and-yellow t-shirt that read, "I slept with Zeo" and many editors wore the shirt to the breakfast briefing.
- Schneider Associates followed up with every editor who attended to thank them for coming, and to begin discussing what other information they needed to write the Zeo story.

"Having the sleepover event at the Standard where editors could sleep with Zeo signaled that this was not an ordinary consumer product but one that warranted major media attention," said Dickinson. "We invested in a big idea and we are confident the investment will pay off in media coverage and buzz." •

TIP 79 Use desk-side briefings.

If a media event is not appropriate for your launch, conducting desk-side briefings with reporters, editors and broadcast journalists is another way to tell your new product story. Once you call or e-mail the reporters you want to meet with (usually numerous times before you get them to say yes), you travel to their offices and make presentations about the new product to convince them to write a story or create a broadcast news piece. Since most of the major consumer news media are in New York, a majority of desk-side briefings are held there. Trade publications are scattered all over the United States, with many located in Chicago.

The most important thing to remember about desk-side briefings is that you are not going to get much time to tell your story. Fifteen to 30 minutes is average; if you have a great story, maybe the media will talk to you for 45 minutes. Here's where you take what you learned from media training and put it into action. Use that Media Message Guide and tell your story succinctly and effectively. The goal is to make editors or reporters care and get them to see why covering this story is relevant to their audience.

Have everything you will need with you to convince reporters this new product is a winner and they have to cover it. If possible, leave them with samples and be sure to offer to send them more proof points if they are still unconvinced. Follow up to be sure the reporters you meet with have everything they need to write the story, and keep calling them to be sure the story gets scheduled.

TIP 80 | Host a virtual event.

With the advent of social media, a new idea in hosting events is to conduct a virtual event on the Web. This is often used when you want to introduce a product to key bloggers and other online media. A webinar or other special event online is created by holding a presentation and inviting participants to call in to preview the new product. With all the sophisticated technology available online, you can create the same drama and feel of a live presentation, but participants don't have to travel to attend.

You can host a question-and-answer period, you can poll the group to ask what they think about the product, you can show video—all the same tactics you would use in a live event, except participants either call in or join a live chat to participate. If a traditional webinar is too static and you'd like to generate a good discussion, hosting a Tweetup on Twitter is a great way to reach a large audience and limit responses to short comments (no pontification). Using a hashtag, a short alphanumeric code that always begins with a "#" symbol, you can identify related tweets so they appear in a thread, which can be copied and pasted for archiving at the end (because the hashtag acts as a code to aggregate tweets). A Tweetup is usually accompanied by an informal gathering at a local restaurant or meeting place. Using a free event hosting site like Eventbrite.com is a good way to communicate the details of the event and manage the RSVP process. If video content is important to your Tweetup announcement, post the video on your Eventbrite page—and if you want to aggregate video taken during your event when attendees tweet out the link, request that they include your unique hashtag for the event.

A virtual microsite was an important destination point for car enthusiasts and consumers during Jack Morton Worldwide's "Discover Genesis Ride and Drive Experience," a 15-city tour that helped launch Hyundai's new luxury car, the Genesis. "Before arriving on site, a select group of potential event attendees were sent e-mail invitations with details and a description of how to RSVP. Other attendees learned about the event from the various Hyundai Web properties including the Hyundai Genesis site [DiscoverGenesisTour.com]," said Liz Bigham, director of brand marketing at Jack Morton Worldwide.

"Discover Genesis" event in California, 2008.

DiscoverGenesisTour.com, developed by Jack Morton Worldwide, included all tour stop dates—invitation-only and public events, tour highlights including photos and video, an interactive game featuring Hyundai and Hyundai Genesis trivia called the "Genesis Discovery Challenge," and links to the Hyundai Genesis Web pages. Visitors to public events could RSVP and sign up to attend or schedule their Ride and Drive directly from the Web site.

Bigham added, "If you create an experience of a product where people can touch and feel it, and where they can directly interact with it, that will be more memorable and effective." The virtual microsite acted as a primer for the experiential tour where consumers could see the car in person.

Another way to achieve virtual participation is to post video, or stream it live. The Apple iPhone allows the capture of video, simple editing and the option to post directly to YouTube after recording. Other camera phones actually allow you to stream the video live and broadcast it on the Web. Of course, that means everyone in the entire world can also see what's happening at your event (gaffes, demo failures and all), since once you broadcast on the Web, it's in the public domain.

TIP 81 Talk to other brand managers to learn what's worked for them.

Sharing information with other brand managers in your company about what has worked for them in terms of events and media coverage is a smart idea. You never know when you'll uncover a strategy or tactic you hadn't thought of that might prove valuable. Also, the media environment is constantly shifting so if you have not conducted a launch in a while, and some of your colleagues have, there are surely new things to learn.

The use of social media to launch new products and promote events is becoming mainstream. The tactics you used last year are just a few of the ones that are now available to add to your launch arsenal. Check out Chapter 10 for tips on how social media can improve your launch.

TIP 82 Be prepared for disaster.

Every launch plan should have a detailed traditional and online crisis communications plan. The plan should spell out how to deal with print, radio and broadcast reporters, but it should also outline how to effectively handle negative online coverage that can spread like wildfire.

High on the list of potential disasters is a high volume of customer complaints about your new product or, heaven forbid, a product recall. But that's only the beginning of what can go wrong. You need to develop a list of all the potential crises that might strike and have strategies in place for responding quickly and effectively.

Speed has never been more important than in today's 24/7 Internet-powered news cycle. If, for example, someone posts a video on YouTube that casts your new product or your company in a bad light, you have to be ready to respond immediately or risk the news of the YouTube video becoming the focus of attention—just when you want all eyes and ears focused on your new product. In this environment, he who hesitates is lost.

To deal with these types of catastrophic situations, companies need to expand their crisis teams to include new professionals who can handle the online aspect of a crisis. Traditional crisis teams comprised key members of the company's executive team (depending on the issue, they could also include someone from marketing, research and development, operations, human resources and in-house counsel), external legal counsel and a representative from the public relations firm. The new crisis team should also include a social media expert and a videographer who can help craft a social media and video strategy to stem the tide of online negativity. Your crisis plan has to include strategies for traditional media and social media responses. Be aware that the timeliness and effectiveness of your response will itself become the subject of news stories and blogs. If your response is sluggish and/or not totally forthright and honest, the story may drag on for days. This is the last thing you need in the middle of a launch, so follow the Boy Scout motto: "Be prepared."

CHAPTER 8:

Real World Launch Tactics

What specific tactics are you planning to bring your launch strategies to life? Today's launch tool kit contains an ever-growing array of methods you can activate to grab consumer attention. New tactics are being invented each day, as are new twists on tactics that have been around for decades. Choosing which tactics (old, new or a combination of both) match your new product's personality and budget becomes increasingly more challenging as the variety of potential campaign elements escalates. All launch choices should be based on your brand's attributes, the dynamics of the marketplace, how your new product fits within today's retail environment, the benefits the new product brings to users, and your target consumers' behaviors and preferences.

To make this discussion simpler, we've divided it into two sections—advice on real world tactics, and advice on how to launch in the cyber world. Of course, most things you do in the real world should be translated into online applications to create a fully integrated launch campaign. For example, if you plan a launch event, you'll be promoting it off-line while talking about it on your Web site, blog, Twitter handle and Facebook fan page, and through other social media channels. Also, your print or TV ads will contain information to drive people to your online properties where they can learn about or buy the product.

It's impossible to discuss every possible real world tactic. Your launch plan is limited only by your imagination, budget and target launch date. The tactics we've highlighted here are those we've witnessed to be highly effective for not only the Most Memorable New Product Launch winners, but for our own clients and other companies as well. In addition to tactics, we've included some general launch advice.

Free samples were the most influential source of information in 2009 at 92% versus 83% in 2008

TIP 83 Sample, sample, sample... then sample some more.

Consumers love free stuff! Sample every chance you get—offer free samples, free downloads, free anything. Sampling is the most effective tactic to get people to try and buy your new product.

Sampling is the perennial consumer favorite in our Most Memorable New Product Launch Survey. In our most recent report, free samples were rated as the most influential source of information about new products, named by 92 percent

of all respondents as highly influential and slightly ahead of recommendations by family and friends, which were rated as highly influential by 81 percent of respondents. Women, who control the majority of household shopping choices, liked free samples more than men did, with

87 percent of women rating them as highly influential compared with 78 percent of men.

Find a way to incorporate sampling into your launch, whether it's distributing free samples at concerts or sporting events, on street corners, in grocery stores, to visitors on your Web site, or through national promotions. Giveaways can also bring new life to existing products and brands, as Denny's showed when it used its first ever Super Bowl ad to announce that it would give a free Grand Slam® breakfast to anyone who came to the restaurant during an eight-hour period on Feb. 3, 2009. More than 2 million people attended, generating publicity from coast to coast that was worth far more than the $5 million the company plunked down for its Super Bowl ad.

Giveaways: Good and Bad

Elissa Elan, an editor at *Nation's Restaurant News*, told us about several recent coupon giveaway promotions from national brands: There is usually some kind of traditional advertising component attached to a successful product launch campaign, although these days you tend to see a bit more inventiveness through tie-ins with television shows or events, movies and the like. And new technologies, such as social media Web sites, are being employed like never before. The real draw, however, seems to be free giveaway promotions that have attracted increased attention, especially given the current economic climate. Twitter and Facebook are inundated by restaurant companies with free coupons for consumer download.

You have only to look at Denny's, Quiznos and KFC to see campaigns that typify successful and not-as-successful promotional programs that were implemented in the past year. Those companies have offered free meals to jump-start sales and brand awareness, but only Denny's, with its Grand Slam breakfast giveaway in February of 2009, managed to pull it off without a hitch. The promotion, which was tied in to the nationally televised Super Bowl broadcast, ended up generating approximately $50 million worth of publicity for the chain as well as an opportunity to attract lapsed users back into the fold.

▶

While giveaway promotions tend initially to lead to increased traffic when executed properly, sustained momentum is often difficult to achieve, particularly after a campaign goes badly. And the main reason a number of these campaigns don't succeed is because they often are poorly planned.

Mark Chmiel, Denny's chief marketing officer, said his company succeeded because they "really preplanned everything before it happened. We were very diligent in planning with our operations people, financial forecasters, and our marketing and franchise partners. We 100 percent didn't want a negative PR disaster to happen to us."

In the case of Quiznos, Trey Hall, the company's chief marketing officer, said its February Million Free Subs promotion backfired after franchisees said they wouldn't honor coupons for free sandwiches because they felt they couldn't afford to participate in the program.

Hall said, "You need at every level—no matter what you do, whether it be a simple or more complex promotion—every 't' crossed and every 'i' dotted. You need a well-thought-out plan and then look at it in every way possible, making sure everyone is thoroughly communicated with. You want to make sure everyone has an opportunity to look at it and smell it and taste it so there are no surprises, that you've uncovered any potential issue. Plan for the worst and hope for the best, but make sure you have a very thorough plan."

In the case of KFC, a tie-in with *The Oprah Show* proved problematic at best. The quick-serve chicken chain, a division of Louisville-based Yum! Brands Inc., ended up having to apologize for being unable to honor millions of coupons for a free, two-piece grilled chicken dinner offered on *The Oprah Show*.

In total, 10.5 million coupons were downloaded from Winfrey's Web site, but only 4.5 million were redeemed because of a combination of supply issues and technical problems. As a result, 6 million customers were left unserved. The promotion, which was used to introduce KFC's new Kentucky Grilled Chicken product line, caused such intense restaurant traffic that "the lines of customers wanting to redeem their coupons [were] out the door and around the block," according to Roger Eaton, the chain's chief executive.

Following KFC's apology, the chain offered staggered rain checks and a free soft drink to those customers who had not yet retrieved their free grilled chicken meals as an attempt to appease the angry and dissatisfied.

Chekitan S. Dev, a professor of marketing at Cornell University's School of Hospitality, said, "Going to *The Oprah Show* was a very smart marketing move, but the devil is in the details." He said to imagine the outcome of having 6 million unserved people angry with them. "Research tells us that when you take a multiple of 10—if those 6 million who are mad at KFC tell 10 people each—my question is would you rather have 4 million people who will be [brand] users or 60 million who say, 'Hey, these guys don't have their acts together.'"

KFC's Grilled Chicken ranked #1 in the MMNPL Survey in 2009

With the KFC launch, the controversial media coverage actually spurred consumer interest. The launch went on to become the best in the franchise's history, and it also earned a No. 1 ranking as the Most Memorable New Product Launch of 2009 in our consumer survey. Talk about turning a negative into a positive. •

When planning sampling, consider new techniques like flash mob brand sampling, where groups of people meet up at a designated time and place after hearing about an event online. Free samples are then given to flash mob participants as well as to the inevitable crowds of onlookers to these seemingly spontaneous but well-orchestrated events.

(For an outstanding example of how sampling can make a product memorable, see the McDonald's case study at the end of this chapter.)

TIP 84 Don't hesitate to give away or lend products to influencers, early adopters and consumers prior to launch.

Not every product category or product price point lends itself to a massive, free sampling program. High-ticket items like electronics are difficult to sample, so consider lending your new product to key influencers instead to obtain direct feedback and generate word-of-mouth buzz.

For some types of products, you need data to prove efficacy. How do you get data if consumers aren't using the product? It's simple. Give away the product to industry experts, celebrities, consumers who are challenged by the problem your product solves, techies who love innovation—whoever will provide testimonials or the type of insight you need to improve the product or marketing. Typically consumers are honored to be the first to try a new product and delight in giving you honest feedback. They are eager to tell you what they liked—or didn't like—about a product, how they used it and what you can do to improve the product. Sometimes you'll find that some people love the product so much they will buy it rather than give it back.

Product seeding not only generates buzz, but gives you valuable feedback and data to review prior to launch. It also introduces you to brand evangelists, who can talk to reporters. So take the first 100 units and give them away to people who will benefit from or enjoy what you're introducing. While you're at it, whenever possible give the product to employees. They will be more than happy to tell everyone they know about your new product and why it's great. And don't forget to promote the product on your Web site, on your intranet and through other internal communications vehicles.

TIP 85 **Speaking of employees, market your new product to them first.**

Companies that do not follow this advice miss out on a great opportunity. Your employees are your best brand ambassadors; they are your resident buzz-generating machine. You'd think that leveraging employee power would be a no-brainer, but Mike Kust, chief marketing officer of the Carlson Marketing Group, a global firm that handles employee morale programs and other related marketing initiatives, told *Brandweek* that less than 50 percent of companies execute internal communications strategies prior to the launch of a new ad campaign.[1]

Letting employees know about a new product and its launch campaign makes them feel special and a part of the brand. They can also serve as valuable campaign message testers. Going to employees first gives you an opportunity to revise any messages that might not be working. Of course, there is always a concern an employee will leak launch information or alert the media before the designated launch date. But with proper communication about the need to keep launch information confidential during specific timeframes, an internal campaign that educates and mobilizes employees can be extremely profitable.

The Internet is also a great way to communicate launch information to employees. McDonald's set up a special employees-only Web site for its Southern Style Chicken Sandwich launch where crew members could talk about the launch, converse with each other and share information. Companies are increasingly using private microblogging services on sites like Yammer.com or technology platforms such as Present.ly, which is offered by Intridea Inc., to quickly and effectively spread important news internally through networks available only to employees of individual user companies. For example, on Yammer.com, employees answer the question "What are you working on?" with a microblog. Present.ly offers private and secure

McDonald's Southern Style Chicken Sandwich

microblogging that is either hosted on Presently.com or deployed by a user company behind its own firewall for added security. Whatever type of private microblogging tool you use, this communication method creates a perfect opportunity for launch team members to disseminate messages about the new product and generate excitement among employees.

TIP 86 Make sure your employees understand your customers as well as the new product.

While you're communicating with employees, include information not only about the product but also about your target customers. Employees are powerful word-of-mouth resources and need to understand and empathize with customers to be able to effectively motivate them to purchase. The messages employees convey will be more authentic if they understand your target customers in addition to the features and benefits of the new product. Your staff needs to know how this new offering fits into people's lives and how it satisfies the "What's In It For Me" (WIIFM) factor. Context is just as important as content when it comes to launching new products. Be sure to provide both.

TIP 87 Use cause marketing to add interest to an evolutionary product or line extension launch.

In an increasingly fragmented media world, audiences "now get their information from three screens (TV, computer and cell phone) instead of one,"[2] said Samantha Skey, executive vice president of strategic marketing at Alloy Media + Marketing. Linking up with a cause that consumers care about is a good way to draw attention to a product even when you do not have something brand new to offer.

Consumers are increasingly more socially responsible and want companies to contribute to making their communities, and the world at large, a better place to live. Just look at this data from the 2008 Cone Cause Evolution Study from Cone, a strategy and communications agency in Boston that has been studying cause marketing since 1993. In 2008, Cone found that 85 percent of consumers said it was acceptable for companies to involve a cause in their marketing, compared with 66 percent in 1993. Seventy-nine percent said they would be likely to switch from one brand to another brand of about the same price and quality if the second brand was associated with a good cause, compared with 66 percent in 1993. Thirty-eight percent have bought a product associated with a cause in the past 12 months, compared with 20 percent in 1993.[3]

Cause marketing helps sell your product and makes it easier to pitch to the media. For evolutionary products or line extensions, a good cause-marketing campaign can be the big idea that drives your launch campaign. It can provide the story line you need to convince the media to cover your launch and help generate word of mouth among consumers.

As Carol Cone, chairman of Cone, pointed out, cause marketing should not be part of every launch. "If indeed your product is breakthrough and has enough of its own story, then think twice about just adding a cause because you need another story angle," said Cone. "It can muddle the revolutionary nature of what you have. Most products are evolutionary, so that's where cause becomes part of the equation. Cause marketing contributes additional points of emotion, new storytelling, and access or links to constituencies and affinity groups."

One of the great things about cause-related marketing is you can do it even if you are launching on a tight budget. Cone recommends finding an innovative nonprofit that has a large base of people who are passionate about a cause that fits with your company. This is where a little money can go a long way in positively impacting a charity and increasing the visibility of your brand and the new product within a key target market. You don't necessarily have to make a big donation to the charity; you can just encourage others to do so on your Web site and in other marketing materials.

| TIP 88 | **Make sure the cause you choose makes sense for your brand over the long term.**

While it's tempting to think of the cause-marketing portion of your launch as a short-term, one-and-done promotion, taking this approach ignores the incredible value that can come with being identified with a cause over time. Think of Yoplait's Save Lids to Save Lives®, which in 2008 celebrated its 11th year of raising money and support for breast cancer. To date, Yoplait has donated more than $22 million to the breast cancer cause. What woman can think of Yoplait yogurt without thinking of the pink lids?

Picking a cause that aligns well with your brand and corporate values enables you to make an impact over the long haul, which can pay huge dividends far beyond your current new product launch. But choose carefully, because you can't just jump in and jump out of a cause-related program without damaging your credibility as a company that really cares about the cause. Plus it takes several years for consumers to connect your brand with a specific cause. If you skip around, they won't be able to value your interest and investment in a particular cause.

One of the important choices you'll have to make is whether you should stick with a well-known cause such as breast cancer, heart disease, childhood obesity or disaster relief, or choose an emergent cause you can own over time. Whichever way you go, make sure the cause and your nonprofit partner relate to your brand and new product. If not, your program won't resonate with consumers. It also won't engage the energies and passion of your employees, and without employee support, cause marketing can fall flat. Try to make this link between your brand, your new product, the cause and the charity as obvious as possible, advised Cone. "You have to look at the customer, the product's features and benefits, the customer's life stage and their needs and find an appropriate cause that will be relevant and help with your launch," she said.

Purex® Asks Customers to Help Change Lives

For the launch of its Purex Complete 3-in-1™ Laundry Sheets, a revolutionary new technology that eases the chore of doing laundry by combining detergent, softener and anti-static all in one sheet, Purex adopted a powerful cause-marketing program under the theme "Purex Changes Lives." The program was designed to empower Purex customers to help women around the world who are living in poverty change the lives of their families by creating sustainable income sources.

Customers who bought the new laundry sheets product could visit www.purex.com/change and, after entering the product bar code number, donate $1 from each purchase to Kiva.org, a global person-to-person micro-lending Web site that helps low-income families create their own sustainable sources of income. On the site, women from around the world describe how they would use money from the program to better their families' lives. Purex customers choose a family to support, receive updates on the loan status, and follow their chosen entrepreneur's activities via e-mails and downloadable widgets.

Actress and mom Angie Harmon teamed up with Purex to be the celebrity spokesperson for the program and was featured in numerous media placements. The program included a Facebook fan page and outreach to bloggers. Also, a Purex Insiders Web site showed videos of women talking about how the new product simplified doing laundry and made their lives better.

What is interesting about this launch is that Purex chose to introduce a new product using a cause-related marketing campaign. According to Jens Bang, CEO of Cone, "Most companies use cause-related marketing once a product is in its evolutionary stage and the product is no longer as newsworthy as when first introduced."

Purex launched its Complete 3-in-1 Laundry Sheets by aligning with a cause that appeals to women and sustains their interest over time. The focus is clearly on the cause and not on the product, despite Purex's claim that the Laundry Sheets feature a revolutionary new technology that makes it easier to do laundry. Could it be that ▶

the proliferation of sophisticated laundry detergents is so great that companies are now finding it difficult to differentiate product features and benefits, and need to turn to cause marketing to appeal to customers? No doubt marketers need to watch this trend as they evaluate whether "revolutionary" is the only product attribute needed to capture the hearts and minds of consumers. ●

TIP 89 | **Avoid superficial cause-related marketing.**

For the first time since Cone began doing its research into cause marketing, the 2007 survey saw a drop in the number of people who said they would tell a family member or friend about a product or company after hearing about that company's commitment to social issues. While 43 percent responded yes to this question in 2004, by 2007 the number saying they would tell someone about the link between a cause and a product had dropped to 30 percent, a precipitous 30 percent decline.

"We realized we're at a tipping point and we've arrived at what we're calling 'ribbonization,'" said Cone. "There is a sea of products out there with ribbons representing different causes but not a lot of depth to the link between the product and the cause. If you just slap a ribbon on something, that doesn't mean it is going to help the cause in any shape or form. This is especially true of all the pink ribbons we see." The way to avoid being superficial and therefore not very meaningful to consumers is to make sure your program has authenticity. "You can't be promoting heart health and selling a high-fat food, for example," said Cone.

Also, integrate the cause into as many aspects of your launch campaign as possible. When people see that you're doing much more than just adding a ribbon to your packaging, they'll begin to believe you really care about the cause.

Don't Run Afoul of the Law with Your Charity Tie-in Campaign

Twenty-some states have "commercial co-venture laws" that impose various degrees of regulatory requirements on for-profit ▶

organizations and charities that enter into partnerships where the for-profit uses the name of the nonprofit in a branded licensing campaign. If you're employing cause marketing as part of your launch, you definitely want to understand and comply with these laws, which are designed to protect consumers from being misled about the exact nature of the relationship between the business and the charity.

According to Ed Chansky, an attorney with the Las Vegas office of Greenberg Traurig, LLP, who specializes in advertising, sales promotion and charitable solicitation law, this area of law is constantly fluctuating. Some states are adding new regulations, and other states are removing them with the belief that regulation is onerous and discourages businesses from getting involved with charities. Chansky also said that most in-house legal departments haven't heard of these laws and find it daunting to comply. "You have to find someone who does know about it," he said, "and for a national campaign it's going to cost you a few thousand dollars to get it taken care of right."

The Basics

Here's a quick look at what it takes to comply with most commercial co-venture laws:

- Write the contract with the charity to include specific state provisions. Make it clear you have permission to use the charity's name, that you are going to pay them the promised amount within a reasonable time and that you're going to document the donation.
- In a handful of states, companies have to register and post bond and then file annual reports showing what has occurred, just as professional fundraisers are required to do.
- In your advertising, you have to disclose the terms of the offer in a way that does not mislead the consumer about the effect that his or her purchase will have on the charity. For example, if you're giving $1 for every product purchased up to a cap of $50,000, then you need to specify the exact amount being donated per unit and the maximum amount the charity may receive from the promotion. ▶

Companies get into trouble when they either ignore these laws or fail to make the offer clear. "For example," said Chansky, "what if I told you that 40 percent of the manufacturer's net profits on a box of cereal is going to a charity? That number is so opaque that it could mean anything between zero and 40 percent of the purchase price, but where on that continuum the amount given to the charity would actually fall is anyone's guess. My advice about disclosure is you really want to simplify the offer so it's crystal clear."

Another area where companies can go astray centers on caps or limits on the offer, such as saying you'll donate up to $50,000. "If you have such a limit, disclose it and limit the offer so that all or substantially all of the advertised items will count toward that amount. Don't put an offer on several million boxes when only the first 50,000 boxes will count; only print 50,000 boxes with the of-fer on it," said Chansky. "Also, don't advertise the program for six months if you know your monthly turn rate means you'll hit the cap after just one or two months. Doing either of these things would mislead the consumer about the impact of their purchase on the charitable donation."

He added: "If all of this sounds too complicated and you can't wrap your mind around it, then change gears and stop making the linkage between a purchase and your donation. Stop saying, 'You do this and we'll do that,' and start saying, 'We are a proud sponsor and are donating X number of dollars this year to XYZ.'" Chansky continued: "If you do that, you are not saying the purchase will benefit the charity—you are saying the company's donation will benefit the charity. The proud sponsor message is a way to be unregulated and move on. Of course, that's a less powerful message, and marketers often want to engage the consumer in the donation process because the percentage of sales is such a powerful message, and that's why it's regulated." ●

TIP 90 Align with an authority.

Whether it's a university professor, someone from a scientific organiza-tion, or another type of expert, find a third party who can speak with authority about your product's efficacy and value. People are skeptical, especially when it comes to buying breakthrough products that are new to the market and do not have a track record. You can't expect consumers to easily believe a revolutionary product will live up to all its claims. And depending on the product, you need to be extremely careful about the claims you make. If it's a food, a health/medical product or an environmental product, the claims may be scrutinized by the Food and Drug Administration, the Federal Trade Commission, the Environmental Protection Agency or other governmental organizations to protect consumers from fraud and dangerous ingredients. Engaging third-party experts will make your launch messages more credible and help people take the leap of faith required to try some thing totally new.

While seeking a "higher power" is a proven tactic, not every launch requires a high-powered expert to vouch for a product's efficacy. You probably won't need a food scientist to tell consumers about a new great-tasting soup unless it includes genetically engineered ingredients, but you might want to use a chef as a spokesperson who can vouch for the product's incredibly fresh and tasty ingredients.

TIP 91   Reach out to influencers.

Every industry has experts to whom the media goes for comment. If you do a literature search on any topic, you'll find several people who are the go-to experts on it. The same is true on the Web. Do a Twitter search or research blogs, and you'll find people active on the Web talking about almost anything imaginable. These influencers are the ones you want to reach out to and educate about a new product related to their expertise and interests.

The hope is that these influencers will like your product and begin talking about it. And if the media happen to ask these influencers if they are familiar with your product, with luck they will offer a positive comment. This "top down" approach is critical to developing buzz about a new product. You introduce the product to people who are in the know to build credibility and speed adoption. Influencers can range from a mommy blogger with a huge following to a famous scientist in a particular area to a celebrity to a physician; the point is to reach these key individuals and attempt to make them early adopters.

TIP 92 | Create word of mouth, both on- and off-line.

Word of mouth is one of the most powerful launch tools you can employ. Generating word of mouth or conversation online about your new product is a quick, effective way to build buzz. Year after year, "recommendations from family and friends" has ranked as one of the Top 10 sources of information that influence consumers in our Most Memorable New Product Launch Survey. Eighty-nine percent of respondents told us that a recommendation from family and friends was one of their top motivators to buy new products in 2009, up from 79 percent the previous year.

BzzAgent founder and CEO Dave Balter sees limitless opportunity in social media for generating word of mouth. "There's thousands of different ways to launch a product and engage consumers with tools that are free," he said. "Everything from building a Facebook fan page to setting up a Twitter account, to building a blog with a lot of content. You don't even have to spend a lot of time. It becomes less about the tool and more about the tactic. How do you find the people you really want to engage with and give them lots of information to share with their networks? Every marketer knows connecting with consumers about a launch is the most effective thing they can do. Customers are building on the media coverage and content that marketers are creating. When something exciting happens, like Gatorade relaunching with Michael Jordan, consumers feel the need to generate their own content about how awesome a new product is—they tweet about it, join the Facebook fan page and even write their own copy."

In 2009, 89% said recommendations by family and friends have an influence on purchasing decisions

TIP 93 | Take your show on the road.

Remember the big purple bus that toured the country to introduce Prilosec OTC? We have no doubt the bus, which was featured in television commercials, was one of the reasons this over-the-counter heartburn medicine earned the fifth spot on our Most Memorable New Product Launch Survey in 2003. Creating a special vehicle that takes your message across the land—or to key emphasis markets—is a great launch tactic.

A visit by a branded publicity vehicle provides local news outlets with a platform for talking about your new product. The vehicle's appearance on the highway and city streets generates visibility and buzz and, of course, provides the opportunity to do product sampling and education at events that relate to your product. In Prilosec's case, health fairs, hospital and pharmacy parking lots, and events that generate massive heartburn, like state fairs or chili cook-offs, were perfect for mobile marketing. Plus, this huge bus with its colorful graphics was a great tool to spread the word on highways and byways.

Outfitting, staffing and operating a full-scale vehicle like the Prilosec OTC bus is expensive and not for every launch budget. But smaller vehicles, such as vans, can be just as effective in drawing attention. Remember, there's nothing like getting out and talking to people about your product. Make sure the staff that operates the vehicle is not only well-versed about the product but friendly and well spoken. It never hurts to run background checks on all employees who represent your company and interface with the public.

Prilosec OTC earned the #5 spot in the 2003 MMNPL Survey

Also, the expense involved with this tactic can be amortized beyond the launch, so don't think of the vehicle as a one-shot tactic. Procter & Gamble and AstraZeneca, the alliance behind Prilosec OTC, extended the use of their big purple bus for at least three years after the product launch. One promotion teamed up Prilosec OTC with the Country Music Association for a coast-to-coast tour that highlighted the CMA Awards' first-ever appearance in New York City. While on the road, the bus crew educated country music fans about heartburn, an ailment that a survey had shown was suffered by 38 percent of country music fans.

TIP 94 **Use the mammoth power of experiential marketing.**

A live event where consumers get to interact with your new product is a powerful launch tool. Seeing is believing for many people, and nothing beats a firsthand experience to turn truckloads of consumers into true believers. Experiential events are great for producing word of mouth about your new product and can help you stand out in a competitive field.

"Experiential marketing includes special events, guerrilla marketing, mobile marketing, pop-ups, trade shows, stealth marketing, viral marketing, street teams and even 'ass-vertising' (messages on butts). Anything that doesn't fit into other categories is often defined as experiential," said Jeff Snyder, president of Inspira Marketing.

"Events that take place at nightclubs and in bars; grassroots marketing; sports sponsorship activation; music and all different forms of entertainment are part of experiential marketing," continued Snyder. "If you find your target customers at the right time, in the right place, you can engage them with the brand. Think of it as relevant lifestyle interventions," added Snyder. "If you are able to understand the mind-set of your core customer, you can create an experience that speaks to that customer. The goal is to make something so sticky, relevant and meaningful for your target consumer that people who agree with what you've created will fall under the brand's umbrella." Snyder said experiential marketing is the fastest way to build brand loyalty.

A consumer survey done by the global experiential marketing firm of Jack Morton Worldwide seems to bear this out. Over two-thirds of respondents said experiential marketing would "be extremely or very influential on their overall opinion of brands and products. Also, 70 percent said that participating in a live event marketing experience would increase their purchase consideration and 57 percent said it would result in quicker purchase."[4]

The beauty of experiential marketing is that nearly anyone can use it, even companies with small launch budgets. Hosting a small party at a restaurant or participating in a community fair doesn't have to be a budget buster. For those who have plenty of resources, you can do it up big and garner not just instant converts but also substantial media attention.

When planning your event, be sure to consider all the senses. You want the total experience to match your brand's promise. For example, if your new product is a deluxe body cream, you want visitors to feel as if they've had a spa-worthy experience. The look, smell and sound of the location should be luxurious. Engaging people's senses on every level will leave a lasting positive impression. "If we aren't appealing to three of the senses, it's not experiential—taste, touch and smell," said Snyder. "Handing out flyers is not experiential marketing. Marketers need to forge that emotional connection, giving the consumer the opportunity to engage with the brand in a sensorial way."

SUBWAY®'s Use of Experiential Marketing Helps Its FRESH FIT™ Menu Make Our Top 10 List

The SUBWAY FRESH FIT menu, which shifted the brand's focus from weight loss to fitness, landed in the eighth spot of our Most Memorable New Product Launch Survey in 2007. Behind this Top 10 performance was an experiential marketing program devised by Jack Morton Worldwide. The firm, a leader in experiential marketing, created a one-day integrated campaign in New York City that gained national press, built buzz and connected with consumers who lead active lifestyles. Then the campaign was made available to SUBWAY agencies across the country who could replicate it in their markets.

The launch began with brand ambassadors riding SUBWAY-branded Trek® mountain bikes into the background crowds of *The Today Show* and *Good Morning America*. The bikers were attired in bright yellow windbreakers that captured the attention of camera crews and anchors, who acknowledged that SUBWAY would be launching a unique event for the day.

Celebrity spokespersons LL Cool J and SUBWAY restaurant's Jared Fogle appeared on *The Early Show* and *CW Morning* to discuss the menu messages about fitness and give away branded mountain bikes.

TOP: SUBWAY FRESH FIT brand ambassadors set off to reward consumers' "random acts of fitness."

BOTTOM: SUBWAY FRESH FIT bike winner celebrates with brand ambassadors.

LL Cool J and Fogle then moved to Times Square for the media reveal atop a SUBWAY branded double-decker bus. They dispatched 150 brand ambassadors to locations such as Grand Central Terminal, Times Square and Bryant Park. The brand ambassadors awarded thousands of SUBWAY Cash Cards to consumers for their "random acts of fitness" such as climbing stairs or power walking and gave 250 branded mountain bikes to 250 lucky consumers.

SUBWAY FRESH FIT launch in New York, 2007: Jared Fogle and LL Cool J pose with brand ambassadors.

As a program follow-on, Jack Morton Worldwide developed an in-school program—"Random Acts of Fitness for Kids"—that was made available to more than 40,000 schools, equipping teachers with curricula and tools to help their students embrace fitness and activity. The program included kits that were mailed into classrooms, a consumer Web site (http://www.randomactsoffitness.com) where teachers and parents could find teaching tools, and a reward system for kids with free SUBWAY meals in exchange for meeting fitness goals.

Subway's FRESH FIT menu ranked #8 in the 2007 MMNPL Survey

The menu launch was a huge success, generating 300 million media impressions with a low cost per thousand (CPM). In the weeks following the launch, SUBWAY restaurants experienced a significant increase in both sales and traffic to stores nationwide. ●

TIP 95 Develop seasonal, holiday and special day tie-ins.

Grab a calendar and identify how to link your new product with a season, holiday or special designated day throughout the coming year. Purchase a copy of *Chase's Calendar of Events,* the authoritative reference guide to special events, worldwide holidays and festivals, civic observances, historic anniversaries, famous birthdays and other celebrations, or browse through a copy at your local library to see if there is a designated day, week or year you can tie your event into to give it more "legs." Whether it is National Ice Cream Month, National Kite Month, or Stress Awareness Month, there is a designated time to recognize almost anything. Creatively linking your product to an established milestone or generating your own special day, week or month is highly effective.

Calendar tie-ins can be particularly good for evolutionary products or line extensions that don't have much intrinsic news value in and of themselves. Journalists and bloggers are always looking for new angles to bring to life a holiday themed story they've written about dozens of times before. The same is true about stories related to the new season or about a special day, week or month such as Earth Day, Breast Cancer Awareness Month, or American Heart Month.

TIP 96 | Create a sense of urgency with pop-up stores.

Pop-up stores—small outlets set up in a vacant retail location in a high-traffic city or mall for a few days, a few weeks or a month—are hot properties. Started in the fashion industry, pop-ups have now moved to other sectors and are increasingly being used in conjunction with product launches. With their short life span, pop-up stores create a sense of urgency among consumers—get it now or it will be gone. They also create news for the media—cover it now or miss the opportunity!

Here are just a few ways the stores are being used. Nike set up a pop-up store in New York for only four days to sell 250 pairs of a special edition shoe named after NBA star LeBron James. Walmart debuted its new fashion line, Metro 7, in a Fashion Cabana in Miami's South Beach for just two days. Electronics giant JVC let people film themselves using its newly launched video camera and make their own DVDs to take home as gifts at its pop-up store.[5]

Clearly, pop-up stores can create a unique environment for your new product. Often found in New York City to capitalize on the massive foot traffic and the proximity to national media, these limited-time-only venues can be pricey. In researching this tactic for a food client whose pop-up store would have required extensive equipment, electrical work and permits, we found a Times Square location would cost upwards of $250,000 for just one month. (Most landlords will require you to rent the spot for at least a month, even if your pop-up store is open for only a few days or a week.) Locations on Fifth or Madison Avenues or in trendy SoHo and the Meatpacking District are equally expensive. Add to that the cost to outfit and staff the store (which will vary depending on the type of product you're offering and the type of events you hold at the site), the cost to put in communication systems and signage, and the cost to purchase other necessities like insurance, and you're investing long-term dollars in what is clearly a short-term situation. But pop-ups can yield the type of media and consumer ROI that can't be duplicated with more traditional strategies.

TIP 97   Make sure your launch contest theme and prize are something to talk about.

Having a launch contest is a great idea, but only if it features an attention-getting, fun theme with exciting prizes that appeal to your target market. Otherwise it will be virtually impossible to motivate consumers to enter the contest, which defeats the whole purpose of the giveaway. Most people have a million things on their to-do lists; getting them to add other items, like going to your launch Web site and entering a bottle cap number to see if they've won a prize, requires a really good contest. What we've also learned is that consumers like cash prizes. Sure they'll take your product, but if you really want to secure lots of entries—think cash prizes.

Also, if you're new to the contest world, make sure you have someone on board who understands the numerous state and federal rules and regulations that go along with running contests, sweepstakes and promotions that include prizes. The last thing you need in the middle of your launch is a state attorney general declaring that your contest does not comply with that state's disclaimer rules. Resist the temptation to have in-house counsel write the rules for the contest. Hire an expert who understands contest rules and regulations and can advise you about the legality of what you are offering on- and offline. No matter how many people enter the contest, you're obligated to give away all prizes or you'll face sanctions for defrauding consumers.

Chris Donnelly, managing director of A&G Brand Promotion, has created highly successful and engaging promotions for national brands. According to Donnelly, a promotional game may face legal problems if it includes both chance and consideration as elements in addition to a prize. Since a prize is inherent in a promotion, marketers need to eliminate either consideration or chance in order to offer a legitimate game. A sweepstakes, for instance, is legal because it requires no purchase, and a contest is also legal because it eliminates chance (contestants are judged).

"I think the key for a contest to be memorable is the sincerity built into it so the contest naturally fits into the new product launch," said Donnelly. "A little humor doesn't hurt either. One experiential contest I developed and executed was for a regional chain of hamburger restaurants based in the heart of NASCAR® and racing country. The contest had a $100,000 prize challenge for two lucky consumers to attend a NASCAR event. Both finalists won a trip to the races, including meet-and-greets with a

NASCAR driver. They also got the chance to unwrap a hamburger at the race event in front of a live audience, and one lucky person was awarded $100,000. There was a lot of publicity, a lot of excitement and everyone was treated like a winner. Plus, the promotion drove in double-digit sales increases to a NASCAR-themed, new hamburger product launch."

One-of-a-kind, experiential grand prize allowed winner to start the Brickyard 400 race event.

TIP 98 | Make sure promotions are exciting and resonate with customers.

What we just said about the need for contest themes and prizes to be exciting is even more important for promotions. They must not only be relevant to your consumers' needs, but also to their lifestyle.

TIP 99 | Don't stint on TV advertising; it's still king.

We'd like to say that launching a new product does not require advertising, but year after year every product on the Top 10 Most Memorable New Product Launch list features a national TV ad campaign. That's not to say you can't create buzz and sales for your new product launch without TV advertising, but it is more difficult. There's nothing like clever 30- or

60-second spots to hammer home the need for your new product with consumers. Maybe that's why major consumer product companies invest in 30-second Super Bowl ads that come with million-dollar price tags. Despite the decline in television viewing and the move toward other media like the Internet, launching a new product with TV advertising not only adds cachet but also drives traffic and sales.

TIP 100   **Leverage the power of money-back guarantees.**

A money-back guarantee is an excellent way to help ease the worry of prospective buyers. This is especially true with revolutionary products, health or "as seen on TV" products, where you may have a difficult time convincing people that your new thingamajig is, in fact, all that you claim it is. By shifting the risk away from the buyer and back to you, you remove a huge obstacle for the buyer.

Dany Sfeir, principal, DS & Associates, explained, "A money-back guarantee (MBG) is essential to the success of a direct response campaign. An MBG works almost every single time and it is part of the success formula. A money-back guarantee is effective as it says you are willing to back up your new product. The longer the money-back guarantee, the higher the chance of getting a greater number of responses. However, it all depends on what the product is and the value of the product you are selling. In general, people send things back at the rate of 10 to 15 percent and sometimes higher, so you need to factor the return rate into your math before you decide on the final selling price."

TIP 101   **Go big, go bold or go home!**

We're not fans of using lots of incremental launch tactics. We favor big and bold over small and safe. Try to have at least some aspect of your launch be unique and noteworthy. Brainstorm to create an attention-grabbing tactic that will shake things up. Sure, there is risk involved, but it's also dicey to go with a launch that offers the same old, same old. Your launch needs to be different to stand out from today's marketing and media onslaught. Do something interesting that will capture people's imagination and interest.

Here's an example of the out-of-the-box thinking we're talking about. To introduce its new Clorox® Disinfecting Wipes Décor Canisters, Clorox Co. signed a multistore deal with Macy's to display the product at flagship stores in Chicago, San Francisco and New York. The colorful Clorox packages, which resemble decorative tissue boxes, were designed as the cornerstone of home kitchen scenes in the windows of the Herald Square store in New York and the Union Square store in San Francisco. In Chicago, where the Randolph Street windows were already spoken for, photos of the home scenes were hung a la mini-billboards on the building's exterior.[6]

Macy's is not a venue that would usually display this type of cleaning product. Why did Clorox choose this high-profile, slightly unusual setting to introduce its new product? Because it realized that in a down economy, retailers are more open to considering new revenue-generating ideas and consumers are more focused and require major stimulation to buy a new product.

Here's another example of going big. Ryan FitzSimons, founder and CEO of the innovation marketing firm Gigunda Group, Inc., masterminded a multiyear experiential campaign to launch new products for P&G's Charmin® bath tissue, including Charmin Ultra, Charmin Fresh Mates, Charmin Mega Roll, Charmin Ultra Strong and Charmin Ultra Soft.

Each year for the past 10 years, the campaign has capitalized on families' universally low expectations for the dreaded public restroom experience. P&G flipped the entire equation on its bottom (pun intended) by bringing luxuriously appointed restroom facilities to event venues to introduce Charmin's new bath tissue products. Gigunda developed the campaign platform and organizing concept dubbed "The Red Cross of Restrooms."

To pay homage to the "Crossroads of the World" location, special NYC-themed stalls were created: Wall Street, Grand Central Station, Empire State Building and Times Square.

As FitzSimons explained, "The test program in 2000 was executed at the largest

Outside the Charmin NYC Restroom Experience at 1540 Broadway, visitors could not miss the 2,000-square-foot brilliant blue billboard exclaiming, "You're in New York... Go in Style."

freestanding facility at the Ohio State Fair with approximately 50 men's and women's restrooms. We renovated the entire building. Every amenity you can imagine was available...from high-energy white-glove greeters, stunning floral arrangements, soothing aromatherapy and cable TVs in every stall, to hardwood floors, beautifully decorated walls and ceilings and even in-stall shelving for personal belongings. And, of course, each stall was cleaned after every use."

He added: "The goal was to elevate the Charmin brand out of the product attribute game and out of the commodity equation. As reported in *Ad Age*, there was a 14 percent spike in sales for Charmin in that designated marketing area. The next year, the program expanded and went to the 15 largest state fairs in the U.S. and permanently renovated the facilities. That year we reached 34 million families, and families stayed an average of 45 minutes longer at an event based on the Charmin amenity, which meant better revenue capture for the venue because parents didn't leave to take their kids home to the bathroom, especially at the end of the day when restrooms typically become deplorable."

FitzSimons continued: "But most importantly, we had the undivided attention of every family in a completely uncluttered and commercial-free environment for an average of three to five minutes where Charmin could tell their story. If you think about how many 30-second TV spots or 60-second radio spots or 8.5 by 11 four-color glossy ads it would take to accomplish the same goal, it's impressive—not to mention laddering the brand up to the higher-order purpose of delivering true value by having families walk away saying 'Charmin looks out for me and my family.' The campaign is truly a game changer in every way.

"Based on success from the first two years, in the third year we added a 53-foot tractor trailer, Potty Palooza, which included 27 home-like stalls that looked like they were decorated by Pottery Barn. Beach board, chair rail, wainscoting, skylights…they were breathtaking. This time we reached 73 million families across the U.S. and we were carried on every national newspaper and every national network, including three consecutive appearances to attend the Super Bowl by request of the NFL as well as a partnership with the Dallas Cowboy cheerleaders. We also produced a 30-foot Potty Palooza truck with 12 stalls to reach the more urban markets."

FitzSimons said his company finally built a permanent, 12,000-square-foot structure in New York's Times Square, which is open during the peak holiday traffic season from the first Monday before Thanksgiving until after New Year's. "The NYC initiative is now going into its fourth consecutive year. It has 20 luxurious stalls, a dance stage for Potty Dances; couches, fireplaces, stroller parking, a kids' tree house and jungle gym; you name it. Each year, 500,000 people go through it and the average stay is 27 minutes. What are they doing in there? It's the ultimate potty party that's all about relief and recharging," he said.

"Located at 1540 Broadway, it truly is Charmin's Broadway show. People get physical relief while also having the opportunity to take a break from the chaos often associated with the holidays and simply recharge. Everything is about having a great time and offering fun events. In fact, in 2007 we threw a wedding in the space with the bride wearing—you guessed it—a dress made entirely out of Charmin."

In the nearly 10 years of this campaign, it has garnered more than 5.1 billion qualified media impressions. The program has won more than 150 awards worldwide, including at Cannes, and is cited in over 15 textbooks. Nothing says "go big and bold" like premium, luxury restrooms in Times Square.

The Sweet Taste of Sampling Success

The launch of McDonald's Southern Style Chicken Biscuit and Sandwich, which earned the fourth spot on the Most Memorable New Product Launch Survey in 2008, shows how powerful sampling can be as a launch strategy. The company declared a National Sampling Day on May 15, 2008, when anyone who came in between 7 a.m. and 7 p.m. and bought a medium-sized drink would receive either a free Southern Style Chicken Biscuit during the breakfast hours or a free Southern Style Chicken Sandwich during the rest of the day. Approximately 8 million samples were given out, and the company experienced a repurchase rate of over 50 percent for the new chicken items. We interviewed Heather Oldani, director of U.S. communications for McDonald's, to get the scoop about this fabulously successful launch.

McDonald's earned the #4 spot in the 2008 MMNPL Survey

How were the Southern Style Chicken Biscuit and the Sandwich developed?

Oldani: We have a dedicated product development team here in the U.S. and globally as well as a head chef who talks with consumers and identifies the food trends and what is going on within the food space. We look at and listen to what consumers say they want to eat when they're eating out. Starting several years ago we saw that the consumption of chicken was increasing dramatically year over year, so we got into the chicken space a couple years ago with the launch of Premium Chicken Sandwiches for lunch and dinner, Chicken Selects®, and McNuggets® Snack Wraps®. Now people can and do want to come to McDonald's for chicken. We are always looking to offer customers a variety of choices and consumers were continuing to turn to chicken more often as part of their protein choice during the day. So we looked at what was popular in the South and ▶

identified Southern-style chicken patties as something that we should test and move forward with. So we tested it in a number of different areas in the country because we need to make sure that whatever we bring to our national members [franchisees] works nationally and not just in one region.

How long was the R&D process?

Oldani: It typically takes several years, so this was at least two years. The marketing piece of that is typically begun six to eight months out from the launch.

Why did you choose to do sampling?

Oldani: We believe in portion size product sampling; we knew that once people tasted the Southern Style Biscuit or the Southern Style Chicken Sandwich they'd like it. So the most significant part of our launch was the National Sampling Day. If I had to pick one thing that accounted for the success of the launch; that was it.

How do your franchisees feel about product sampling?

Oldani: Our franchisees buy into the notion of sampling and a lot of them do it alone on an ongoing basis—they know it's important and have seen the success of it.

What role does the Internet play in your launch?

Oldani: We have the traditional www.mcdonalds.com, which is our corporate Web site and we provide food information there. Whenever we launch a new product we put up a dedicated page with a fun way to engage with the product and give information about it.

For this product, we also felt there was a possibility to engage people virally with the chicken or the egg debate so we put up a site called WhatCameFirst.com, which added a layer of fun. People could go on and have some fun with the chicken and the egg and a dance-off challenge.

Did you use social media?

Oldani: We had a variety of social media initiatives. We had a blogger relations program where we had categories of bloggers that we reached out to with information on the National Sampling Day. This included people who were identified as chicken aficionados, people who cover our business and restaurant people looking for deals on a regular basis.

We also communicated with employees. We have about 700,000 employees, both in our home office, regional offices and divisional offices as well as restaurant managers and crew. There is huge potential for them to be ambassadors for the brand. We sent an e-mail out to the entire U.S. system. We also put information on stationM.com, a special site for our crew, and gave them an opportunity to upload their videos doing the Chicken Dance for a chance to win prizes.

We also had guerrilla street teams that directed people to the WhatCameFirst Web site and handed out [prepaid, reloadable] Arch Cards. And we had a team of people to go out and do videos asking people which came first, the chicken or egg.

Did you do any celebrity tie-ins?

Oldani: As a brand we have a variety of sports alliances with NASCAR, Olympics, and the WNBA [Women's National Basketball Association]; as a result of those alliances we frequently have the opportunity to do a variety of things like sponsor the WNBA All-Star Game. We also get an opportunity to have the stars come into the restaurants and serve up products, so for this launch we had WNBA players in certain markets to serve up the Southern Style Chicken Sandwich. We also had a NASCAR car with a paint scheme related to Southern Style Chicken.

What do you think it takes to launch a memorable new product?

Oldani: I think it takes a comprehensive, collaborative effort. We have all the disciplines coming together and asking, "What is the one thing that we all feel is going to make this product successful?" Then we ask how the disciplines can work together to make that happen. Having everybody with a seat at the table and collaborating together is the biggest thing that has made a difference. ●

CHAPTER 9:

Tactics for a Wired World

Every marketing department ponders three questions *on an ongoing basis*:

1. Where are my customers?
2. What is the best way to communicate with them?
3. How do we stay relevant?

More and more, the answers to these questions are that customers are online, they are talking and exchanging ideas and the best way to engage them is through relevant dialogue.

In the early years of the Internet, the focus was on one-way delivery of information. Now, it's on having two-way communication with consumers in which you both exchange important information. Consider everything from online banner ads to mobile taxi-top advertising that features

text message promotions. Know your demographics and how to reach them multiple times by intersecting their lives from dusk until dawn using a variety of creative marketing vehicles.

If you are not moving in lockstep with consumers, and communicating with them as part of their daily lives, there is a real possibility your company and new product will be left behind. To avoid this situation, we suggest devoting time, energy and enthusiasm to building a robust on- and offline brand presence, which will help position your company to succeed in today's rapidly changing marketplace.

Here's what you need to do to establish a powerful brand image online that will support your new product launch:

TIP 102   Develop a world-class Web site.

What if your Web site is the only source of information consumers use to determine if they will purchase your new product? When consumers arrive at your site, do they immediately notice something distinctive about your company as well as compelling reasons to buy your product? Are they able to communicate directly with a real person and get a quick response? Can they find out what experts are saying about your company and its products? Can they view feedback from other consumers? Can they sign up to receive updated news and information about your product? Is your Web site "sticky"—filled with useful information, tools and entertaining material that encourages people to come back time and time again? Will this information and the Web site be so powerful that consumers will be compelled to buy your new product?

As the focal point of all online branding, advertising and social media, your Web site is one of the most important pieces of the marketing puzzle. Your priority should be moving beyond Web 1.0 and brochure-ware toward Web 2.0, where your Web site is an engagement tool that differentiates your brand. It's critical for your site to allow interaction with your customer base and promote participation. Then you will be ready for Web 3.0, which is fast approaching. Web 3.0 could make the Web a seamless part of everyday life and much more intuitive to users, in the same way that GUI (graphical user interface) technology changed the way people interact with computers.

Chris Pape, principal of the digital agency Genuine Interactive, says, "A good Web site is not a monument. It's not a brochure. It creates a two-way dialogue with the consumer. The social media movement is part of a larger Web site strategy. When Web sites were first launched in 1996, it was brochure-ware, and now Web sites of successful companies contain elements of social media within their sites, not just outside their sites.

"If you go on zappos.com, you can talk about the shoes, the styles, if you like them or if you don't, and even tell others if the heels wear too quickly. And of course, you can look at the shoe and purchase it. It's an open format. You might think they are in danger of people bashing the products, but people—shoe enthusiasts included—feel they are a part of something larger. Plus, it has benefited their search engine optimization because they have created a consistent way to build quality content around their products."

Your Web site should incorporate appropriate widgets, blogs, linking tools, videos and wikis, as well as establish connections with related online sites like Facebook and Twitter. The goal of your site is to be professional and uniquely engaging.

TIP 103 | Capture consumer information for continuous communications.

Two of our favorite words when it comes to managing customers are "opt in." When you are able to engage customers—whether on your Web site, Facebook, Twitter or a microsite, or through mobile campaigns—an important part of the process is capturing consumer contact information. This allows you to develop a customer database that can be used for direct e-mail programs and to continue the dialogue you've established.

It is critical to have an opt-out option, including a process for managing requests to be removed from your marketing database. Web-based direct e-mail programs like Constant Contact provide many of the tools for efficiently managing customer outreach and databases.

TIP 104 | Use search engine optimization (SEO) to push your launch to success.

SEO is vital to ensure that you are included in the conversation. When consumers are researching products or services in your category on search engines such as Google or Bing, they will review (and click on) only a limited number of links. Consumers are savvy enough to know the difference between paid and organic search results, just as they know the difference between advertising and editorial content in *The New York Times*. Blending your paid SEO with a savvy organic SEO program that incorporates social bookmarking can help you market more effectively in new media channels.

Well-executed SEO strategies, performed with organic keywords and linking methods and/or with paid keyword marketing, help ensure that your brand and product appear early in the search results, ideally on the first page.

Three of the most important components of SEO are:

1. **Keyword optimization.** Make sure your site has searchable text that contains an appropriate number of keyword mentions that best describe your product/brand type, category and features.

2. **Link structures.** Ensure that your site is well connected with industry news and other affiliated or supporting sites through hyperlinks.

3. **Evolving content.** Not only does new, growing content make your site more dynamic, it also indicates to search engines that your site is actively producing new information and updates. Constant content updating increases your site's value and importance in search engine standards, and means a higher indexing and resulting search ranking.

It is important to consult with SEO technology experts who can manage the technical aspects of optimization and ensure that your code methods are search-engine friendly. Code methods can be white hat, which means they are accepted SEO tactics that are part of good design, or black hat, which means they are gimmicky, risky, unaccepted and potentially damaging.

Mike Troiano, president of Holland-Mark Digital—a marketing firm that helps businesses connect with, respond to, and benefit from the external truth about their customers, products and brand relationships—says, "The best way to drive traffic to your site is to deliver content that is worth looking at."

Is it really that simple? Yes. Troiano added, "That sensibility should be consistent with a strategy, rather than getting into an SEO arms race or trying to game the system with Google. It's better to try and build something of value, to deliver content that people find valuable that encourages conversation. With all of that pointed at your destination hub, it's a more sustainable way to optimize search engine traffic."

SEO also benefits when all of the weapons in your marketing arsenal are working hard in a cohesive manner. An aggressive public relations campaign, for example, is also a good way to enhance your organic search engine optimization. Newly posted optimized press releases, new articles in the media, and new blog posts all move your product and your company higher up in the organic search.

To optimize new product press releases (and all your press releases, for that matter), start by using words that are commonly searched. These words may be drastically different from the words the brand team uses in other marketing materials. By aligning the commonly searched terms with the words in your press releases (common search terms can be researched with Google AdWords), you will create a library of optimized pages that will help drive your organic traffic numbers.

TIP 105 Create a launch Web site with content management capabilities that is easy to update and interesting to consumers.

When consumers are excited about your brand, they want to be able to obtain a great deal of information in one place, particularly when your launch campaign is building excitement and interest for the upcoming new product release. By creating a launch Web site, you can offer timely, relevant information about your product that can be updated frequently using content management software. If your content becomes stale, you risk losing both consumer interest in your product and momentum for your launch.

With a launch microsite, the story of your new product, its features and the early reviews can be rolled out as a separate but supporting communications campaign. Whether you incorporate this microsite as a blog on your main Web site or create a separate site for the new product, you give consumers a reason to come back. An important SEO tactic for launch microsites that are posted for more than two months (the approximate time for search engines to crawl the Web and identify links and new content) is to link the launch site back to the main Web site. Also, link the launch site to relevant articles, reviews or information on other sites—again to maximize SEO.

TIP 106 **Make the URL of your Web site or microsite memorable.**

This seems like a no-brainer, but it is becoming increasingly difficult to secure memorable URLs that support brand differentiation, brand equity and campaign themes. URL searches frequently turn up existing sites that can create brand confusion (another company in a different industry is already using the same URL), or the site name you develop may have already been purchased by a third-party holding company (a company independent from the URL registration company that owns the URL name and is holding it to make a profit).

As more names continue to be spoken for, it's trickier to find a URL that meets four important criteria: memorable/unique; branded; consistently available across multiple platforms (for example, as names for your Facebook vanity URL and your Twitter handle); and concise. All four criteria are important when selecting a URL, but consistent availability is critical to campaign effectiveness since you want consumers to recognize the campaign across multiple types of media. It is also important to consider URL naming during campaign and brand development because a $1 million logo and name is not worth much if it can't be marketed effectively. Make sure your agencies check if the URLs they are proposing are available before they present an entire campaign using that Web site address.

In a program for Sweethearts Conversation Hearts, produced by New England Confectionary Company (formerly NECCO), we invited consumers to go online and create sayings for a new line of Sweethearts by submitting their own ideas to replace the iconic "Hug Me" and "Kiss Me" messages. Not only was our first URL choice, Sweethearts.com, being used

by a different organization, but our second choice, MySweethearts.com, was owned by a holding company. We ended up negotiating an acceptable fee to purchase MySweethearts.com from the holding company. It was more than a regular domain registration site would charge, but the expenditure was worth it to make sure the name satisfied all four criteria for URL names.

TIP 107 Maximize the effectiveness of mobile media in your launch by designing a dedicated, mobile-friendly Web site.

Consumers' use of mobile technology is growing at astronomical rates. It won't be long before mobile marketing becomes a mainstay of launch campaigns and is ubiquitous in marketing programs. But mobile marketing will pay off only if you take into account the limitations of mobile devices. In Web guru Jakob Nielsen's user testing of Web sites on mobile devices, the 36 "full" sites (those designed to be viewed on desktop computers) received very low scores. Nielsen concluded, "If mobile use is important to your Internet strategy, it's smart to build a dedicated mobile site."[1]

A mobile-friendly site focuses on features that people are likely to use in a mobile scenario and eliminates everything else. Keep in mind that consumers do not want to perform tasks on their mobiles that involve heavy interaction or in-depth information. Pare down your mobile launch site to the bare minimum and make the link to it very prominent on your main Web site.

TIP 108 Consider the value proposition of mobile campaigns for the customer.

Mobile campaigns are effective when the effort and the number of steps required to participate in your application/promotion are minor compared with the value consumers receive from it. Remember the CueCat device given to new subscribers of *WIRED* magazine? It was designed to scan UPC codes after articles and stories in print magazines, which would then deliver more information on the topics of interest from the Web. What went wrong? The setup took too long and the entire process was difficult compared with simply searching on the Web the old-fashioned way. Based on some of the message board comments from users, people were also wary of submitting all their purchasing data to a Big Brother tracking entity. The bottom line with mobile marketing, which is aimed at people on the go, is the tried-and-true KISS: Keep it super simple!

Right now, when marketers consider mobile marketing they tend to look at the numbers. "Three to 5 percent of users are accessing the Web on mobile applications," says Pape of Genuine Interactive. "They are the early adopters who are younger, and they appreciate good creative ideas and useful applications. They are more apt to be the real influencers. They are only 5 percent, but that 5 percent are the ones who are going to scream and yell about a brand."

Zak Dabbas, co-founder of Punchkick Interactive, a design firm focusing on full-service mobile marketing, says, "Mobile marketing doesn't stand alone. It needs traditional media to promote it. The apps that are working well have traditional components in the campaign. It is a great measurement tool, and the most engaged consumer you will ever find is one who can see an advertisement and then act on it. Plus, everything has to be opt in. Mobile phones are the most personal devices, so if I am willing to let a brand communicate with me, they are going to have to give me something of high value."

A long-range view of mobile marketing and usage comes from Dror Liwer, principal of the digital agency Zemoga. "It's exploding now, but it is in its infancy," Liwer explained. "The U.S. is two to three years behind Europe, which is a leading indicator of what will happen here. The marketing campaigns are all about creating an experience. In Europe, people do everything with their phone. They browse the Web through their phones more than through their computers. They chat, do Facebook, social networking, buy movie tickets, pay for gas, and receive geo-located offers."

The newspapers, television and mail of tomorrow are going to be accessed through the next generation of the iPhone, BlackBerry, and Palm—and through gadgets we haven't yet seen. All will have powerful computing devices with lots of local storage and great data input capability, and will be Web enabled. Within three to four years, people will have even more-powerful Web phones in their pockets. Instead of toting laptops, they'll take their iPhones and use them to search for products and services. Geography-based targeting is becoming more prevalent as technology improves and consumers become more receptive to receiving marketing messages on their phones. Are your marketing materials enabled for use on these mobile devices?

TIP 109   Understand that video is not inherently viral.

If we had a dollar for every client who asked us to create viral video like Burger King's "Subservient Chicken" or OfficeMax's "ElfYourself," we could retire rich. It is nearly impossible to set out to make a viral video and actually succeed in creating one. By nature, a viral video is something that takes off on its own. It has an impromptu or improvisational quality to it and involves unusual, surprising and often unexpected humorous material. In other words, it's not scripted or produced. Still, marketers have tried to capture this lightning in a bottle, with only moderate success. These types of videos are difficult to produce because people are less likely to forward along a branded, produced, professional video as opposed to a surprising moment authentically captured.

Bud Light Lime was able to create a moderate buzz among younger demographics with the "Behind the Lime" mock documentary featuring the character Limey, a 4-foot-tall creature with the body of a giant lime and the arms and legs of a human, who happens to be an amazing break-dancer and skateboarder. The Doritos Super Bowl XLIII commercial featuring the "crystal ball" was also a YouTube hit.

But in general, these are the exceptions, and in the end they probably didn't perform as well as true viral videos.

While it is important for marketers to use produced video on their Web sites and in campaigns, outrageous and successful viral video is not something that can be created with any consistency. The best way to foster genuine sharing of video content related to your brand is through a contest or promotion calling for customers to generate video content, preferably using a public site like YouTube or Flickr. A video contest encourages customers to engage with the brand as they show their friends and relatives the videos they create. It also demonstrates that the company values their opinions and comments.

The makers of K-Y® YOURS + MINE® Couples lubricants used YouTube and Flickr as a successful part of their marketing campaign.

The K-Y Brand, which landed at spot number six in our 2008 Most Memorable New Product Launch Top 10 list for its YOURS + MINE Couples lubricants, generated interest on Flickr and YouTube with its commercials. K-Y introduced the product with humorous, scripted testimonials from couples in bed describing the exhilarating effects of the lubricants. The sheer novelty of a traditionally taboo couples-oriented product drew people in.

Video also holds the power to change the way consumers and marketers interact. Consider this excerpt from our interview with Steve Garfield, an expert on all things video and a consultant to major broadcasting companies, about the launch of the Ford Fiesta:

> Product uniqueness propelled K-Y YOURS + MINE Couples lubricants to #6 in the MMNPL Survey in 2008

"Look at what Ford is doing with the Fiesta—that car isn't even out yet, and they have already seeded 1,000 bloggers with cars. They are all putting up YouTube videos, and you can see the car before it even comes out. You know Brooklyn Hillary? She drove from Detroit to L.A. with the car and went to Ford and met people at Ford. She is doing a video a day on Flickr. They gave them all video cameras, gave them all cars, and gave them one challenge a month that they have to video. This is a Fiesta movement. [Bloggers] are Twittering about it, and ... they got 4.7 million impressions from 100 bloggers about what happened. They are really happy. There are many different stories. It is very grassroots, very Americana. People on the Web were interested in hearing about this stuff beforehand and it is a great project as a pre-buzz thing. They could have user groups and meet-ups and then car clubs for people who like the car."

Garfield also believes that as remote video upload to the Internet becomes more common (currently the iPhone 3GS allows instant video upload to YouTube), citizen journalism and firsthand reporting of events will grow, along with opportunities for consumers to express their views on products through video, as in the Ford Fiesta example.

Mastering new media becomes even more important as you plan your entrance into social media, the topic of our next chapter.

CHAPTER 10

Social Media: Redefining How Consumers Engage with New Products

The emergence of social media is radically changing the way new products are launched. This new medium is not only influencing the tactics used to introduce products, but it's also driving the discussions about who should be the first to see or try a new product. No longer is it mandatory that a

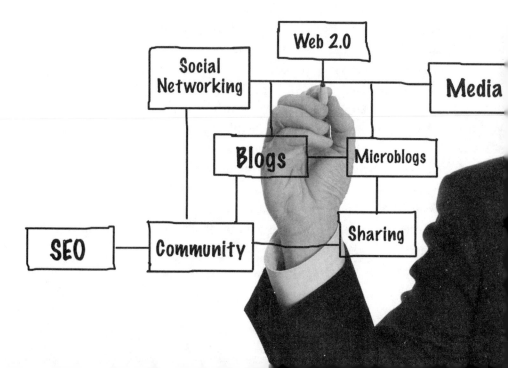

major daily newspaper or a broadcast television network gets a product preview or an exclusive announcement about a new product launch. Influential bloggers and other online "reporters" and special interest Web sites are now part of the mix when defining a new product launch strategy.

One of the most difficult things for marketers to accept is that consumers are now in control and are perfectly willing and able to mount their own positive or negative campaigns about a new product. When long-standing brand leaders make critical missteps in product development, marketing, advertising or at events, consumers take notice—and tell others. They talk, share information, vent their outrage, and create a virtual firestorm of feedback—a firestorm that can derail a launch, create a negative aura around the product and its features, and assault the very integrity of—and affinity for—your brand. Conversely, when this consumer power is harnessed, it can be used to encourage valuable word-of-mouth marketing and impact search engine optimization prior to a new product launch.

Social media allows marketers to engage customers in a conversation—a real, live dialogue that has the power of thousands of focus groups. This dialogue can help you develop products that fulfill *actual* consumer needs and gather valuable feedback on what potential customers have to say about your product. In addition, social media can drive customer acquisition, generate "buzz," and disseminate new product news faster than a news release as people quickly pass along information to their friends on Facebook or their followers on Twitter.

Here are tactics to consider when crafting a social media campaign to augment traditional launch strategies:

TIP 110   **Engage brand ambassadors online.**

People who love and trust your brand are often willing to discuss it openly, both on- and offline. Marketing agencies and organizations should include brand ambassador programs as central components of their new product launch and social media strategies. A brand ambassador is a consumer who is an active advocate for a brand and has been recognized or endorsed by the brand, usually for his or her product knowledge and/or passion. These brand aficionados are part of an exclusive community that has a privileged relationship with the brand, and they are recognized by other consumers for that relationship.

Brand ambassadors can be excellent sources for creating a dialogue about your product during the development, launch and distribution phases. How can you find them? Start by listening. Track what consumers who love your brand are saying online and also listen to what consumers who love your competition's brands are saying about them. Once you understand what is being said, begin to develop one-on-one relationships with consumers to set the stage for your product launch. Provide these key influencers with advance information or seek their opinions. These ambassadors can seed the market for you and create demand at retail.

The Microsoft Most Valuable Professional Award program is a great example of engaging customers to serve as brand ambassadors in a credible way. Through this program, Microsoft has developed relationships with hundreds of communities and discussion forums where customers are interacting with and supporting each other. MVP participants are recognized and respected because of their relationship with Microsoft. They are often sought out by other forum members for their advice. Some MVPs have even garnered more respect and credibility with customers than their Microsoft employee counterparts. While MVP is not a marketing program, it is an excellent case study demonstrating the power and effectiveness of using customers to represent a brand via social media engagement.

Walmart's Elevenmoms program shares some similarities with Microsoft's MVP program in its approach to social media engagement. The particulars are different, but both oft-criticized organizations may face fewer bumps in the road because of these brand ambassadors. Walmart's Elevenmoms are a group of bloggers who write regularly on the many challenges facing moms raising kids and running households. Walmart specifically chose these bloggers for their content quality and influence. They enlisted these Elevenmoms to build a community of other moms who share advice and insights on saving money and living better— Walmart's mission.

Walmart's Elevenmoms are not paid but receive "soft incentives" like travel expenses for meetings with Walmart's team and product promotions. The Elevenmoms believe in what Walmart is trying to do and that's what makes it work. The Elevenmoms and the community built around them provide invaluable feedback to help shape Walmart's business, and offer a place for customer interaction. This model has been extremely successful for Walmart, according to Robin Neifeld, a writer for ClickZ.com.

"The dynamic of such a giant brand as Walmart actually allowing this kind of program to progress organically without strangling control is an example to both small and large players out there. If you've got nothing to hide, social media can be a tremendous ally," said Neifeld.[1]

| TIP 111 | **Use social media to generate instant feedback.**

Unsure of how a particular product feature will test with your customers? Imagine if you could get the best development or marketing ideas from people who actually use your product. Instant, real-world responses from social media users can help guide both major and minor decisions required to create and fine-tune product features. This is the benefit of "listening" to the social Web. You can:

- **Find conversations that are already happening and pull ideas from them.** Twitter—which enables companies to "listen" for brand mentions and respond to users in real time—is great for listening to all types of conversations.

- **Create opportunities for communities to offer and edit their own ideas about your product.** For instance, gearing up to ship Windows Mobile 6.5-powered devices in fall 2009, Microsoft planned a large-scale worldwide advertising campaign starting in October 2009 to introduce the new Windows phone brand. But first, they asked consumers for innovative ways to promote Windows phones. Microsoft teamed up with Zooppa.com, a Web site that allows companies to publish creative briefs and crowd source freelance graphic designers, directors, animators and writers to develop innovative, creative ideas in return for cash prizes. Microsoft offered anyone the opportunity to contribute video, print, radio or Web ads or even ad concepts with a total cash prize of $14,000 up for grabs.

- **Launch a "beta" version of your product.** Many of the most forward-looking companies, like Google, launch new products in beta form to gain valuable information and feedback while developing and tweaking product features. Google's Gmail, an e-mail program with coveted accounts that was one of Google's most successful launches, was a beta product offering. As Google gained more Gmail users, the company learned valuable information about people's usage and interaction patterns. With that input, Google was able to refine the product.

- **Leverage opportunities created by your product.** The introduction of Apple's revolutionary iPhone—2007's Most Memorable New Product Launch–demonstrates how to launch multiple new products using social media to generate instant feedback. The iPhone's "App Store" features hundreds of free applications ("apps") that essentially are free trials of games or products for which users might eventually pay. The iPhone apps are great ways to make consumers aware of new products and promote trial before an official launch.

> **The iPhone earned the #1 spot in the 2007 MMNPL Survey**

- **Gain additional, positive brand impressions.** Another great social media example is FedEx's introduction of its online "Launch a Package" program. FedEx wanted to participate in social media but needed a relevant way to begin. So they studied how people use various social media tools, looking for an opportunity. They found it on Facebook. FedEx built "Launch a Package," which allows Facebook users to customize a virtual package with messages, video, virtual gifts and photos to send to Facebook friends. The application met a need and fit FedEx's core brand perfectly; plus, the results were immediate: 100,000 installs in 48 hours. It was the first branded app to make No. 1 on Facebook's Most Active page, with over 50 percent of users returning more than 10 times after installing it.

TIP 112 Set up online focus groups to get unbiased data about your new product and launch campaign.

Instead of using traditional focus groups that can be skewed by one or two highly opinionated, vocal participants, you can gather open, honest feedback from online consumers who are free to form their own thoughts. An additional benefit is that people can offer their initial responses, then come back later with more feedback once they've had time to think things over. Anyone who has ever participated in a focus group knows the feeling of walking out and realizing later that you had something more to say.

With an online focus group, you can easily gather these important second thoughts and more unbiased views from participants.

Lynda Gordon of Decision Metrics is a proponent of the holistic approach: "You should use more than one methodology. There is nothing like cross validating different methodologies to confirm you are asking the right questions. Do a focus group to get some initial responses, and follow that up with an online purchase survey to see if consumers, when not talk-ing about attributes and designs, will still make choices. In the case of an unlimited budget, I would always do focus groups, then phone or online surveys and finish it with in-store intercepts. Those three methods, when used together for testing product launch, are highly reliable."

The Power of Social Media in a Launch – The TweetDeck Story from Founder and CEO Iain Dodsworth

How did the idea of the TweetDeck come about?

Dodsworth: I was a contractor and my background was in developing and managing financial dashboards, displays of fast-moving informa-tion, which were rather dry in content. When I looked at Twitter, origi-nally I felt there was no value there for me and not enough conversa-tion. But when I came back to it a year later, it had changed radically. There was a lot of conversation. I was following 30 to 40 people and keeping up with them was rather difficult. I was starting to miss tweets from real friends, and my colleagues were being drowned out by oth-ers. One day I was in Starbucks thinking about this as a problem, and I felt like I could fix it myself.

I wanted a dashboard, a full-screen view, and an external monitor application. I didn't just want it off to the side—I wanted to have ▶

it running all the time. So I built it. I took my friends and I segmented them from the stream of information that was flooding by. It was easy to come up with all kinds of ideas around this. What if I wanted more than one grid? How about 10 grids? How do I display this? That's how the concept was born. That was the eureka moment. That is where innovation comes from—when somebody looks at something from left field without constraints.

I built the TweetDeck in three weeks, and I built it purely for me. It was a solution to my problem but I still had to go and find a job. I finished the basic demo and sent it to 10 friends. I told them not to send it to anyone as it wasn't finished, but they did. And they were

blown away with it as a concept. That's when I knew it was something more than just a solution for me. It was amazing. I built it for me, it was a niche product and I thought, "If people really wanted a Twitter dashboard, why wasn't it built?"

So I created a Web page, made it a private download, and I got flooded with e-mails and tweets desperate to get a hold of it. Louis Gray, who was an early adopter and major tech blogger from Silicon Valley, said it was amazing, and asked if he could be the first person to blog about it. The demand from that blog post was so large, and they (his blog followers) were able to go get it from the Web site. That is how it launched, July Fourth, via a blog post on someone else's blog. In terms of a launch strategy, there wasn't one. Instead it was me battling against the torrents of demand for the product. I was in a nice position because TweetDeck was the first to market, the first of its kind and it also hit a vocal, techie niche market. They promoted the hell out of it, which helped it really make a splash when it was launched.

I just kept updating and adding things, making it faster, broader and broader. A few months later, after it was out in the marketplace, I started to find the way I was using the Internet was changing subtly. I was using TweetDeck every day and it was the first thing I did ▶

in the morning. I kept it running so I could keep up with the U.S. overnight. It was interesting—my primary source of information was moving from e-mail and RSS to my TweetDeck, this stream of real time data that was coming from Twitter, Facebook and MySpace. Now it comes from everywhere, from eBay, Amazon, online news sites. This dashboard of short, punchy, fast-moving data was a new way of consuming information that was replacing e-mail, Web pages and RSS feeds. Early in 2009, I had a crystallized vision for the TweetDeck. We were building a browser, not just a Twitter application, but in a real time way.

I didn't spend a penny on launching the product, and I haven't spent a penny in pushing the product in any way. I am very proud of the fact that we used the medium (Twitter) to push the product (which was about Twitter) out further. Every time you do a tweet from TweetDeck, it says "via TweetDeck." We are currently in the lovely position to be the number-one application on Twitter, and we are going to get the same status on Facebook, all free.

As a social media company, was it natural for you to beta test the TweetDeck with your users to fine-tune the product before full launch?

Dodsworth: We've done many updates of TweetDeck and they've all been called 'beta,' so it's always in beta testing. It's a continually moving goal post. New ideas came in, new suggestions, so we've been trying to innovate further. It's incredibly difficult to pin down a point where you aren't in beta. It's a useful label for a technology company, if you want to get out to market very quickly. Rather than spending a large amount of time with closed sessions of testing to make the product 100 percent effective, you get the first mover advantage.

Has the process been worthwhile? Did you gain meaningful user insights that helped you build a better product?

Dodsworth: We get an absolute ton of information in the form of hundreds or thousands of tweets per day from the community. We have a mass of information, but the vision for TweetDeck stays the same: ▶

building the browser. That is where we are going and where we will end up. When we put out updates, or our own ideas about functionality, half the people love it and half think we should do it a different way. There are always differing opinions and all of it generates feedback. •

TIP 113 Use social media to identify the "right" product messaging and positioning before launch.

Engaging customers through social media to gain insights into what they want in a new product is a great way to strategically position your product before launch planning even begins. Often, the most vital feedback you can get is negative criticism, as it helps identify potential product, feature and marketing issues prior to the actual launch.

Some marketers fear that online communities can be risky because they may backfire and become a liability: What if they bash you in front of all the other customers? What if it turns into a complaint forum? How can you make sure it doesn't turn negative and change the perceptions of all your customers? These concerns are common at many companies that consider engaging their customers in their new product prior to launch. The idea of bringing together customers and giving them the ability to be critical in public sounds like a recipe for disaster. In some cases, it certainly can be. But other times, what companies instinctively want to avoid can be their greatest asset. The book *The Cluetrain Manifesto*, a 1999 harbinger of the importance of social media, sums it up best:

> *"Online markets will talk about companies whether companies like it or not. People will say whatever they like, without caring whether they're overheard or quoted—in fact, having one's views passed along is usually the whole point. Companies can't stop customers from speaking up, and can't stop employees from talking to customers. Their only choice is to start encouraging employees to talk to customers—and empowering them to act on what they hear."*[2]

If customers choose to be critical, don't try to hide or divert their comments; share them at your company because they may represent a silent majority that is looking for a voice. By giving customers that voice and responding to them in a community, companies can build a valuable and irreplaceable foundation of trust and open communication. Using this foundation, customers can help companies make real improvements. Negative reviews can have a positive side. Negative product feedback typically is a byproduct of a poor product or poor customer service. These negative reviews can be an extension of your market research or customer care efforts, and can help drive change and improvement of product design, assortment and service.

The retailer eBags is an example of a company that leverages consumer reviews to make its purchasing decisions. The online seller of handbags, backpacks, business cases, urban bags, luggage, and travel accessories creates vendor scorecards that incorporate feedback and data from its product reviews. eBags uses these scorecards to make buying decisions, such as which items to continue or discontinue, which items to fix, and which vendors to avoid.

Customers appreciate being "courted" during the development process because everyone likes to believe their feedback is important and valued. Be sure to thank and reward consumers who provide input and advice. Whether you offer them a special "friends and family" discount, a chance to provide input for new features in Version 2 of your product, or an opportunity to be the first to try the next version, be sure to reward consumers who serve as your advocates. Even customers who complain should be acknowledged, as there's nothing more detrimental to a brand than an irate customer.

TIP 114 Establish a real online dialogue with customers—the effort will pay off handsomely.

For decades, marketers and advertisers have focused on developing a "voice" to use in speaking to consumers about their brand. They communicated this "voice" through catchy 60-second television ads, radio spots and outdoor billboards that told consumers what they were expected to know and think about the brand. Breaking through with an effective message to specific target audiences is the Holy Grail of branding. Now, social media mavens are turning marketing monologues into two-way conversations. More than ever, marketers are dependent on what consumers think, what they want, and what they believe about their brands and products. Conversely, the opportunities are limitless to capitalize on this new access to consumers and the dialogue you can create about a new product.

"Social media by definition is almost 100 percent locked in, right?" said Jason Baer, social media strategy consultant and founder of Convince & Convert. "People have to subscribe to your Twitter feed, they have to 'friend' you on Facebook; they have to want to go to your Web site, your YouTube video, your social outpost. It's all about communicating with those who have indicated they care about you. Social media is a sort of a backstop, so you use other, more traditional tactics like media relations, blogger relations, direct mail, print, trade show, TV, radio, outdoors—whatever the product and strategy calls for. You use these elements as the tip of the spear, but the shaft of the spear is social media. So perhaps you drive people to Facebook and to YouTube, you encourage them to follow you on Twitter, etc., so the call to action is, engage with us on social media, learn more about this product not only from us, obviously a biased communicator, but from other customers. I would use traditional tactics to drive people to social media outposts, then make it more of a conversation about the product as opposed to, 'Here is our brochure, here are our bullet points about this product that we think you need.'"

Engaging consumers in authentic discussion is a sure way to build brand loyalty and buzz. (See "5 Key Steps Required to Master the Social Media Engagement Cycle" on page 215 for ideas on how to start your dialogue.)

TIP 115   Leverage the power of bloggers by sampling.

The power of a product review written by the right blogger can be astounding. But the important thing is identifying the right blogger, with the right content and readers, so you can make reasonably accurate predictions about how your product sampling will be received.

Choosing a blogger based simply on scope of reach can be dangerous. Assuming the wrong things about a blogger can make your brand look foolish or out of touch, and many bloggers won't hesitate to tell their readers about your mistake. When you fully understand the medium and the message of the blogger you are eager to engage, you are ready to approach him or her about sampling and reviewing your product.

Bloggers, or "citizen journalists," are much more likely to review a product favorably when it is the right "fit" for them and their audience, and of course, when it is offered for free (still one of the most powerful words in marketing). Reviews of products by bloggers create positive brand impressions in their communities and help fuel marketing efforts. Simply put, word of mouth is fast, but word of net can be 100 times faster and reach much further. According to Jason Baer, "If somebody writes a negative blog post, a negative comment, or even a tepid or lukewarm piece of information about the product, companies are going to have to get on top of that because [it can damage the brand]."

It is important to note that the Federal Trade Commission (FTC) has reviewed the use of product sampling with bloggers and instituted new rules, plus penalties for nondisclosure. Under the new regulations, bloggers are required to disclose whenever they receive a product for free to review, or both the blogger and the company providing samples could face prosecution and fines. The rules are aimed at creating greater transparency, not just for bloggers and reviewers, but also for celebrities making product comments and endorsements. The ruling even states that individuals could personally be held liable if they do not disclose that they are being paid, or that the product they are reviewing was provided free of charge.

These new rules could lead to a sea change in the way that products are reviewed if bloggers want to retain their authenticity. Instead of mostly positive product reviews with only minor "suggestions" instead of "dislikes," bloggers will have to make a choice: Either discontinue accepting products for review (no more free stuff), or write product reviews with a focus on credibility, honesty and yes, more negativity. Unfortunately for marketers, the obsequiousness of near-perfect product reviews may go away—but the opportunity to gauge real feedback will no doubt return.

A great example of blog marketing gone wrong in the pre-FTC-ruling era is the Walmarting Across America campaign, where Laura and Jim, folksy lifelong Walmart fans, traveled across the country in an RV. They visited Walmart stores along the way, talking to joyful employees while, of course, keeping a blog about their adventures. While their story met with initial enthusiasm, news quickly spread that the bloggers were being paid by Walmart to carry out the promotion.[3] Despite being an interesting idea, the campaign was no longer compelling to the American public and had the feel of being disingenuous.

Walmart rival Target initially had its own social media challenges. Target received a complaint from a blogger representing the group Shaping Youth, about a Target ad that she thought could have a potentially negative latent message about the image of women. Target offended not only this particular blogger but all bloggers with its e-mail response: "Unfortunately we are unable to respond to your inquiry because Target does not participate with nontraditional media outlets. This practice is in place to allow us to focus on publications that reach our core guest."[4]

After a considerable backlash, much of which came from incensed bloggers, Target shifted its position and has since begun focusing on engaging consumers on the Web and collecting their feedback.

Rules of Pitching a Blogger for Marketing Purposes

1. The rules of blogger engagement in many ways mimic the rules of friendship. Be very knowledgeable about both the blogger and the content written on the blog.
2. Make sure the product or service you are marketing is appropriate for the blog.
3. Don't be robotic—the more personal you are, the better response you will receive from the blogger.
4. Whether you're dealing with a newspaper journalist blogger or a niche hobby blogger, as a marketer you will most likely need to connect with that person again, so develop a relationship and maintain it. Stay in touch and don't contact a blogger only when you need him or her to review your product.
5. Realize you may encounter resistance and even negativity from a blogger about what you are proposing, so be prepared to manage the discussion tactfully. •

TIP 116 Respect mommy bloggers.

The estimated 100,000-plus mommy bloggers (moms who post blogs and/or participate online) are the thought leaders for the 34 million moms who are online, as well as all the other moms who are offline. Since women collectively make approximately 80 percent of household purchasing decisions, mommy bloggers are a very powerful group. Mommy bloggers are, in essence, the "Oprahs of the Internet." These highly influential women are not only spending a large amount of time blogging but also sharing opinions and ideas online. Because of their power, mommy bloggers are targeted more than any other group for their insights, reviews and opinions.

When you're developing a product for moms or planning a product launch that reaches the mommy blogger audience, there's no excuse for ignoring the opportunity to test market and sample online. Mommy bloggers are available, eager to participate, discerning and vociferous in their comments. If you make a critical misstep, mommy bloggers will respond in full force. Our advice: Avoid their wrath at all costs by being thoughtful and respectful in your approach.

For a prime example of how much fury this group can generate against a marketing campaign gone wrong, look no further than Motrin. Its ill-advised online and print ads claimed some moms tote their infants around with baby body carriers as a "fashion statement" and summed it up with, "Supposedly it's a real bonding experience ... but what about me?" The outrage rocked the social media world. Twitter tweets on Motrin went berserk as moms interpreted the ads as a slam against parenthood and parent/child bonding. Within two days, the ad campaign was pulled and Motrin's Web site featured this apology: "With regard to the recent Motrin advertisement, we have heard you. On behalf of McNeil Consumer Healthcare and all of us who work on the Motrin Brand, please accept our sincere apology. We have heard your complaints about the ad that was featured on our website. We are parents ourselves and take feedback from moms very seriously ..."

"Many people with small networks have just as much influence as a few people with large networks," explained David Armano, now a senior partner at Dachis Group, in *Ad Age*. What has been dubbed the "Motrin Moms" debacle is a reminder of not only the power of Mommy Bloggers but also the importance of consumer engagement in your messaging.[5]

Vroom Solo Cleans up with Mommy Bloggers

Through its social media offering called Mommies Clique™, Schneider PR turned a new product into a Web and social media success story. During June 2009, Mommies Clique members engaged in online communication with mom bloggers about Vroom Solo, an under-the-cabinet, mounted, stand-alone vacuum system that makes it easier to clean high traffic areas in the home. Over the course of the month, after developing authentic and credible relationships with bloggers, Mommies Clique members asked the bloggers if they would like to review a Vroom Solo.

The online communications program was extremely well received. Vroom Solo product samples became a highly sought-after product to review on the Web. More than 70 bloggers received the product, generating 61 organic blog hits, with all blog posts linking directly to the product Web site (Vroomyourroom.com), thereby increasing unique monthly viewership significantly.

Vroomyourroom.com saw a significant spike in its traffic, boosted by blogger product reviews that were 100 percent positive and authentic, including personal videos and photos of moms and their children quickly cleaning up spills and messes with the Vroom Solo. Blog readership numbers totaled more than 660,000—all within an extremely targeted demographic of moms following their favorite mom blogger.

The Vroom Solo outreach is a great example of a brand's effort to creatively target its message to a specific demographic in a cost-effective manner. The effort generated brand recognition and raised awareness of Vroom Solo in a short period of time. •

TIP 117 Build a social media newsroom on your Web site.

As social media strategies continue to prove their relevance and importance, it is no surprise that the traditional online newsroom—a set of static Web pages that support one-way information delivery, protected by passwords and available to only "official" journalists and industry analysts—is about as relevant as a typewriter. Taking the place of the old-fashioned newsroom is a new social media newsroom, a more dynamic, open and flexible Web-based newsroom encouraging two-way communication and information sharing among diverse audiences. A social media newsroom's content is easily accessible to media but also to other important constituents—customers, business partners and investors. These groups can subscribe to, review and use relevant news from the organization, as well as find related images, audio, video and other multimedia files.

A social media newsroom can drive referral traffic by creating consumer advocates. Genuine Interactive, a digital agency, creates social media newsrooms that help increase natural search ranking and the proliferation of news through social media channels. According-ing to Genuine's founder, Chris Pape, "A true social media friendly newsroom can help consumers post your company's news, tools and content on their own social media sites. By giving consumers an easy way to share your content, you empower an army of mini PR mavens in the form of consumer brand advocates."

Pape believes there has been "a large shift in power from newspapers and publishers to the consumer … it's a reshuffling of the power base. You can share content through a new group of powerful people, who are the influential, active, social media public. Before, PR people had to pitch your story to editors or reporters. Now, a story that truly resonates with consumers will make it to the top of Digg and Google News and be posted on Facebook pages. The power is shifting from a few large media companies to millions of influential consumers."

Take, for example, Ford's Digital Snippets social media newsroom, with RSS feeds, Flickr photo sharing, links to blog reviews with video and lots of opportunities for user feedback, comments, conversation and republishing.

Unfortunately, many social media newsrooms start out with a flash and then stop. They are not updated for months, if at all. Granted, it takes a lot of hard work to pull together all the content, multimedia and social news sharing capabilities. But why is that any different from creating in-store point of purchase, print advertising and television spots—all of the "old" marketing tactics that marketers have employed in the past? By keeping your online newsroom fresh, you jump higher in the search rankings. If you are releasing something to the media, just add it to the social media newsroom too, since you've already done the work. Plus, when you write press materials using the same keywords consumers use when they search online for products or brands in your category, you can ensure that the information is optimized for search engines, moving it higher up in the results.

TIP 118 | Use social bookmarking to spread the word.

With social bookmarking, "citizen journalists" store, organize, search and manage Web page bookmarks. Social bookmarking is an excellent way to link content—either blog content, or Web content that's related to your product or industry—back to your Web site and social media newsroom, thereby increasing link structures and strengthening SEO.

Does social bookmarking really matter? Yes, but only to the extent that you're interested in search engine rankings and organic traffic, which most marketers are. Some of the social bookmarking sites like Digg and Delicious carry a pretty heavy weight, and are definitely worth the "link juice" if you're fortunate enough to get a link from them. When content is linked to the community at Digg or Delicious, others link to the content and comment on it, so the link structure to your own Web site strengthens and SEO is boosted. Combining social bookmarking and search engine optimization can help market your company or product better through different channels.

Most marketers don't have time to manage all their social communities, plus participate in the bookmarking community. So unless you have an assigned "content captain" on your team, you may want to use social media just to help strengthen your own content and SEO. Bookmarking enthusiasts aside, it's also important to be selective and establish criteria for choosing which emerging social media technologies to adopt. "You could spend half your life trying every technology that comes down the pike, and still be hopelessly at sea," commented Alexandra Samuel, CEO of Social Signal, a social media agency. "What is available is choice: choice among social networks, choice among software programs, and choice among hardware options. But most crucial of all, the choice to stop keeping up with all the shoulds and must-haves, and to start choosing technologies that support the goals and priorities that matter to you."[6]

TIP 119 **Tweet about your product to build buzz.**

These days it is difficult to pick up a newspaper, listen to NPR or watch your local TV news without hearing about Twitter. Everyone from pro athletes to celebrities to reporters has joined regular folks to communicate what they are feeling at that particular moment in 140 characters or less. Despite the millions of people using Twitter every day, most people just don't get it: "What's the big deal over this Twitter thing? It's just another way to send a text message."

Mark our words, years from now when we look back on the Twitter-wave that swept across the world in the early 21st century, it will be recognized for what it is—the most important marketing revolution of our lifetime. At first glance, Twitter seems to be just another in a long line of technology tools. But look again. Having lost trust in traditional media sources, people are turning to one another for recommendations and referrals. Texting is fast, but it reaches only one person at a time. With Twitter, you can send out a single 140-character tweet, and everyone who is following you receives it. They, in turn, can re-tweet (RT) your message to their followers, and so on.

Dunkin' Donuts is ahead of the curve when it comes to incorporating Twitter into its product marketing. Just ask David Puner, communications manager at Dunkin' Brands, who is better known as Dunkin' Dave. "The expectations are, if a person likes a brand, they should be able to find them on Twitter," he said. "Dunkin' Donuts on Twitter is a voice representing the company, which is nothing without our franchisees and shops and, of course, our customers. When I'm on Twitter,

David Puner, Dunkin' Dave

among other things, I'm looking for unique questions to which Dunkin' fans will be interested in having an *insider* answer. Or sometimes I'll play off our new products. Any day, at any time, in real time, the conversation can go in a surprising branded direction based entirely on direct interaction with the customer in this digital space. The amount of traffic for one person to handle is enormous, so it's impossible to answer everything, but I try to engage with as many people as I can who want to be engaged."

TIP 120 Treat social media as another form of online customer service.

The potential for providing good customer service through social media such as Twitter is enormous and offers huge opportunities for creating a positive brand experience. When you're launching a new product, it is particularly important to have a plan for responding to tweets and other feedback where people might express displeasure with your new offering. Dunkin' Dave added, "This is going to change the way consumer care is handled. We haven't yet increased the human resources on Twitter to make it a consumer care vehicle. But the more Dunkin' Donuts talks on Twitter, the more it seems people expect from the space. We're keeping an eye on it."

Customer Service the New-Fashioned Way

By now, you've probably heard of Frank Eliason, the director of Digital Care at Comcast. Charged with responsibility for customer service, Frank used a Twitter account to show the gentler side of this giant media corporation. Frank discovered there were myriad negative tweets about Comcast on Twitter, so he took it upon himself to begin responding to, and fixing, the issues he was equipped to handle.

After responding to more than 22,000 tweets, plus a great many direct phone calls to customers in distress, Comcast's "Twitter Man" is still providing

Frank Eliason   subscribers with unprecedented access to everyday help with service, while giving the organization a much more personal feel.[7] Now there's a legion of people at Comcast who troubleshoot customer questions and complaints. (A colleague of ours recently tweeted to Frank and within one minute was contacted by @comcastsheila to handle the problem.)

It helps that Frank follows the doctrine of being "Frank" first, or in other words, "be yourself." He speaks in the same manner that he would to his friends and coworkers, and gets "on the level" with ▶

his customers, treating them with respect, courtesy, friendliness and discretion. Sometimes Frank simply tells customers that everyone at Comcast is trying their best, and sometimes that personal engagement is all it takes.

There is no substitute for speaking as a real person with another real person, and that's how customers should feel when you interact with them online. •

TIP 121 Don't expect to measure social media campaigns the same way you measure traditional media.

Social media provide fragmented, multifaceted delivery points for brand messaging and product information that are difficult to isolate and correlate with sales numbers. Common ROI questions that are still difficult to answer include: How many blog comments does it take for a blog post to be considered effective? How many fans are required to declare your Facebook fan page a success? What's an acceptable number of Twitter followers for a brand? How many brand impressions (and in which media) will generate sales results for the new product? Can you compare social media results with traditional GRP (gross rating point) metrics? Do these new measures and media translate into sales? Or are they just discussions that ultimately could lead to sales?

Some experts say social media cannot be measured. As Katie Paine, founder and CEO of KDPaine & Partners, a leading marketing and public relations measurement firm, explained, "Some of the most popular outlets don't tell you your CPM (cost per thousand). Shel Israel, who writes a well-known blog titled 'Global Neighbourhoods' about social media topics, has 20,000 readers of his blog, but there's no information available to check. How do you calculate CPM for that? What is the volume and reach?"

New media will lead to new metrics, one would assume. But while television advertising has enjoyed the GRP standard for decades, how can one assume that eyeballs are actually watching the ad and how can one assume the same eyeballs are reading a blog or tweet? Marketers are accustomed to getting data from the media department outlining "reach," said Paine. "If we reach 50 million people, we will sell X cases of shampoo," but this is not true of social media. The process is still being sorted out. Where television ratings and data tracking have established a track record of reliability, marketers are still trying to identify not only what to measure in social media, but also *how* to measure it and correlate it to sales.

Mike Troiano, president of Holland-Mark Digital, offered this opinion on measuring social media: "A lot of the efforts to measure social media are misguided. The energy around measuring social media marketing is to try to assign value to engagement. What is the value of a re-tweet, the value of a follow? As a brand, the price of entry is [maintaining] a two-way dialogue with advocates and potential advocates. That part is a fixed cost, an infrastructure cost, measuring customer service, staying engaged. Once you've engaged with them and have a relationship, you need to do activation, sending out special offers, activities to help you prioritize feature A versus feature B, for instance. These are the kinds of activities that have tangible value in the real world."

He continued, "It is less about unit volume and more about key themes, offering great insight into whether your message is penetrating the masses or going unheard."

In measuring social media, the goal is to understand the return on investment. We need to know how specific programs paid off and how they compare with more traditional marketing disciplines and channels. We are driven by clients to compare output performance in social media with output performance in advertising. Many major consumer packaged goods (CPG) companies require ad-equivalency measures in traditional PR programs so they can compare "apples to oranges." WOM (Word of Mouth) Units—an actual term used by the Word of Mouth Marketing Association—are considered more valuable than ad impressions. Dr. Walter Carl, founder and chief research officer of ChatThreads, an independent word of mouth research company, believes that "depending on the type of product, and typically for CPG products, 80 to 90 percent of the consumer conversation takes place in face-to-face venues or publicly unavailable venues like e-mail, phone or mobile conversations. At ChatThreads, when we look at conversations, we look at multiple people in the conversation. One person might tell us about the conversation, then others will tell us about the conversation, and we can match up the reports. We can see conversations that are reported by people we couldn't access, and we get insights about what people are doing afterwards. Trying the product? Purchasing?" Dr. Carl concluded, "The challenge in analyzing conversations on blogs, online forums and Twitter is closing the loop between conversation and subsequent action."

Our research shows that if you recommend a new product to a mom, that recommendation is far more valuable and actionable than the ad she sees in *Parents* magazine. But how much more valuable? These are the metrics that the best and the brightest in the social media stratosphere are working to determine.

5 Key Steps Required to Master the Social Media Engagement Cycle

Step 1: Educate and immerse yourself prior to leaping into social media.

It is incredibly important for you and your team to familiarize yourselves with all aspects of social media and developing technologies that can impact your brand. Focus on not only formal knowledge of how a particular product/site/technology works, but on the various ways it is being used, the demographics of the users on the site, and the social context(s) of its use. Each online social network has its own unique vibe and its own unwritten rules about what is acceptable and what is not. You need to be well versed in these before entering into the conversation.

Step 2: Employ a listening campaign.

Customers are constantly offering valuable information about where they are, where they go, what they do, what they think, feel and want. By listening with a focus on what you're thinking and planning for your product launch, you'll gain insights that can lead to creative, innovative ways to tailor the launch to specific audiences. Develop a well-defined list of places to listen, then a well-defined method for recording the information so it can be analyzed and organized to use in launch planning and implementation.

▶

Step 3: Establish communications protocols to respond to consumers quickly and accurately in both positive and negative situations.

When you decide to engage consumers, you'll be entering a fast-paced, emotionally laden, content-overloaded environment where your communications will be highly scrutinized and possibly way over-analyzed. That's why it is important to determine the person within your team, or at your public relations or marketing firm, who is best equipped to manage your communications protocol. That person will need to decide how various types of feedback should be handled: Online or offline? Publicly in the media where it occurred? As a separate, private conversation in e-mail/chat? When confronting negative feedback or comments, you'll want to follow a defined protocol to stay on message and protect your brand. The contents of the Media Message Guide, particularly the Q&A section where both positive and negative questions have been addressed, can help you formulate appropriate messages.

You'll want to gauge where the naysayer is coming from and determine what kind of person he or she might be. Is this an impassioned consumer or a blog rabble rouser? A target customer or a reviewer who had unreasonable expectations and is better served with an entirely different kind of product? Consider questions like: Is this person credible? Is he or she influential in your space? Has the community supported or condemned this person's comments previously? If the community doesn't support this person, do we even need to further engage him or her? Sometimes the best thing you can do is let the negative comment go unanswered, but it's important to have a very good sense of when you can and can't use that strategy. Knowing your audience can help you anticipate how your responses to negative comments might be received.

On the positive side, never let a great comment go unrecognized. Fan the flames of excited, engaged customers and make the most of their endorsements by spending as much time thinking about the plan for when things go right as you do for when they go otherwise. Have a defined set of the kinds of responses you'd like to provide to ▶

those offering positive feedback, from enthusiasm about upcoming launches to excitement over new features.

Step 4: Engage, engage and engage some more.

There's really no such thing as too much of a good thing when it comes to social media engagement. By frequently interacting with individuals or groups of people within an environment, you establish a presence and rapport that is personal and effective. If someone comes across your discussion threads, posts or updates in multiple locations, not only do your posts translate to additional brand impressions, but they also affect search engine optimization in an organic and credible way. But be warned: Social media is a fast-growing, fluctuating and diverse environment. When engaging, consider the following:

- Develop a Facebook presence (fan page, group, "quiz" or "sticky" presence) to engage consumers.
- Become involved with other communities that are aligned with your brand.
- Create a Twitter handle to provide information and updates, and connect with like-minded "friends."
- Tell product stories and hold contests on splash pages.
- Tie mobile phone campaigns to event promotions and use geotargeting to help drive traffic.
- Entice membership by providing easy signup and positive reasons to return to your site such as drawings for free products and interactive games.
- Bring your online presence into your traditional advertising. Be sure to include your Web address, Facebook fan page address and Twitter handle.
- Recruit product evangelists and ambassadors to advocate for your new product and brand.
- Stay abreast of the next big thing in social media. Research the tactic and include it in your next launch campaign.

▶

Step 5: Organize, analyze and use consumer social media feedback.

It's important to remember the goal of social media engagement is not just brand impressions and dialogue, but obtaining feedback that can help fine-tune your new product and launch plan. While organizing and analyzing online feedback data can be a monumental task, it's well worth the effort. Online tools like Google Reader, which organizes personally chosen news feeds from all over the Web, or Radian6 and Crimson Hexagon, two different tools to help monitor feedback on social media sites, make the data management process less time consuming. ●

CHAPTER 11:

Measuring Launch Results

A new product launch is one of the most visible activities within any company—big or small, publicly traded or startup. Intensely scrutinized both internally and externally, the launch is quickly labeled a success or a failure by traditional media, influential bloggers, competition, retailers, consumers and, ultimately, management and stockholders. An unsuccessful product launch can not only cause a dip in the stock price, but can also throw a promising brand or product manager's career off track.

Savvy launch managers understand how important it is to establish parameters that will gauge launch success. With what we call Launch Success Parameters in place, the definition of success is determined in advance rather than by industry pundits or Monday morning quarterbacks huddled around the corporate watercooler.

Unfortunately, a surprising number of companies fail to heed this advice and therefore have nothing in place to measure how well the launch program has performed. In a survey conducted by Schneider Associates with Babson Executive Education's Center for Business Innovation, 62 percent of the 100 B2B marketers we polled rated their product launches as only "moderately successful." Almost 10 percent of respondents never set any success metrics at all. Twenty-nine percent said they set launch metrics during the launch, and 13 percent said they didn't set metrics until post launch. These are dubious practices since success parameters set after a launch is under way or completed are likely to be heavily influenced by the results, thus skewing the data.

Just as going into a product launch with little or no pre-planning is a recipe for disaster, so, too, is conducting a launch without metrics or a launch analysis methodology in place. When you don't develop Launch Success Parameters and measure against them, others will fill the vacuum and judge success based on their own parameters. Instead of being able to assure senior management that a new product is meeting its goals, you're left in a defensive position without any clear data to cite. Cynical senior managers who were never in love with the new product can quickly undermine your bargaining position when you have no hard metrics to measure success. Plus, additional launch dollars required to ensure success can quickly disappear.

Similarly, when senior executives are left to create their own expectations about how quickly a new product should take off, they can be overly optimistic if goals are not forthcoming from the launch team. This, too, is a recipe for failure; once it's clear their pie-in-the-sky expectations are not being met, they may pull back on launch program resources.

Consider these key issues when measuring new product launch success:

TIP 122 | Set success metrics before the launch starts.

To help ensure success, launch managers should consider involving management, finance and the cross-functional team working on the launch to determine what should be measured and why these factors are critical. "You need to check what other people's goals are and get consensus on the metrics to be sure everyone is on the same page regarding the metrics," said Katie Paine, founder and CEO of KDPaine & Partners, a leader in PR and marketing measurement.

Setting up systems to gather data before and during the launch, and then taking the time to analyze the data following the launch, is critical to understanding and measuring new product launch success. Developing the criteria to measure a launch campaign should be part of the program development process. That way, product and brand managers can confidently say, "My product launch was successful!" and produce the data that unequivocally proves it met key success parameters.

Michael Guggenheimer, vice president of business development at Radiator Specialty Company, discussed his methodology: "Marketing is an area where people tend to think of it more as art than science. But if you are not clear on what results you hope to achieve from a marketing campaign, and you don't make it part of your cost model—then you are more likely to be disappointed at the end."

Guggenheimer added, "You have to ask: What could the market opportunity be? What is a reasonable investment? What investment profile would be required over several years? Who are other players in the space? Can we determine what the other competitors are spending?"

TIP 123 | **Measure the right success metrics.**

The companies in the Schneider/Babson College study used two types of launch success metrics. Some used results-based measures, which focused on business outcomes such as sales or profits, and stock price or market valuation. Others used process measures, which capture activities that contribute to business outcomes. These include such factors as time to market, percentage of sales from new products, and number of retailers penetrated.

Process measures can be tracked on a monthly or weekly basis to provide quick feedback to markets. In contrast, results metrics are lagging indicators because by the time these results are in, it might be too late to change the launch course.

"Process measures tend to be predictive; they are forward looking," said Eric Mankin, director of Professional Services for the Corporate Learning Division of Harvard Business Publishing. "You can get a sense of what your results are going to be by looking at process measures, but they won't tell you definitively what the results are going to be. For instance, your pipeline is a good process measure. If you have 40 leads in your pipeline, you can make a determination of how many of these might turn into clients. Whereas results measures tend to be backward looking. They are critical because they measure business performance, but they don't have predictive ability. Sales goal tracking is a results measure. You can do well in one quarter, but without process measures (what's in the pipeline), you can't predict how you are going to do in the future."

Added Mankin, "In great organizations, there is a strong link between process and results goals. You need to be able to bear down and have a few process measures that are linked to the success of the business."

TIP 124 Create "musts" at the beginning of the campaign that outline what must be achieved.

Every campaign has goals that must be met and criteria by which the program will be judged. Create a "must" document as part of the launch overview that articulates what the launch campaign must accomplish. For instance, here is a list of "musts" that might be included in a campaign overview document for a food product being launched in summer:

- Showcase (name of product) and raise awareness of availability.
- Drive traffic to stores.
- Create relationships within local communities.
- Engage key audiences including (specify key groups).
- Feature a cause-marketing element.
- Drive national and local media exposure and traffic in crucial (insert the selling season) months.
- Leverage existing national partnerships and encourage new ones.
- Engage consumers during prime time—i.e., before (insert name of holiday, such as July Fourth) while they are still planning their holiday weekend.
- Use radio promotions and food drops two weeks before the holiday to build buzz.
- Focus on emphasis markets: (specify markets).
- Engage mommy bloggers two weeks before the holiday.
- Activate conversation on Twitter the week of June 29 with giveaways for July Fourth celebrations.
- Maximize exposure on Facebook fan page and include July Fourth product photo.

Be strategic about the number of "musts" you set out to accomplish. The goal with "musts" is to be sure that the program you've designed accomplishes the "musts" you've outlined.

| **TIP 125** | Set several stretch goals. While the goal is to create launch success metrics that are within reach, you should also establish a few stretch goals that are ambitious.

For example, what is your dream retailer—the one that is possibly a stretch for you to penetrate now but might become more feasible after you have solid sales data to report from others? What is a high-profile media opportunity that could speed your product to success overnight? Thinking big in two or three areas will force you to start laying the groundwork for achieving these home-run results.

As the oft-quoted saying goes, "Aim for the stars, because when you aim for the stars, you will reach the moon." Just be sure you label these as super-hard-to-reach goals so that everyone—especially senior management—is clear that they represent over-the-top success. You wouldn't want to be judged a failure because you didn't reach these stretch goals in the final analysis. On the flip side, you want to put rewards in place should you and your team achieve the stretch goals.

| **TIP 126** | Conduct benchmarking studies both before you begin and afterward to understand if your campaign increased consumer awareness of your product and category.

If you don't know the baseline from which you're starting, you can't judge whether your launch tactics helped you penetrate consumer consciousness or whether attitudes toward your product or brand are improving or deteriorating.

One benchmark you might consider using is the Net Promoter® Score. Net Promoter is a customer loyalty metric developed by Satmetrix, Bain & Co. and Fred Reichheld, first popularized through Reichheld's book *The Ultimate Question*. Companies obtain their Net Promoter Score by asking customers a single question on a 0 to 10 rating scale: "How likely is it that you would recommend our company to a friend or colleague?" Based on their responses, customers can be categorized into one of three groups:

NPS® Loyalty Forum

Promoters (9-10 rating), Passives (7-8 rating), and Detractors (0-6 rating). The percentage of Detractors is then subtracted from the percentage of Promoters to obtain a Net Promoter score. A score of 75 percent or above is considered quite high.

Companies are encouraged to follow this question with an open-ended request for elaboration, soliciting the reasons for a customer's rating of the company or product. These reasons can then be provided to frontline employees and management teams for follow-up action. Proponents of the Net Promoter approach claim the score can help motivate an organization to become more focused on improving products and services for customers. They also say that a company's Net Promoter Score correlates with revenue growth. We like using the Net Promoter Score because it provides a quantitative approach to gathering consumer insights that doesn't involve laborious focus groups and consumer insight sessions. And using this as a benchmark before and after a launch can help you gauge whether your launch tactics moved the dial in your favor with consumers.

TIP 127 Track your success in reaching targeted influencers in your industry and in target market groups.

Create Launch Success Parameters for educating key audiences about your new product. For example, for the Zeo Personal Sleep Coach, we identified 25 of the top sleep industry influencers who needed to know about this breakthrough product. Part of our strategy included setting target dates for getting the product into the hands of these VIPs.

There will also be influencers in your various market segments who can help you drive buzz about your new product within those markets. Set target goals and deadlines for these people as well. Then, for both the industry and target market influencers, monitor the success you're having in your outreach. By closely tracking results, you'll be able to identify if something isn't working in your outreach strategy and fix it. And of course, you'll also want to monitor the feedback you're receiving from influencers and use it to recalibrate your launch plan.

TIP 128 Measure how well you're doing with sell-in against your distribution plan.

The effectiveness of your various launch marketing tactics can be seriously disrupted if you're not getting the anticipated sell-in with retailers or on the Web. For example, you don't want your big ad spend to drop before your top-tier retailers have your new product on their shelves. Closely tracking how actual distribution is matching up with your launch plan is essential. If things are not going as quickly as you'd hoped, you may want to rework your launch timetable or rethink the distribution plan. All team members need to be aware of how sell-in is progressing so they can consider the implications for their portion of the launch if things aren't proceeding according to plan. Avoid the temptation to launch early just because a good media opportunity surfaces. If the product is not on the shelf, or available online, do not speak to the media until you are ready.

TIP 129 Calculate advertising, direct response, Web, PR, word-of-mouth, and social media success using a variety of media metrics.
Set metrics for each media tactic in your launch tool kit, including the newest Web 2.0 channels. Setting these metrics and tracking success against them as your launch progresses will enable you to turn up the heat on the tactics that are working well and retool those that aren't producing the desired results.

Colin Angle, co-founder and CEO of iRobot Corp., portrays social media as an ongoing process and struggle. "We have various services we monitor. Our PR firm and our internal team use tools to discover what's going on with the Web, and we try to efficiently keep track of it. We have enough scale to afford some tools and people to perform monitoring, but as a smaller company, it's going to be hit or miss. Online advertising is getting more and more of our dollars because it's quantifiable, as opposed to social media, where it's more difficult to quantify the benefit. With direct response on the Home Shopping Network, we had to try different strategies to make it work. When it comes to home shopping and online sales, you're never optimized when you start out. You have to refine the message and treat it as a math problem rather than a marketing problem. It's a grand optimization challenge, and you will learn things that surprise you."

In the 2009 MMNPL Survey, 80% of respondents watched content online

On top of response monitoring, evaluating the content of media coverage to see whether your key media messages are being included in stories is an important way to measure campaign success. Amassing a boatload of press clippings and broadcast placements is great, but quantity doesn't necessarily trump quality. If your key messages aren't included in the coverage you're getting, you need to fine-tune your media strategy. Maybe additional media training is required to make spokespeople more proficient in delivering the messages. Maybe the information you've labeled as key is not ringing true with the media so they are substituting their own messages. Whatever the cause for coverage being off target, closely monitoring which messages are getting through and which are not allows you to make content corrections.

Our Measurement Tool

The Schneider Associates Metrics Model (SAMM™) is a four-part measurement tool providing a comprehensive snapshot of a campaign's performance from both a quantitative and qualitative perspective.

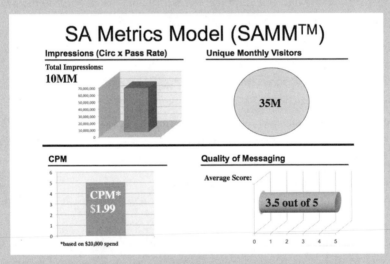

First, the total PR impressions or viewership of a campaign is measured using print and broadcast circulation figures. "PR impressions" are industry standards for measuring a program or placement's "reach" based on these circulation numbers.

Second, data from Compete or Quantcast is compiled to determine the number of Unique Monthly Visitors (UMV) to a Web site. (Compete is an online competitive intelligence service that combines ▶

site and search analytics and monitors more than 2 million opt-in Internet users. Quantcast is another option for measuring traffic because it allows marketers to opt in and have key information about traffic strength published publicly. Quantcast also takes into account actual visitor habits at work and home through an opt-in user panel.)

The third step is calculating CPM (cost per thousand), which is determined by adding impressions (10 million in the following example) and monthly unique visitor data (35,000 in the example), and then dividing by 1,000. That figure is then divided into the campaign cost ($20,000 in the example).

$$(10 \text{ million} + 35,000) \div 1,000 = 10,035$$
impressions and visitors per thousand

$$\$20,000 \div 10,035 = \$1.99 \text{ CPM}$$

The fourth and final step incorporates a Quality of Messaging analysis, the criteria for which must be established at the beginning of a program. Each print and online media placement is compared with the Single Overriding Communications Message (developed in the media messaging session) and the supporting key messages from the Media Message Guide. Depending on the accuracy and completeness of the placement, each is assigned a qualitative score between 1 and 5, established with client input. (A strong campaign will score in the 3.5 to 5 range, meaning that the key messages are being communicated effectively by the media.) The multiple scores are then averaged together.

This process works because it fuses client goals and expectations with quantitative and qualitative analysis, thereby delivering a snapshot upon which all stakeholders can agree. •

In essence, every tactic in your launch plan should have a success metric attached to it. Here are some traditional ways to measure campaign success:

- Product sales
- New retailers carrying the product

- New SKUs being carried by existing customers
- Alternative distribution channels carrying the product
- Meetings with new buyers
- Meetings with influencers
- Advertising impressions
- Desk-side briefings with the press
- Number of news articles in key publications
- Total media impressions
- New investors
- Greater quality and quantity of contacts
- Number of speaking engagements
- Number of bylined articles
- Hits to Web site or microsite
- Requests for product information
- Downloads of a coupon or promotional offer
- Blog postings mentioning new product
- Positive reviews by consumers
- Testimonials by influencers
- Agreement by major retailer to carry the product
- Videos posted by consumers
- Posts on Twitter mentioning the product
- Number of fans on Facebook fan page

Sampling was the most influential source of new product information in 2008 and 2009

TIP 130 Set a number of samples to distribute to key audiences, employees and the media.

Establishing target goals for your sampling campaign provides a basis for determining what you expect this tactic to achieve. Effective sampling takes planning and resources. Set targets and budgets in advance for this tactic. Be sure the product has a track-back mechanism that drives consumers to the Web or to a store so you can measure the effectiveness of the campaign. Whenever possible, capture names and e-mail addresses so you can continue to communicate with consumers.

TIP 131   Be realistic about your metrics if you have a breakthrough product.

If you have a breakthrough product that requires considerable consumer education, it can be tough to gain traction on some success metrics, such as aggressive first-year sales. When we launched a mosquito abatement product, we achieved gangbuster results in terms of media coverage the first year the product was available. But sales were much slower to materialize than anticipated. Part of the problem was that previous products had failed to deliver on their promise to eliminate mosquitoes. We had to conduct a comprehensive consumer education campaign to educate and convince skeptical consumers that this new product was based on science and actually delivered on its promise.

One thing is for sure: Consumer education takes time. We spent almost a year winning over skeptical influencers in the mosquito-abatement product category (who initially bashed the product) and then convincing early adopter consumers of its efficacy. But once we secured a number of brand ambassadors, the word of mouth on this product was terrific and sales began to take off. So if your product is establishing a new category or includes breakthrough technology, factor more time into the launch plan for education and adoption when setting your metrics.

iRobot's Colin Angle said, "We get all the early adopters for free. They like robots and will buy from us. The gadget press adores us, but the challenge is to find the early majority—the people who make up the belly of our target market—and make the product work for them."

TIP 132   Determine ways to measure when you've achieved category leadership.

No matter where you're starting from, every company's long-term goal is to achieve category leadership. In some cases, that leadership objective will be limited to a certain region of the country. Or, you may have aspirations to be the nationwide or even global leader. Whichever is the case, how will you know when this goal is in hand? Set metrics now to determine when you've penetrated people's consciousness enough so they're thinking and talking about your brand and products.

For instance, is your company included when national business or trade publications write major stories about the industry? If they're talking about a relevant product category on *The Today Show*, is your product included?

Do top reporters contact the company CEO for a quote when important news breaks in your industry? Being included in trend and roundup stories often signals that your company is a category leader. Calculating the ROI of being named in numerous articles about a category, or more important, having your product featured prominently in these types of stories, is an important measure of campaign success.

TIP 133 **Track actual timelines and budgets compared with the original launch plan once the launch is completed.**

As part of the process of continual launch improvement, analyze delays that occurred in the time line and major variations that occurred in the budget. What part of the launch took longer than originally anticipated? Do you need to allow more time for some activities, or were there delays that could have been avoided? Were some launch tactics clearly underbudgeted? How would you alter future budgets to make them more realistic?

CHAPTER 12:

Sustaining Launch Success

As we discussed in Chapter 2, our definition of launch includes success-fully propelling your new product into the marketplace...*and sustaining its success over time*. Once you are in the Post-Launch Phase, it is tempting to breathe a big sigh of relief—but don't do it just yet. You are coming to the end of your launch and sales are humming, but the cold hard truth is that your work has just begun.

As we have pointed out, in today's constantly changing business environment, successfully promoting and launching new products requires coordinating multiple factors. With consumers becoming more sophisticated and demanding, organizations need to launch unique products and services that anticipate the rapid shifts in consumer preferences.

How will you assure that things keep going well after your major launch activities are put into play? How will your product continue to grab your key audiences' attention, so that you don't have a Rocket Launch in which sales soar and then quickly fall back to Earth? What's your plan for examining what you've learned from the launch, and how are you going to apply those insights to the post-launch period? You'll need to answer these questions and more. Here are key actions we recommend for sustaining success beyond the initial launch.

TIP 134   **Conduct an After Action Review.**

It is imperative that you bring together key members of your team and various agency partners for an After Action Review, as we suggested in Chapter 3. In the U.S. Army, after each day of battle the generals gather their direct reports to discuss what worked, what didn't work and what they are going to do differently tomorrow. In the same way, consumer product manufacturers need to carefully review what's transpired during launch and what needs to be done to win the marketing wars. The incremental learning achieved by this method, which is a different process than the traditional postmortem review, will help your team grow to become best in class at launching new products.

TIP 135   **Create a SWOT analysis.**

It's also helpful to conduct a SWOT analysis, where you outline the Strengths, Weaknesses, Opportunities and Threats created as a result of the launch. This is another technique to help dissect the launch effort and enable the team to understand where it stands as a result of the initial launch campaign.

TIP 136   **Recalibrate the launch plan.**

From the After Action Review and the SWOT analysis, you'll learn things that may alter or inform what you were planning for the Post-Launch Phase. Obviously, it's a good policy to consider doing more of the tactics that work exceptionally well and eliminating those that turn out to be duds. It's also fine to add new tactics that emerge when potential partners come forward, when influencers bring new opportunities to the table, and when additional media placements surface as a result of the initial coverage.

TIP 137   **Repurpose press coverage.**

To make the most of the media coverage you've received to date, find new ways to repost, repurpose or reuse it. Re-tweet it on Twitter, post it on your Facebook page, add it to the newsroom on your Web site or send an html e-mail to your prospect list with an article embedded. Provide your sales-people with copies of press coverage so they can give it to retailers when they go on sales calls. Add it to brand affinity sites like BzzScapes, an online community where fans post information about their favorite products.

According to Dave Balter, founder and CEO of BzzAgent, "With Bzz-Scapes, consumers do something that is unlike anything before. They collect and create content about the brand from around the Web. In the first eight weeks of BzzScapes, 6,000 communities were formed around popular consumer brands. Two hundred thousand pieces of content were collected in these communities. Cou-

pons, material from corporate sites and testimonials were posted. We also gave consumers the tools to search through the information at BzzScapes,

filter the best of that content, and bring it into their Web sites or blogs." Balter continued, "Brands can get content found authentically (as consumers created this new content on BzzScapes and other sites). The brand can then distribute the content where they think consumers are talking—Facebook pages, Twitter, their corporate site. The authenticity of consumers telling a brand what is important—that's the stuff that other consumers will want to consider."

TIP 138   **Tune up press and collateral materials.**

Now that you've conducted numerous press interviews and talked to consumers, it might make sense to tune up your press and collateral materials. As you talk about your new product with reporters and consumers, you'll learn more about what resonates with

56% of Twitter users in 2009 chose Twitter over traditional media for new product information

them. This allows you to refine the messages and tighten up what you are saying and writing about the product, the company and the market.

For maximum optimization of new product launch press, integrate new images and graphics on your launch Web site, Facebook fan page, Twitter handle and in your social media newsroom to promote launch messages. Online demos, brochures, video and press releases about the new product serve as online sales support while offering consumers the opportunity to familiarize themselves with the product from the comfort of their homes. E-newsletters, blog updates and e-mail campaigns can inform consumers about new product launches and product improvements. Creating links to industry-related sources and partners can add credibility to the new product. Be sure your online materials match the offline materials you are distributing; if you make changes to one set of materials, remember to make the same changes on all sets. Re-circulate the documents to the internal team and sales force to be sure everyone is speaking in the same voice using the latest information.

TIP 139   **Continue to scan the horizon for new emerging trends.**

With luck, the trends capitalized on during your initial publicity push are still current and you can continue to use them as a platform for developing additional news that relates to your product. Since new trends are constantly emerging, it is important to monitor the consumer, business and industry media every day. Provide other launch team members with the news you've scanned so they too can understand what's happening that relates to your product and post-launch plans. Lynn Dornblaser, Mintel International Group's leading new products expert, believes, "Whether or not your new product appears on the market at the beginning of a trend, in the middle, or toward the end will significantly impact how successful that product may be. Similarly, new products that tie in with long-lasting trends usually perform better than those that are positioned against a short-lived fad."

TIP 140   **Plan for other milestone sales opportunities.**

Many products have a "sales season" when consumers are receptive to buying it and the media is receptive to writing about it. Does your product tie in with a holiday? Many products are marketed throughout the year in one way and then again with a new story line for the holidays. How are you going to promote your product as this year's must-have holiday gift? If your product relates to self improvement, weight loss or health, the December/January period is the time for launching or re-launching it because everyone wants to make a fresh start for the New Year.

"Retailers are looking for new products, new ideas and new concepts, but they are being much more selective about the offerings they are making," according to Stanford Weiner, principal of the import company Sterling Inc. "We launched a palm tree in a Christmas motif. It was a tree we had seen in a factory that we thought would look great when lit up. We took it to a wholesale Christmas environment and it was accepted so well that people wanted it right away and didn't want to wait for Christmas. So we created an everyday line of palm trees and it went to the biggest distributor in the U.S. It started as a Christmas item, became an outdoor/indoor patio item, went through the channels, matured, and then when sales declined, it went back to being a Christmas item."

Consider launching and/or promoting your product in the time frames that make sense for the category. If you are marketing a Valentine's Day candy, introducing it to consumers in June will be an uphill battle. If you are marketing ice cream, consumers and the media will expect to hear about it in the summer—unless it's a better-for-you product that would fit right into a New Year's resolution story. Subway, for example, has done an excellent job of introducing products that reflect consumers' interest in eating healthier or slimming down after they've overindulged during the year-end holidays.

TIP 141   **Identify new ways to keep your product newsworthy.**

There are two adages that apply specifically to new product launch that you cannot ignore. The first is, "To make the news, you have to make news," and the second is, "The first three letters of the word 'news' are N E W." To keep your product fresh and top of mind with consumers and the media, you constantly need to be developing new ways to showcase it. Entering your product in awards competitions is a sound strategy for generating positive attention and getting others to say how great it is. Also, with awards comes publicity, and often recognition at prestigious events—other ways to extend the value of your brand.

Major conferences and trade shows also showcase new consumer products and recognize their industry's most innovative products for the year. These shows also attract national media people who walk the aisles in search of new products to feature in print, broadcast, online and social media.

Here's a fun example of guerrilla marketing at trade shows: For the Wellness® brand, a natural dog food manufactured by Old Mother Hubbard®, we created attractive gift bags and delivered them to the rooms of participants in the Westminster Kennel Club Dog Show in New York. The Hotel Pennsylvania, directly across the street from Madison Square Garden where the show takes place, is dog friendly, and management was happy to deliver our gift bags to the canine guests and their owners. Wellness was the only pet food company to treat these canine stars to "celebrity VIP gift bags," which created amazing buzz among the owners and the media covering the show.

Think out of the box when you're developing ways to introduce your product to new audiences. Once you've exhausted all the tactics in your original launch plan, what's next? Are you going to tie into a charity? Would a celebrity spokesperson bring excitement to the brand? As your product moves from revolutionary to evolutionary, you'll have to add tactics that "borrow" interest from others.

TIP 142 | Capitalize on breaking news.

Breaking news can provide fresh ideas to pitch to the media because reporters, editors and bloggers are always looking for new sources of information. While it is time-consuming to scan consumer, business and industry publications, along with blogs and newsletters, these media provide a wealth of information that could be just what you need to keep your product in the news. Remember, the news cycle is always changing, so if there is a story that relates to your product, move quickly. The more you can insert your content into the context of the news, the more exposure you will generate.

TIP 143 | Launch new SKUs, features and benefits.

It's important to think about what new features and benefits you are going to add to the next version of the product. Consumers and the media love "new and improved," so be sure to have another SKU or a different version of your product in the wings. Is there a related product that is going to follow this product? If so, when? How is it different? How are you going to position the newer product if the original is still on the market?

It's also important to think about the next launch while you are still deep in the throes of the original launch. An effective launch requires constant planning. Competitive analysis should be performed at regular intervals—at least every six months—because the competition is always ready to unseat you by using new or better positioning.

Clair Sidman, marketing manager for Ian's Natural Foods, a leading creator and manufacturer of all-natural and organic foods including Red Banner allergen-free products (no wheat, gluten, milk, egg, nut or soy), commented on the company's experience bringing products to market rapidly: "Last year, Ian's launched 24 new items in one year. It had to be done because a lot of competition was entering the children's space. As a leader, we had planned to enter many new categories and we said this is the year we had to do it. With the Red Banner line of allergen-free food products for children, we believed Johnny wants to feel like his friend Jimmy. He wants to be able to eat  the same products and feel like a regular kid despite the fact that he has life-threatening food allergies. We looked at core products that we had in our natural and organic line, non-allergen free, [and] then we looked at whether we [could] make a 'sister' allergen-free food product. For instance, we have an organic chicken nugget. Well, we were the first to market with a wheat-free, gluten-free, dairy-free, egg-free, nut-free, soy-free chicken nugget. What is one of the Top 10 items on a list of products that kids like? Chicken nuggets!"

TIP 144 **Create the new launch plan.**

There is no such thing as a completed launch plan. It's all about creating the new launch plan, a road map that is constantly evolving based on the market and your product's evolution. What worked today might not work six months from now. As marketers, we need to keep the tactics that we use to launch new products just as relevant as our products. The constant changes in consumer behavior, economic conditions, shifts in the media environment and the emergence of new communication technologies require constantly perfecting the launch course to ensure you are on track.

The goal is to be new to someone all the time. That means you can introduce an SKU that suddenly makes you relevant to an entirely new group of people. Or you might discover that the audience you thought would buy the product—women, for instance—is not the audience at all, but that men are buying the product in droves. That type of demographic shift requires a new plan detailing how you are going to build and sustain interest.

According to Dave Dickinson, president and CEO of Zeo Inc., "Never lose new—that's why you have line extensions. Always have something new to talk about to keep your product fresh and newsworthy. Make sure you are thinking about new audiences. If it's a consumer product, is there a business-to-business market as well? The secret of new products is always having something new to sell to somebody."

CONCLUSION:

Summing It All Up

We've given you a lot to ponder. You may even be feeling a little overwhelmed by the myriad of choices and decisions that lie ahead. So it seems appropriate to conclude *The NEW Launch Plan* with a few pieces of practical advice. Here are some fundamentals that should always drive your launch plan. Follow this advice and you can't go wrong with the launch strategies and tactics you choose to deploy.

TIP 145   **Remember, launch is both an art and a science.**
Successful launch veterans will confirm the truth of this statement. You can do all the research in the world, plan meticulously and execute flawlessly, and still not have a successful launch. It's the flash of creativity that transforms an ordinary launch into an extraordinary one. Don't get so tied up mining the research data for new insights or duplicating tactics from earlier launches that you neglect the creative spark that can bring the entire launch plan to life in new and exciting ways. Remember, what is newsworthy about new products is the word "new." Make sure your launch campaign is as fresh as the product you are introducing.

TIP 146   **Allow for serendipity and be ready to take advantage of it.**
A great launch sometimes benefits as much from serendipity as from careful planning and hard work. If you have a health care product, for instance, breaking medical news may put your product in the spotlight as a potential solution to a health problem. Or, a media darling might fall in love with your fashion product and decide to anoint it as one of his or her new favorite things. These things happen—be ready to respond and capitalize on your good fate.

TIP 147   Don't do anything distasteful that will turn off consumers.

Our Idea Camp facilitator likes to say: Every idea is a good idea when you're brainstorming, but not every idea is a great idea when you are planning a campaign. In fact, great ideas can turn into nightmares if they are not appropriate for the product or are poorly executed.

Take this example from another part of the world. When McDonald's Japan was launching the Quarter Pounder in Kansai, the company's CEO pointed to the long lines outside one particular branch as a sign of huge demand. But it turns out that about 1,000 of those in the queue had been paid to stand there by a company that McDonald's hired to do "product quality monitoring."[1] Credibility went out the door and the launch story became more about misrepresenting demand for the new product than about the product itself.

Avoid such embarrassing situations by thoroughly vetting launch ideas and every aspect of how they will be executed and perceived by customers. Coordinate every launch team member's activities so there are no unpleasant surprises.

TIP 148   Pay attention to details.

Remember that every detail counts. All your hard work can quickly evaporate if you're not on top of everything—and we do mean *everything*. For example, just because *your* staff thoroughly understands what you're trying to accomplish at your launch event doesn't mean everyone you've hired for the event is on the same page. Have you briefed the catering staff and the venue staff so they know what's expected of them? Do the entertainers and spokespeople you've hired to interact with the audience understand the product, who it is geared to, and what you consider appropriate and inappropriate material and behavior?

Things can go wrong in an instant—especially at events. What if people leaving your "green" event witness the cleanup staff throwing materials from the recycling bins into a regular trash dumpster? In this environmentally conscious age, that's what people will talk about on the way home or on their blogs, not your great new product. What if the comedian you've hired to be the master of ceremonies at a family-oriented event uses off-color language? The parents will blame both the company and the funny guy for not being family friendly.

If you're holding a launch event, don't leave anything to chance. Prepare a comprehensive time and action plan that covers the smallest details. Make sure everyone who will be working the event understands its purpose and the type of image and messages you want to convey. This includes your own staff as well as the venue personnel, catering staff, musicians, photographers and others. Be specific about things that need to be done before, during and after the event that require flawless execution. Make sure you tell people what to wear, including comfortable shoes, so there is no question about what is appropriate dress. Our advice, in fact, is to button up all aspects of your launch campaign, not just events. Think through the implications of every choice you make so you can avoid surprises that can be detrimental to your brand and the launch.

While it can be annoying to have someone on the team always playing devil's advocate, we all need that kind of objectivity to avoid potential pitfalls. You might consider giving the infamous naysayer the official job of pointing out challenges you face with the launch and the campaign ideas you've selected. Then make sure you listen to what that person says, even if it temporarily puts a damper on what you're planning. Better to find out before the launch rather than during or afterward that one of the key elements is flawed, so you have time to make adjustments.

TIP 149　Have a backup plan.

Run through what-if scenarios to be sure you've thought through all launch eventualities. What if the product is delivered late? What if the testing comes back negative? What if consumers in the focus group don't like the product? What if the buyer at Walmart tells you he hates the taste of your new line extension and you should reformulate? What if TMZ digs up some dirt on your celebrity spokesperson and releases it the day of your launch? All of these scenarios—and scores more—have happened to our clients. Be prepared to be flexible and willing to change the course of your launch if necessary. Think of all the negatives *before* the campaign is launched so you've covered all the bases.

TIP 150　If you can't do it right, just don't do it.

Sometimes you fall in love with a tactic that doesn't match your budget or your time frame and you just can't let it go. The result: You rush your planning or you try to execute the idea with fewer resources than are required to make the tactic work. You end up with a launch component that doesn't meet expectations because the execution was hurried or flawed.

It is far better to accept from the get-go that not every cutting-edge tactic will work with your schedule or budget. Sometimes you need to make tough choices. Doing a handful of things perfectly is far better than having many different launch elements executed at only 75 percent.

TIP 151   **Have a sense of humor about launch.**

We recommend you keep a sense of perspective about your launch and remember that it's not brain surgery. As dire as it all may seem at the moment—and believe me, there are times we all wonder if the launch is ever going to happen—the most important thing is to remain flexible and calm. No matter what happens, there are always ways to recalibrate and put the product and the launch back on course.

Sure, your company has a lot riding on this launch, and you and your team want it to succeed. The best thing you can do is to stay focused on the plan, the budget and flawless execution. When failure is not an option, staying the course takes the day. In addition, maintaining a sense of humor and perspective will enable you to rationally engage with management, colleagues, consumers and the media.

Let's be honest—consumers love new products and that's what we're selling. Hopefully, we are selling it in a way that piques consumer interest and engages them in conversation and trial. One lesson we've learned is that if you stay true to the heritage of the brand and develop new products or features that make sense for the brand, consumers will respond.

If it's ice cream, it's about fun. If it's beer, it's about socializing. If it's a lifestyle product, it's about any number of things, such as wellness, reducing stress, being able to do something faster or better, or adding a little luxury to your life. In a world where social media increasingly allows us to interact with consumers on a one-to-one basis, maintaining this realistic and authentic focus is especially important.

TIP 152   **It's better to be lucky than smart.**

As Len Schneider, author Joan Schneider's father, often says, "I'd rather be lucky than smart." It's a trait that propelled him through a long and successful sales career, so we can't help but mention that a certain amount of luck plays into launch success. The truth is, all marketers secretly wish their products will launch on a day when there are no palace coups, plane crashes, fires, deaths of famous people, or other catastrophic events that take over the local and national news. We all hope to choose a time of year when the eyes of the world are not drawn to hurricanes, parades, fireworks, elections or flu scares. We keep our fingers crossed that the celebrities we select will not be arrested for substance abuse or sexual misconduct—at least not while under contract. And we pray that the bloggers who try our products will like them, the sites that review them will endorse them, and that the Consumer Reports reviews are favorable.

As you can see, launching new products is the nexus of luck and intellect. Do everything you can, but it doesn't hurt to light a few candles along the way.

We love talking about launch and welcome the opportunity to talk with you about your launch challenges and what you've learned from launching new products that might be useful to others. We encourage you to contact us at jschneider@schneiderpr.com or jhall@schneiderpr.com with your questions or comments. For constant updates about exciting new launches, please visit our blogs at www.LaunchPR.com and www.MMNPL.com. In the meantime, we wish you great success with your next launch!

FOOTNOTES:

INTRODUCTION:

1. "Q: American Advertising in the Media," Google Answers, http://answers.google.com/answers/threadview?id=56750.

CHAPTER 1:

1. Internet World Stats, "Top 20 Countries with the Highest Number of Internet Users," Miniwatts Marketing Group, http://www.internet worldstats.com/top20.htm.

2. IDC, "IDC Finds Online Consumers Spend Almost Twice as Much Time Using the Internet as Watching TV," press release, February 19, 2008.

3. Brat, Ilan, Ellen Byron, and Ann Zimmerman, "Retailers Cut Back on Variety, Once the Spice of Marketing," *The Wall Street Journal,* June 26, 2009, http://online.wsj.com/article/SB124597382334357329.html.

4. Ibid.

5. Barbara Grondin Francella, "Private Label Programs Take Off," *Brandweek*, July 9, 2009, http://www.brandweek.com/bw/content_display/news-and-features/direct/e3i70172e607ddc1be9960f59b1a9371187.

6. The Pew Research Center for the People & the Press, *Internet Overtakes Newspapers as News Outlet,* survey, December 23, 2008, http://people-press.org/report/479/internet-overtakes-newspapers-as-news-source.

7. The Nielsen Company, *Global Faces and Networked Places: A Nielsen Report on Social Networking's New Global Footprint,* March 2009, page 3, http://server-uk.imrworldwide.com/pdcimages/Global_Faces_ and_Networked_Places-A_Nielsen_Report_on_Social_Networkings _New_Global_Footprint.pdf.

8. Ibid.

9. Michelle McGiboney, "Twitter's Tweet Smell of Success," The Nielsen Company, March 18, 2009, http://blog.nielsen.com/nielsenwire/ online_mobile/twitters-tweet-smell-of-success.

10. Nielsen Wire, "Social Networkers with Multiple Profiles Skew Young, Tech-Savvy," The Nielsen Company, March 24, 2009, http://blog. nielsen.com/nielsenwire/tag/online-demographics.

CHAPTER 3:

1. Jefferson Graham, "Facebook's a Great Friend to Businesses," *USA Today*, August 5, 2009.

2. Rob Gonda, "Bewitched by Twitter," *Adweek*, April 23, 2009, http:// www.adweek.com/aw/content_display/community/columns/othercol umns/e3i888016761f9ec8244cc028a0e687de81.

3. comScore Media Metrix, March 2009.

4. Ned Roberto and Ardy Roberto, "Popcorn and Lindstrom on Marketing Trends," Inquirer.net, November 3, 2006, http://business. inquirer.net/money/columns/view/20061103-30283/Popcorn_and_ Lindstrom_on_marketing_trends.

5. Mintel, "Mintel Identifies Trust as Crucial Issue of 2009," press release, February 27, 2009, http://www.mintel.com/press-release/mintel-iden tifies-trust-as-crucial-issue-of-2009?id=330.

6. Bonini, Sheila, David Court, and Alberto Marchi, "Rebuilding Corporate Reputations," *McKinsey Quarterly*, the Online Journal of McKinsey & Co., June 2009, http://www.mckinseyquarterly.com/Rebuilding_corporate_reputations_2367.

7. Geoff Northcott, "Ford Fiesta Movement and Social Media Participation Points," May 16, 2009, http://www.geoffnorthcott.com/blog/2009/05/.

CHAPTER 4:

1. Knowledge@Wharton, "Beware of Dissatisfied Customers: They Like to Blab," The Wharton School of the University of Pennsylvania, March 8, 2006, http://knowledge.wharton.upenn.edu/article.cfm?articleid=1422.

2. Geoffrey A. Moore, *Crossing the Chasm: Marketing and Selling High-Tech Products to Mainstream Customers* (HarperBusiness, July 1999).

CHAPTER 5:

1. "eMarketer Projects Online Retail Sales to Fall in 2009 and Rebound in 2010," *Internet Retailer,* Vertical Web Media, March 5, 2009, http://www.internetretailer.com/dailyNews.asp?id=29655.

2. Business Wire, "CPG Companies Face Merchandising Crisis, Turn to New Solutions," August 29, 2007, http://www.businesswire.com/portal/site/home/permalink/?ndmViewId=news_view&newsId=20070829005734&newsLang=en.

3. Jim George, "Club Stores: Show Us the Value," *Contract Packaging,* December 2006, 12, http://www.packworld.com/article-22428.

4. Adam Diamond and Ricardo Soto, *Facts on Direct-to-Consumer Food Marketing: Incorporating Data from the 2007 Census of Agriculture,* U.S. Department of Agriculture's Agricultural Marketing Service, May 2009, 3, http://www.scribd.com/doc/16562250/USDA-Farmer-to-Consumer-Sales-Charts.

CHAPTER 6:

1. Miriam Marcus, "The Death of the Fad," Forbes.com, September 6, 2007, http://www.forbes.com/2007/09/06/fads-styles-crazes-forbeslife -trends07-cx_mlm_0906fad.html.

2. Ibid.

3. U.S. Census Bureau, "An Older and More Diverse Nation by Midcentury," press release, August 14, 2008, http://www.census.gov/Press-Release/www/releases/archives/population/012496.html.

4. Christine Esposito, "Be Smart about Changes in Shopping Behavior," Happi.com, http://www.happi.com/articles/2009/01/online-exclusive-shopping-behavior.

5. Gail Tom and Codruta Catanescu, "Types of Humor in Television and Magazine Advertising," *Review of Business*, March 22, 2001, 92.

CHAPTER 7:

1. Jakob Nielsen, "Press Area Usability," Jakob Nielsen's Alertbox, January 20, 2009, http://www.useit.com/alertbox/pr.html.

CHAPTER 8:

1. Kenneth Hein, "Employees Can Help to Make or Break a New Campaign, So Why Not Market to Them First?", *Brandweek*, February 16, 2009, http://www.brandweek.com/bw/content_display/current-issue/ e3i6266a3e7e491921cc8e5b3a0a41903b4.

2. Libby Copeland, "High-Water Marketing: Climate-Change Clothes, a Little Smug on the Hip," *Washington Post*, February 18, 2007, http:// www.washingtonpost.com/wp-dyn/content/article/2007/02/17/AR 2007021701686.html.

3. "Past. Present. Future. The 25th Anniversary of Cause Marketing," Cone, LLC, http://www.volunteermatch.org/corporations/resources/ cone_research.pdf.

4. Liz Bigham, "Experiential Marketing: New Consumer Research," Jack Morton, http://www.jackmorton.com.

5. Pallavi Gogoi, "Pop-Up Stores: All the Rage," *BusinessWeek*, February 9, 2007, http://www.businessweek.com/bwdaily/dnflash/content/feb2007/db20070206_949107.htm.

6. Sandra M. Jones, "Macy's New Ad Campaign: Decorative Canisters of Clorox Wipes," *Chicago Tribune*, March 20, 2009, http://archives.chicagotribune.com/2009/mar/20/business/chi-fri-notebook-0320-mar20.

CHAPTER 9:

1. Jakob Nielsen, "Mobile Usability," Jakob Nielsen's Alertbox, July 20, 2009, www.useit.com/alertbox/mobile-usability.html.

CHAPTER 10:

1. Robin Neifeld, "Social Media Advice for Brands from a Wal-Mart Elevenmom," ClickZ, April 22, 2009, http://www.clickz.com/3633473.

2. Levine, Rick, Christopher Locke, Doc Searls, and David Weinberger, *The Cluetrain Manifesto* (New York: Basic Books, 2009), 144.

3. Pallavi Gogoi, "Wal-Mart's Jim and Laura: The Real Story," *BusinessWeek*, October 9, 2006, http://www.businessweek.com/bwdaily/dnflash/content/oct2006/db20061009_579137.htm.

4. David Burn, "Target Doesn't Engage with Non-Traditional Media," AdPulp, January 17, 2008, http://www.adpulp.com/archives/2008/01/target_doesnt_e.php.

5. Michael Learmonth and Rupal Parekh, "How Twittering Critics Brought Down Motrin Mom Campaign," *Ad Age*, November 17, 2008.

6. Alexandra Samuel, "Don't Keep up with Social Technology," *Harvard Business Review*, August 3, 2009, http://blogs.harvardbusiness.org/cs/2009/08/dont_keep_up_with_social_techn.html.

7. Rebecca Reisner, "Comcast's Twitter Man," *BusinessWeek,* January 13, 2009, http://www.businessweek.com/managing/content/jan2009/ca 20090113_373506.htm.

CONCLUSION:

1. "Hundreds Paid to Wait in Line at McDonald's Product Launch," Japan Probe, December 25, 2008, http://www.japanprobe.com/?p=7966.

INDEX